DATE DUE

MAR 27 1995	
JUL 10 1997	

Niles Public Library District

6960 Oakton Street
Niles, Illinois 60648
(708) 967-8554

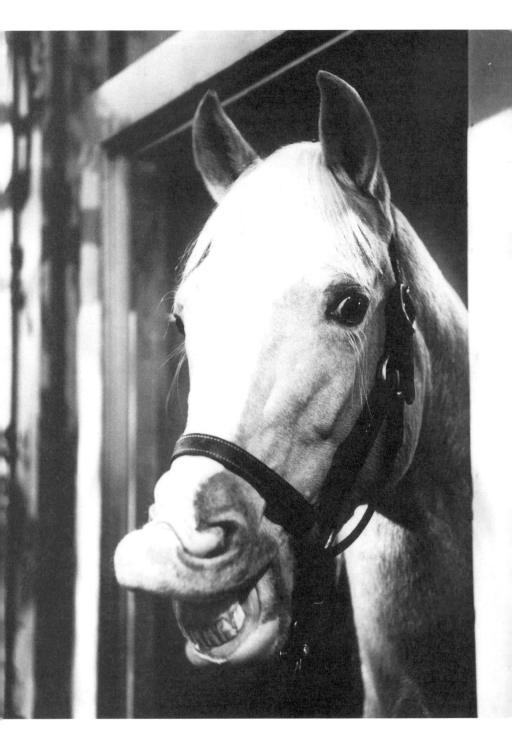

THE FAMOUS MISTER ED

The Unbridled Truth About America's Favorite Talking Horse

NANCY NALVEN

WARNER BOOKS

A Time Warner Company

Warner Books, Inc., 666 Fifth Avenue, New York, NY 10103
W A Time Warner Company

Printed in the United States of America
First printing: September 1991
10 9 8 7 6 5 4 3 2 1

Library of Congress Cataloging-in-Publication Data

Nalven, Nancy.
  The famous Mister Ed : the unbridled truth about America's favorite talking horse / Nancy Nalven.
    p.   cm.
  Includes bibliographical references and index.
  ISBN 0-446-39296-0
  1. Mister Ed (Television program)   I. Title.
PN1992.77.M59N35   1991
791.45'72—dc20   91-11982
                                                            CIP

Book design by Giorgetta Bell McRee
Cover design by George Corsillo
Cover photo by Gari Rona; from the Motion Picture and Television Archives

In loving memory of my grandparents, Mollie and Morris Berger, and Katherine and Leon Nalven

Acknowledgments

....

Many heartfelt thanks to the individuals who were directly involved with *Mister Ed*, who shared their time, memories, photos and incredible hospitality, and who *truly* made this book possible: Al Simon, Alan and Gini Young, Arthur Lubin, Herb Browar, George Burns, Connie Hines Savin, Edna Skinner, Larry Rhine and Hazel Shermet, Ben Starr, Marty Ransohoff, Jim Aubrey, Dave Kahn, Jay Livingston, Arch Dalzell, and Janie and John Nicolaides.

I am also extremely grateful to the following people: Jim Spegman for his inspired illustrations, Barry Felsen, Esq., Trav Livingston, Dennis Dalzell, Marty Silverstein and Shirley Jones at CBS Photos, Herb Stott, Big Bucks Burnett, Gene Yusem, Jack Langdon, Gene Trindl, Richard Hewitt, Fred Seibert, Alan Goodman, Len Fischman, Bob Zeltmann, Elliot Krowe, Bill Black, TV book authors Stephen Cox and Joey Green, James O'Donnell and Charlex, Barbara Greenberg, Jill Tarnoff and Joe Robinowitz at *TV Guide*, Dawn Snyder and Bob Oswaks at Orion, Mary Suggett, Charlie Stoddard, Jeff Cook, the New York Public Library, and the Library of Congress.

Love and affection to my family for all their patience and cheerleading. A special thank you to David Burd for his *immense* contribution to this project, from soup to nuts (or is it from "oats to hay"?). Thanks also to Derek Tague, future TV-book author, and Ray "Rocky" Meola for above and beyond the call of duty Mister Ed-related research and photos.

Thanks to Eleo Hensleigh, Herb Scannell, Rich Cronin, Lisa Blanck, Larry Jones, Maggie Shearman and Scott Webb at Nick at Nite, and may your mighty *Mister Ed* flagship forever sail! Thanks to my agent Vicky Bijur for believing in the project. Thanks to my editor Rick Horgan for repeatedly cutting "the show was in the best of hooves," and to Mauro Dipreta and my copyeditor Durba Ghosh at Warner Books.

And finally, thanks to Erica Schoenberg, Tom "the dear sweet" Pomposello, Nancy Menna, Steve "Mac" Diamond, Sarah Nemetz, Tish Megerdichian, Steve Thomas, Jill Gershon, Jessica Wolf, Carol Forsythe, Dave Landesberg, Alysa Kadin, Mark Chesnut, Cindy Tendler, Troy Ellen Dixon, Ed Levine, Noel Frankel, Lillie Cuadrado, Rich Mines, and Ken Murphy.

Contents

• •

Mister Ed *Theme Song Lyrics*

A horse is a horse
Of course, of course
And no one can talk to a horse of course
That is of course
Unless the horse
Is the famous Mister Ed

Go right to the source
And ask the horse
He'll give you the answer that you'll endorse
He's always on a steady course
Talk to Mister Ed

People yakkity yak a streak and waste your
time of day,
But Mister Ed will never speak unless he has
something to say.

© *Orion Television.*

A horse is a horse
Of course, of course
And this one will talk till his voice is hoarse
You never heard of a talking horse?
Well listen to this:
I AM MISTER ED.

Reprinted with permission. Written by Jay Livingston and Ray Evans.
Copyright renewed 1988 Jay Livingston and Ray Evans.
Assigned worldwide to Jay Livingston Music (ASCAP)/St. Angelo Music (ASCAP).

Courtesy of Alan Young.

Foreword by Alan Young

•••

Records tell us that horses began carrying men as far back as 3000 B.C. Mister Ed told me the same thing, adding that he personally had carried *me* for over five seasons. I thought this comment was beneath him and so gave no response. However, I felt it was a little petty, considering the fact that I *memorized* my lines and did not use cue-cards the way some horses did. But, far be it from me to reveal family secrets, or air old grudges. Besides, he was always lording it over me because his Latin name is *Equus Caballus* which has a lot more ring to it than Young. Also, because he has eight more teeth than I have, which doesn't mean a thing unless you smile a lot.

Oh, I guess I could have just swept this dirt under the rug and written a sugary foreword for Nancy's book but with today's "Tell it like it is" tendency, Nancy Nalven deserves the truth. So—here it is: like many comedy teams, off stage Ed and I never spoke to each other! We never socialized nor double-dated. He went his way and I went mine. We'll leave it at that. Besides, three of his teeth were capped.

Introduction

•••

Mister Ed was *high concept* television at its best, with a rather simple story: "a talking horse who only talks to one guy." The horse is called Ed. The guy is named Wilbur. Stuff like that only happens on television. No pun intended, *Mister Ed* is really a completely different TV *animal*. It's TV that's obviously born from TV (a nutty variation on classic shows such as *The Honeymooners* and *I Love Lucy*), and made exclusively for TV (the show made no pretense of being real), with a great deal of heart, talent and wit. The "comfortably numb" nostalgia the show evokes is only part of the pleasure. The real satisfaction comes from acknowledging *Mister Ed*'s craft and—dare I say it—*genius*. I grew up watching *Mister Ed* every week and loved it, especially the scenes in which Ed wore giant eyeglasses and read the paper. But it wasn't until rediscovering the show on Nick at Nite that I realized how sophisticated many of the jokes were. To this day, the main criticism against *Mister Ed* is that the humor is so "low brow"—you know, cheap laughs. Well, don't worry, palomino pals. *Mister Ed* was Jack Benny's favorite TV show. And the original *Mister Ed* pilot was financed by George Burns himself. So, as you can see, we're in very good company.

Those near and dear to *Mister Ed* whom I interviewed for this book delighted in recounting their experiences working on the show (delighting me thoroughly in the process). This book is as much for them as it is for the horse, a remarkable creature named Bamboo Harvester, whom *Mister Ed*'s writers endowed with a rich and engaging spirit. Guaranteed, if Mister Ed took out a "Personals" ad in *New York* magazine, he'd get a flood of responses from eligible fillies everywhere.

I doff my proverbial hat to *Mister Ed*'s zany, visionary writers, and regret that I never had the opportunity to meet Lou Derman, head writer, who passed away in 1976 while still working on *All in the Family*. His delightful scripts will continue to be enjoyed by those of us who grew up with the show, as well as a whole new generation of "Ed-Heads"—the official name for *Mister Ed* fans.

If you've ever been remotely intrigued by *Mister Ed*, how they made the horse talk, drive a truck and surf, how they got away with it for—count 'em—six seasons, rest assured that the answers to these questions are but a canter away. And if you truly loved the show, and remember watching it every Sunday night in your p.j.s, then gather up a cozy bed of hay and fasten your saddle, because you're in for a real *Mister Ed*-fest.

And they're off . . .

Nancy Nalven
New York, 1990

"It's Been a Long Time Since I Was a Pony"

MISTER ED'S BEGINNINGS

In January 1991 *Mister Ed* celebrated the thirtieth anniversary of its debut on American airwaves. It was quite a milestone—few TV stars have kept talking to their audience that many years—and quite ironic. *Mister Ed*'s creators had a heck of a time getting the show out of the stable and into American living rooms. But once it hoofed and clawed its way to the TV set, *Mister Ed* turned horse power into staying power, and thirty years later, the series is undeniably one of America's best-loved TV classics.

There are at least two big reasons why *Mister Ed* merits a closer look. Big Reason One: In front of the camera, *Mister Ed*'s producers provided pure viewing joy, utilizing two key ingredients—exaggeration and innovation; and Big Reason Two: Behind the camera, *Mister Ed* is equally as intriguing, not only with its unique production challenges, but with a fascinating history. *Mister Ed* was the very first show to go from syndication (airing locally in individual markets) to network television, as well as the first TV venture for Filmways TV Productions, which went on to produce some of the most successful and imaginative TV shows of the 1960s: *The Beverly Hillbillies* (CBS, 1962–71), *Petticoat Junction* (CBS, 1963–70), *Green Acres* (CBS, 1965–71) and *The Addams Family* (ABC, 1964–66). Cumulatively, these

1

© *Orion Television.*
Alan Young and Mister Ed mug to the camera for a 1961 publicity shot.

facts suggest *Mister Ed* was a TV landmark, not your average, garden-variety talking-animal sitcom you can dismiss at the drop of a hoof.

Looking back on it, *Mister Ed* seems to fit in perfectly with the early 1960s TV landscape, combining just the right elements of fantasy and comedy while upholding honest-to-goodness American values. But even in 1960, the year *Mister Ed* finally got the green light from its sponsor, the show was considered a radical concept for television—maybe too radical. Obstacles ranged from getting a financial backer, to convincing the Hollywood community that a show about a man and his talking horse wasn't one big joke, to finding the right leading man, to finding the right leading horse . . .

Fortunately, there were enough people in Hollywood with the horse sense to realize that *Mister Ed* was a winning idea, but it all started with director/producer Arthur Lubin, who first envisioned a *Mister Ed* TV series.

Courtesy of Arthur Lubin.
Director Arthur Lubin discusses the next scene with his horse star in this publicity photo from 1963.

Arthur Lubin: A Wild Guy With a Vision

A most interesting *Mister Ed* connection—in fact, the biggest "Aha!" of all —is that Arthur Lubin directed for Universal the first six Francis the Talking Mule pictures (1949–55), which would serve as a prototype of sorts for *Mister Ed* ten years later. If Lubin had not enjoyed directing a talking mule and his human sidekick, it's doubtful *Mister Ed* would have ever seen the light of day.

Arthur Lubin was born on July 25, 1901, in Los Angeles. He studied film at Carnegie Tech, where, interestingly, several *Mister Ed* alumni also schooled—associate producer Herb Browar; Scott McKay, the star of the *Mister Ed* pilot; and featured character actress Hazel Shermet.

Although Lubin began his show biz career as an actor, performing in the Pasadena Playhouse during the mid-1920s, he soon switched to directing —first on Broadway, then back in Hollywood. When asked recently why he switched from acting to directing, *Mister Ed*'s director replied, "There are some things in life to which one is fated. I was meant to be behind the camera."

Francis and *Mister Ed* aside, Lubin is every fantasy-film junkie's director. Although his sixty-two feature films run the gamut from comedies to westerns to suspense dramas to fantasy/adventures, his trademark film was either a comedy or lush fantasy. He directed the first Abbott and Costello comedy for Universal, *In the Navy* (1941), and lists as his all-time favorite project *The Phantom of the Opera* (1943), which starred Claude Rains. His other fantasy pictures include *Ali Baba and the Forty Thieves* (1944), starring Maria Montez; *Night in Paradise* (1946), with Merle Oberon; *Lady Godiva* (1955), with Maureen O'Hara as the first-recorded streaker on horseback and Clint Eastwood as "first saxon"; *It Grows on Trees* (1952), with Irene Dunne; and *Thief of Baghdad* (1961), with Steve Reeves (lensed during the first *Mister Ed* season).

What do all these works have in common? Imagination and atmosphere. Lubin was skilled at the delicate art of layering in magic and fantasy, while preserving the audience's suspension of disbelief—a talent that would prove particularly useful once his attentions were fixed on transforming a talking mule, and later, a talking horse, into compelling family entertainment.

Francis the Talking Mule chats it up with Donald O'Connor in *Francis Joins the WACS,* a 1954 feature for Universal.

Francis the Talking Mule

Today Arthur Lubin is considered one of the great masters at directing nonhumans for film and television. But back in 1948 was it any surprise that Hollywood was as stubborn as a *you-know-what* in accepting Francis the Talking Mule? Lubin compares his initial struggle getting Francis to the big screen to the resistance he met later on, selling the "talking horse" concept: "*Mister Ed* was probably the hardest show to get on the air. No one wanted it. It was the same argument when I was doing *Francis*. I brought the script to the agent, one of the biggest in town, Mike Levee, and he said to me, 'If anyone buys this script, I'll eat it.' " Well, Mr. Levee had to develop a taste for manuscript quite quickly, because Universal produced Lubin's first Francis picture in 1949, and followed that with six more installments over the next seven years. In Levee's defense, he represented many of Hollywood's most glamorous at the time, including Greta Garbo, so it's easy to understand why he wasn't immediately spellbound by a script starring a talking mule.

The seven Francis films made from 1949 to 1956 (Arthur Lubin directed all but the final one) actually saved Universal Studios from financial ruin. Sounds like a perfectly plausible Francis story line: "Talking Mule Saves Bankrupt Hollywood Studio!" The Francis films were intended to generate quick income and made no pretense of being high art. All were shot on Universal's backlot, filmed in black and white, and were relatively short in length, from eighty to ninety-one minutes.

Donald O'Connor starred as Peter Stirling in all but the final Francis film. A second lieutenant stationed in Burma during World War II, Stirling becomes the human compatriot to Francis, a talking army mule. The Francis films were based on the 1946 novel *Francis*, by Peter Stirling, who wrote under the pseudonym David Stern.

Movie critics were surprised that even the most sophisticated audiences were enthralled by the magic of Francis, which held itself together with the simplest, most contrived premises. The series made millions.

Finally in 1956 the producers of the by-this-time lackluster Francis series were waiting for the other hoof to drop. And drop it did. The final Francis feature, *Francis in the Haunted House,* was a bomb. Donald O'Connor refused to star in it, despite the fact that the Francis series gave him better visibility than ever, bringing him fame not even realized from his performance in the 1952 sensation *Singin' in the Rain* (which he did on outside loan to MGM).

Arthur Lubin recalls that O'Connor, although "young and bright and cheerful" at the beginning of the Francis series, became more difficult to work with toward the end. It was partly attributable to boredom (the cast and crew were all growing tired of the series by now). Maybe, too, O'Connor's frustration stemmed from the realization that the mule was getting most of the fan mail!

For the last film Mickey Rooney was recruited as Francis' new human sidekick, but he wasn't received with open arms. The film lacked more than O'Connor's charming presence. Arthur Lubin hadn't directed it, nor had veteran cowboy actor Chill Wills provided the voice of Francis, as he had in the previous six ventures. Wills' place was taken by cartoon voice man Paul Frees ("Boris Badenov").

_____ FRANCIS FILM FEST _____

1949	*Francis*	Director: Arthur Lubin
1951	*Francis Goes to the Races*	Director: Arthur Lubin
1952	*Francis Goes to West Point*	Director: Arthur Lubin
1953	*Francis Covers the Big Town*	Director: Arthur Lubin
1954	*Francis Joins the WACS*	Director: Arthur Lubin
1955	*Francis in the Navy*	Director: Arthur Lubin
1956	*Francis in the Haunted House*	Director: Charles Lamont

Trivia Corner

What tall-in-the-saddle movie star made one of his earliest film appearances in a Francis the Talking Mule film, and seven years later guest-starred on an episode of *Mister Ed*? *Answer:* **Clint Eastwood** was directed by Arthur Lubin in both film and television, each time with a talking animal. He appeared in the 1955 movie *Francis in the Navy* and guest-starred on *Mister Ed* in 1962 (which certainly served as a nice cross-promotion for *Rawhide*, Eastwood's concurrent western series on CBS). Incidentally, Lubin also directed Eastwood in three more films during the 1950s.

The Original Story of *Mister Ed* . . .
"The One Hollywood Didn't Dare Make!"
(as Ed would say)

So what exactly is the Francis–Mister Ed connection? "I had completed a series called Francis and was anxiously looking for another comedy because I enjoyed directing them," explains Arthur Lubin. "Sonia Chernus, a secretary whom I knew at CBS, had read some short stories by Walter Brooks, in *Saturday Evening Post* and *Liberty* magazine, about a talking horse named

Mister Ed. But while the horse spoke, he also drank a great deal and got drunk."

Little did the director know that at the time he discovered David Stern's novel about a talking mule, *Francis*, in 1946, there was already in existence a whole library of stories—twenty-eight to be exact—about a talking horse named Mister Ed. In fact, Francis is modeled very closely after the original Mister Ed character created by Walter Brooks. Both animals are not only

© *1990 CBS Inc.*
Clint Eastwood and Connie Hines (Carol Post) twist something fierce on the Filmways lot as Ed looks on in a publicity shot for "Clint Eastwood Meets Mister Ed," 1962.

talkers but drinkers and carousers. The TV Ed we know and love is a regular gentleman compared to these two scoundrels. Lubin, knowing a good story when he read one, contacted Brandt and Brandt, the agency representing Brooks in New York, and took an option on the idea of *Mister Ed*. Eventually, he purchased rights to the *Mister Ed* characters from Dorothy Brooks, who had inherited the properties from her husband.

In exchange for first introducing Arthur Lubin to the Walter Brooks stories in 1957, Sonia Chernus received "Format Developed by" screen credit as well as a small percentage of the show's royalties. In addition, Lubin gave her a shot at cowriting one *Mister Ed* episode with head writer Lou Derman. In 1962 they scripted "Clint Eastwood Meets Mister Ed," an agreeable assignment for Chernus, who had become friendly with the rugged young film star through mutual association with Lubin. Sonia passed away in July 1990.

THE ORIGINAL WALTER BROOKS CHARACTERS

○ Mister Ed (remained Mister Ed in the TV series)
○ Wilbur Pope (this name was kept for the 1958 *Mister Ed* pilot, but changed to Wilbur *Post* at an early Filmways script meeting)
○ Carlotta Pope (again, this was her name for the pilot, but became Carol Post for the Filmways series)

OTHER BROOKS INCIDENTALS

○ The Popes reside in Mount Kisco, New York, not Hollywood, California.
○ Wilbur Pope is an architect just as in the TV series, but he's with the firm of Lamson, Camphire, Leatherbee & Wallet (sounds like a name out of Dickens). In the TV show, Wilbur is self-employed, working project to project. Alan Young recalls that his character needed a profession which kept him close to home—and therefore, to the horse—so they made him an architect.

SIMILARITIES TO OUR MISTER ED

Brooks' Mister Ed, like our Mister Ed:
○ Recites Hamlet
○ Speaks Latin
○ Is patriotic
○ Has spy-phobia (fear of spies!)

The *Mister Ed* Pilot

What good is an idea for a TV show unless it gets produced? Once Arthur Lubin had an option on the Walter Brooks stories, he brought the *Mister Ed* project to his agent to be shopped around to various studios. In 1958 Maurice Morton at McCadden Productions, the production company owned by George Burns, was introduced to *Mister Ed*. To this day, Lubin claims it was a simple case of horsemanship that got the pilot produced. The comedian's manager "loved horses and recommended it to George," Lubin explains, "and George agreed to finance a pilot. He liked the idea but I think he was influenced a great deal by Maurice Morton, who had his own horses in the Valley. A deal was made between myself and George Burns." George Burns remembers that his interest in the *Mister Ed* project stemmed from Lubin's proven success with the Francis the Talking Mule film series for Universal earlier in the decade. Whatever the reason, George invested $75,000 to produce the *Mister Ed* pilot.

The McCadden pilot, entitled "The Wonderful World of Wilbur Pope," was written by a group of four writers, including George's kid brother, Willy Burns. These were the same four who went on to adapt the script for the first TV episode of *Mister Ed* ("The First Meeting"), which premiered in syndication almost three years later.

The pilot took between three and four days to make, recalls Lubin, and starred Scott McKay as Wilbur Pope. McKay's previous TV credits included the role of Hank Merlin on *The Stage Door,* a live dramatic series on CBS from February to March 1950, as well as Bob Wallace on *Honestly Celeste,* another short-lived CBS series starring Celeste Holm (Oct.–Dec. 1954).

Sandra White, whom Lubin says "disappeared after the pilot," played McKay's wife, Carlotta Pope. Her very black hair is a real contrast to Connie Hines' (Carol Post) very blond bob. At this point, the *Mister Ed* team was still two horses away from Bamboo Harvester, the palomino that came to be known as *the* Mister Ed. The equine used in the pilot, a palomino quarter horse owned by horse trainer Les Hilton, was "a horse of a different color," a bit darker in hue than the ultimate Ed. Alan Young recalls that the darker horse didn't photograph as well on television.

The voice of the horse in the McCadden pilot is played by Allan "Rocky" Lane, the same man who played Ed's voice for Filmways TV. When casting for the horse's voice, Arthur Lubin naturally wanted to hire Chill Wills, the voice of Francis. But when approached for the part, Wills was not interested.

There are a few notable contrasts between the original pilot and the eventual premiere episode of Filmways TV: Scott McKay as Wilbur was an unassuming, likable type, but not nearly as funny or appealing as Alan Young, who was extremely skilled in comedy. The Popes moved into 1046 Valley

Spring Lane, not too far off from 17230, where they ended up as the *Posts*. Wilbur Pope is employed as a lawyer, not an architect. Additionally, in the McCadden script, the Popes were married eight years prior to moving into their new house. In the first TV episode, you assume that Wilbur and Carol are newlyweds because Carol insists that Wilbur carry her over the threshold of their very first house. It's not until a couple of episodes later that you learn they've been married for three years. The threshold gag was also used in the pilot, as well as *very* enthusiastic laugh tracks. The next-door-neighbor Addisons do not show up until the Filmways TV series. Instead, the Popes have lots of nosy neighbors. (See Appendix B for more details.)

The pilot's credits give coproducership to Arthur Lubin and George Burns, and sign it a "McCadden Productions–Lubin Pictures" production. Neither Al Simon nor Herb Browar, future *Mister Ed* producers, had been directly involved with the McCadden pilot in 1958, though they did work with George Burns at General Service Studios. "I remember being interested in it and watching some of the dailies," Herb Browar recalls, but neither man had a direct hand in it. MCA, the distribution company for McCadden Productions, was unsuccessful in selling "The Wonderful World of Wilbur Pope" to any of the networks or to a sponsor, and to this day, the pilot has never appeared on television.

The Birth of Filmways TV Productions

At the same time that George Burns produced the *Mister Ed* pilot at General Service Studios, Al Simon, vice-president of McCadden Productions, was busy making shows like *Burns and Allen* (CBS, 1950–58), *Panic* (NBC, 1957) and *21 Beacon Street* (NBC, 1959). In 1959 Marty Ransohoff, chairman and CEO of Filmways, a very successful New York–based company which produced commercials, came to Hollywood and started up a television division, Filmways TV Productions. Ransohoff brought Al Simon on as president of the newly formed company.

Simon's TV background was impressive. Before working with George Burns, he was associate producer on the first season of *I Love Lucy* as well as *I Married Joan*. With McCadden Productions, Simon associate-produced *Burns and Allen* and *The Bob Cummings Show*. *Mister Ed*, like these other TV shows, was to be filmed out of General Service Studios on Las Palmas in Hollywood. Simon was actually the first person to bring a TV show, *I Love Lucy*, to a movie soundstage, in 1951. He was also the first to use the three-camera system to film *Lucy* in front of a live studio audience, which revolutionized the shooting of all television. When asked about his innovation of the three-camera technique, Simon, with characteristic modesty, claims that he was simply "at the right place at the right time. I just liked television."

Herb Browar (associate producer) and Johnny Nicolaides (V.P. business affairs), who both worked with George Burns at McCadden, also joined the staff at Filmways TV. They were a public company, listed on the American Stock Exchange, employing the best in the business. Now all they needed was a show . . . and a sponsor.

Meanwhile, the *Mister Ed* pilot, though unsold to date, had not gone completely unnoticed. George Nasser, who owned General Service Studios with his brother James, had seen the "The Wonderful World of Wilbur Pope" pilot and thought it would make a good short film to play in his movie theaters up north. One day, purely by coincidence, Nasser asked Al Simon to take a look at the *Mister Ed* pilot, and see what improvements might be made to it. "George Nasser was a big champion of *Mister Ed*," recalls associate producer Herb Browar. He believed, more than any other thing he had seen, it had possibilities, and so did Al Simon and I."

Courtesy of Herb Browar. Associate producer Herb Browar today, holding a Mister Ed promotional horseshoe distributed by Filmways, with his dog Morgan.

"I looked at the pilot, and I thought there were a lot of very good elements in it, but it had an enormous deficiency," recalls Simon. "There were a lot of production errors in it." For instance, "there was too much in the show that did not involve the horse, and it took far too long to actually introduce the talking horse. The characters were dull. There were a lot of people in the opening who weren't very important." Despite the pilot's weaknesses, Simon believed there was enough potential for a very funny TV show.

The real architects on *Mister Ed*: executive producer Al Simon and director/producer Arthur Lubin, July 1990.

Birth of "The Mister Ed Company"

George Burns was more than happy to enter into a deal with Filmways TV Productions to resurrect *Mister Ed*. If for no other reason, he "just wanted to get his $75,000 back!" Marty Ransohoff agreed to recast "The Wonderful World of Wilbur Pope" pilot right away. "I liked the basic concept and felt we could go with it with fresh casting." And so, "The Mister Ed Company" was born, a joint venture between Filmways, George Burns and Arthur Lubin.

The Studebaker Connection

So now Filmways TV Productions had their precious colt of a show, *Mister Ed*, but they still needed a buyer. They peddled it to the three networks, who all said no to the idea of a sitcom about a talking horse. Ransohoff learned that the Studebaker Corporation was looking for a show which would give them an identifiable personality, like the Dinah Shore–Chevrolet connection (*The Dinah Shore Chevy Show* ran on NBC from October 1956 to May 1963). Ransohoff presented the *Mister Ed* idea to Studebaker. They were interested in sponsoring the show, but knew they would have to sell the idea to all the Studebaker dealers across the country if they were ever to finance its production.

At that time George Burns came up with the idea of casting Alan Young in the lead as Wilbur Pope. As a result of the meetings that were held with Studebaker over the first half of 1960, Filmways prepared a presentation film for the company's annual sales conference in Chicago. The original Mc-Cadden pilot was edited down to contain the twelve funniest minutes. In addition, Filmways made a customized three-minute film short to precede the *Mister Ed* pilot. It was directed by Arthur Lubin and featured George Burns, who introduces the new cast—Alan Young, Connie Hines and Mister Ed, a different horse from the one in the 1958 pilot, who had been sold by this time. The sales film was a hit . . . but could enough money be raised to finance the show?

Steve Mudge, the man who managed the Studebaker account at the D'Arcy Advertising Agency, loved the presentation film that Filmways had shown at the sales convention and decided to follow through on the initial enthusiasm shown that day in Chicago. As his personal grail, he took on the task of selling *Mister Ed* to each of the dealers individually, traveling across the country over the next few months. He worked out a deal in which each Studebaker dealer would contribute twenty-five dollars for every car that was sold, and the Studebaker home office would match that contribution, meaning they would have fifty dollars per car sale toward the production of *Mister Ed*. Little did the consumers who bought a Studebaker in 1960 realize that their purchase was helping a talking horse get off the ground. TV stations in over one hundred markets agreed to run the Studebaker-sponsored show, starting in January 1961. Production on *Mister Ed* would begin in October 1960.

In Search of a Horse . . .

Trainer Les Hilton had sold the horse used in the Studebaker sales film. With only five weeks to go before shooting commenced, and with no star, things were a bit tense in expectation of finding a horse who could "hoof" the bill. "If anyone knew the horses in this town, Les did," Herb Browar boasts. "He knew every horse in the Valley." About a month before production, Hilton invited both Al Simon and Browar out to the San Fernando Valley to see a

© *1990 CBS Inc.*
A portrait of Ed with his trainer, Lester Hilton, from 1965.

palomino he had his eyes on. "All I cared about was, could Les train him, could he be ready?" admits Browar. "It was like casting, I was casting a horse!" Filmways paid $1,500 for the palomino, whose name was Bamboo Harvester. He had been a parade horse so he was used to crowds. Hilton had the horse gelded and took him back to his ranch to begin training.

Lester Hilton admitted to *TV Guide* in June 1962 that it was love at first sight: "I kept looking for the right horse in California, Arizona, Oregon and Washington, and finally found him 3½ miles from my home in San Fernando Valley. He was eight at the time, but he had the right kind of eyes and he sure was sensitive." The horse's vital stats, according to Orion Television, *Mister Ed*'s syndicator, were 1,100 pounds, fifteen hands high.

Al Simon recalls that his initial hesitation about the $1,500 price tag could have proved disastrous. While viewing the horse that afternoon, Hilton discreetly whispered to Simon that the wife of Carl Ward, Bamboo Harvester's owner, clearly did not want to sell the beautiful palomino. Upon hearing this, Simon immediately replied, "Sold, for fifteen hundred!" at which point the woman burst into tears. So Filmways finally had their new blond star (besides Connie Hines), and Les Hilton could get to work training the soon-to-be television idol.

Finding Mister Ed's Voice

The story surrounding the discovery of Mister Ed's voice is almost as mystical as the effect he had on *Mister Ed*'s fans, particularly the young viewers. Filmways did not reveal the actor's identity, former cowboy star Allan "Rocky" Lane, until well after the series was canceled. Alan Young tells a charming tale about how the producers first discovered Mister Ed's voice: "George Burns was listening to all these voices and he finally said, 'Stop ... Horses wouldn't talk like that.' Well, who knows what horses would talk like, but he knew that's how they wouldn't talk, so one day, there were a bunch of us out at Lester Hilton's little tiny wee house, he had a typical cowboy's house, and we were out there looking at this horse he had purchased, Mister Ed, and suddenly a voice came out of Les' little old house. There used to be a man called Allan 'Rocky' Lane who was a B-picture cowboy star, but then he came upon tough times, they stopped making those pictures, and now he was sleeping at Les Hilton's, on the couch, he had no place to go, and this voice came booming out of the little house, 'Hey, Les, where do ya keep the coffee?' and Al Simon turned and said, 'That's Ed's voice.' "

Although Simon doesn't claim to be the one who first discovered Rocky Lane that afternoon at Hilton's cottage, he does remember approving of his voice: "I was looking for a deep voice, Rocky's was right," the executive producer recalls. "Rocky truly thought he knew how a horse would react." Ironically, if things had been going better for Rocky when Filmways was casting *Mister Ed*, he might never have been asked to audition for the part of Ed's voice. Filmways needed an actor who didn't already have a full-time commitment to another studio, since the voice of Ed would need to work late hours, several days a week. That's why more famous "voice men" like Mel Blanc couldn't be seriously considered. Rocky, out of work, was perfect for the job.

In the 1940's Allan "Rocky" Lane was a dashing star of B-westerns for Republic Pictures.

"And They're off!"

Mister Ed premiered on January 5, 1961, in New York (airdates and times varied slightly from station to station). Approximately 115 stations across the country carried the show that first season (the first twenty-six episodes). Marty Ransohoff marvels at Studebaker's interest in *Mister Ed*: "Here was a show whose major appeal was four-to-nine-year-olds, we thought, being sponsored by an automobile company! Their hope was that the kids would bring their parents to the TV set, the young couples who were probably twenty-five to forty years old, whom they wanted to sell the cars to. Studebaker was gambling that the parents would be watching, too, and I think it paid off." An additional ironic twist was simply the fact that an automobile company was sponsoring a show about a *horse*. Astute viewers of *Mister Ed* will notice that Wilbur drives a Studebaker in some of the episodes.

To the Networks: The CBS Deal

It was June 1961. *Mister Ed* had just completed its first season in syndication, and although the series was successful, Studebaker did not want to fully finance the show for another season. It seemed only natural for Filmways to try the three networks next. "Marty and I went around to everybody, and the answer was no. We tried everywhere, we had special meetings," Al Simon recalls. And then one day, everything changed. Jim Aubrey, at that time the president of CBS, had seen *Mister Ed* in syndication and thought it was "the type of show that would appeal to the people who watched television." He contacted Marty Ransohoff and expressed interest in acquiring *Mister Ed* for his network. "It was a very flattering offer, because if the show were on the network instead of syndication, it would give him an additional run," explains Aubrey. "After the show came off the network, of course, he could have the syndication rights too, which he realized."

On June 22 William H. Hylan, CBS vice-president of sales administration, publicly announced that *Mister Ed* would debut on CBS in the upcoming fall season, and would be sponsored by Studebaker-Packard Corporation and Dow Chemical. *TV Guide* wrote in 1962 that CBS had been "hard-pressed for something lively to catch the kiddies (and their elders) in the 6:30 (ET) Sunday time slot," which was fine and dandy with Filmways. According to *TV Guide*, once the show moved to CBS on October 1, 1961, it immediately garnered a 20 Nielsen rating.

Before acquiring *Mister Ed,* Jim Aubrey had done his homework and knew that the syndicated series had been a thoroughbred winner in the local ratings during its first year. "Once I was attracted to the show, I had complete research done on it, which verified my impressions. I was amazed, as we went from market to market, to find out how appealing it was, which just convinced me more than ever that my liking *Mister Ed* wasn't in any way freakish, but it was something that the general public seemed to like just as well. So the research findings made the decision to buy the show that much easier."

Suspending Disbelief: The Critics

The press did not receive the new TV series about a talking horse with affection. Nor did the Hollywood community. It's not surprising, considering how much trouble Arthur Lubin and Al Simon had getting *Mister Ed* on the air to begin with. Alan Young remembers that when the Studebaker auto dealers first sold *Mister Ed* into syndication in 1960, the commercial paper called it "the freak sale of the month." Simon admits that members of the television community, especially those in New York, seemed "embarrassed" by the idea of a show starring a talking horse. When *Mister Ed* first appeared on television, "people thought it was a kids' show." And it took a long time to develop a faithful audience, one that appreciated the sophistication of the writing.

The cognoscenti just weren't getting it. Director Arthur Lubin told *TV Guide* that in the beginning he was "busily explaining to anyone who would listen that the trick was to really believe that the horse could talk." Today, it's hard for any fan of *Mister Ed* to imagine there would be any difficulty "suspending disbelief" in the theatrical sense. Sure, a horse can talk.

Variety had not been kind to *Mister Ed* in its January 11, 1961, review of the show's syndication premiere, "The First Meeting": "The sponsor hopes to repeat the success of Francis, the talking mule. Mister Ed is a talking horse, who has four gag writers. . . . The net of their efforts wasn't worth it. . . . Ed has a baritone voice, but he's built like either a gelding or a mare. . . . The frau of the roll-eyed Young is pert but unsure Connie Hines and as the customary caustic neighbor there is the abused Larry Keating. . . . Once in a while a good line gets across, but the laugh track for this maiden voyage into video program production by Filmways is paced far faster than most of the dialog. Examples of Mister Ed talking: 'How Now Brown Cow' and 'It's bigger than both of us.' Example of the ensuing laugh track: Uproarious. Maybe a talking horse is commercial, but there has to be more than an idea to put it across."

Didn't sound too promising. However, amid all the skepticism, *Mister Ed* was quietly winning its time period in practically every market that carried it. CBS' decision to buy *Mister Ed* for its 1961 season certainly lent prestige and credibility to a show that, just five months earlier, had been perceived as a big joke.

Variety's review of the October 1 premiere on CBS was far more hopeful. The trade publication was now calling *Mister Ed* "entertaining fare for this [family] audience." Though a talking horse was still deemed "a gimmick" by *Variety*'s reviewer, the show "is not entirely limited to the one joke pattern. Also supplied by scripters Lou Derman and Bill Crewson is some humorous material in the family comedy groove and several sly one-liners for the grown-ups in the audience." The premiere episode, "My Son, My Son," has "its funny moments." The cast "all perform in true situation comedy style, mugging and exclaiming effectively under producer-director Arthur Lubin's guidance. *Mister Ed* is a cute show in the family entertainment scheme."

Ahhh, now that's more like it! The show had paid its dues—it would never win an Emmy—but it was no longer the laughingstock of Hollywood, and more important, it had found its audience. Of course, these early critics did not have the benefit of time to know what a cult classic the show would become.

In March 1962, the series now firmly on the right track, *TV Guide* referred to *Mister Ed* as "one of the more pleasant phenomena of present-day TV." The show's dialogue is "surprisingly crisp" with "enough built-in humor to do credit to Noel Coward."

The Infamous *Mister Ed* Theme Song

Much of *Mister Ed*'s perennial success might be attributed to the sheer contagiousness and universality of its theme song, composed by the team of Jay Livingston and Ray Evans. Even if you're just a casual fan of the show, chances are you can recite the *Mister Ed* theme song in your sleep. Director Arthur Lubin marvels that no matter what cruise ship he's on in any part of the world, the band always seems to be playing the *Mister Ed* theme song for the amusement of passengers. That the tune caught on should be no surprise. The *Mister Ed* songsmiths weren't exactly chopped liver. Jay Livingston was the best in the business, with three Oscar-winning credits ("Mona Lisa," "Buttons and Bows" and "Que Sera, Sera," Doris Day's big hit) as well as the TV theme music to *Bonanza*.

Herb Browar describes the first time Filmways heard the theme song in 1960: "Jay came over himself and sat down at the piano. He sang the song for us; it was a demo and it had a catchy melody. We were going to have

Rocky Lane sing it—that is, until we found out he couldn't sing." Jay Livingston picks up the story: "Some time later, I received a call from Al Simon. Filmways sent a man named Raoul Kraushaar to Rome to record the score for a number of their pictures. It was a money-saving device. Al said that Raoul had gotten an Italian opera singer to do the [theme] song, and it was so bad—as you can imagine—that they couldn't use the track."

That explains why the first six *Mister Ed* episodes have theme song music only, and no lyrics. The producers were frantically trying to find someone who could do the words justice. So who finally ended up singing the *Mister Ed* theme in those velvety tones? "They had their first airdate coming up," Livingston remembers, "and Al said he liked the way I sang the song and asked me to sing it to the instrumental track they had made in Rome so they could go on the air." "Suddenly I remembered how Jay sang it," Browar adds. "I asked him to come down here. And I had a piano brought onto the sound stage, and I told Jay, 'We'll reverb [electronically echo] the areas that we have to reverb.' And we played it back. And it was terrific. And I said to Jay, 'You're gonna sing the song!' "

Although Livingston was told "they would find a professional singer in a week or two to replace my voice . . . they never [did], and that is me singing the theme song on all the *Mister Ed* episodes." Even the very deep "I am Mister Ed" at the end of the song? That's Jay too, courtesy of reverb!

Jay Livingston's daughter, Trav Livingston, explains that Ray Evans was the lyrical collaborator for the song. He and her father were lifelong friends and partners. To this day, the rights to the theme song are equally split between Jay Livingston Music and St. Angelo Music, Ray Evans' company.

Incidentally, Raoul Kraushaar is credited as "Music Supervisor" for the first *Mister Ed* season only. Browar explains that Kraushaar "didn't work out, so we got ahold of Dave Kahn, who is a very talented guy. Dave played clarinet with Clyde McCoy's band in the thirties when he must've still been a teenager." Kahn went on to be music supervisor for all the Filmways TV shows, overseeing the music on as many as five series at once.

THE FAR SIDE

By GARY LARSON

The famous "Mr. Ed. vs. Francis the Talking Mule" debates

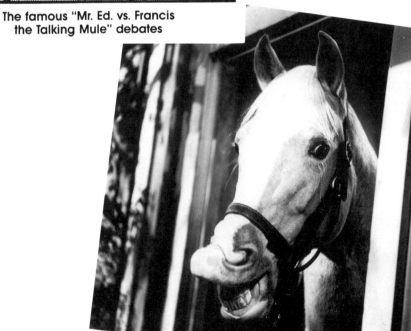

HOOFNOTES
Francis the Talking Mule vs.
Mister Ed the Talking Horse

SIMILARITIES

1. Both Francis and Ed have one human buddy—Peter Stirling and Wilbur Post respectively.
2. Both Francis and Ed are touts; they psychoanalyze racehorses for their mental blocks and befriend influential horses (those belonging to police and spies), to help their human cohorts succeed at romance and finance.
3. Both enjoy mouthing off to cops and swindlers, thus getting their human compatriots in deeper trouble.
4. Both stars are assisted, at times, by nylon string, tied to their bridles, and visible to the naked eye.
5. Both are enlisted by government agencies to solve top-secret cases, the U.S. Army for Francis and the "SIA" (Secret Intelligence Agency) for Ed. Francis credits the "FBI"—that is, "Feed Bag Information"—for his ability to tout!
6. The voices for both Francis and Ed were provided by veteran cowboy movie actors. Chill Wills spoke for Francis in six of the seven films, and Allan "Rocky" Lane for Ed.
7. Both Francis and the early Ed (1961–62) are crabby. (Note: Allan "Rocky" Lane mellowed his interpretation of Mister Ed with time. As the series progresses, the readings become goofier and play more to the audience; the voice becomes more aware of itself within the context of sitcom TV.)
8. Both Universal Studios (Francis) and Filmways (Mister Ed) kept the identity of the animals' voices secret, thus beefing up the mystery and adding to their fan-mail quotients.

9. Francis won the first Patsy Award (the Oscar/Emmy equivalent for animals) in 1951 (the award was actually inspired by Francis and was presented to the team of mules that played him); Mister Ed swept the TV Patsy Awards during his Hollywood reign, claiming victory in 1962, 1963, 1964 and 1965.
10. Francis and Ed were both trained by the marvelous and gentle Lester Hilton. Hilton was responsible for everything from getting the star mule to lose weight before the second Francis film commenced shooting, to teaching Ed how to exercise with Jack LaLanne.
11. Both Francis and Ed become football mascots—Francis of West Point's team in *Francis Goes to the Races,* and Ed for State U. in episode 6, "Sorority House."
12. Both Francis and Ed got more fan mail than their human costars.
13. Both stars talk with their mouths full; Rocky Lane, for the record, does a better job at depicting Ed's "hay gab" than Chill Wills does Francis'.
14. Both Francis and Ed act with the same supporting cast: Hayden Rorke (also Dr. Bellows in *I Dream of Jeannie*), Larry Keating (Ed's Roger Addison), Barry Kelly (Wilbur Post's less than endearing father-in-law, sans mustache as Roy Mallory in *Francis Goes to the Races*) and Clint Eastwood.

DIFFERENCES

1. Obviously, Francis is a mule (hybrid of a horse and an ass), and Ed is a horse, of course (though he thinks he's an ass in episode 101, "Ed the Donkey").
2. Francis "dislikes talking in front of strangers," but when push comes to shove, and Peter Stirling's neck is on the line, the words fly. Ed, of course, will only talk to Wilbur Post. This is no small point—*Mister Ed* gets its life from the built-in dilemma of Wilbur's "secret."
3. Peter Stirling emerges as a national hero, because he can reap the rewards of Francis' talents openly before the

rest of the world; Wilbur Post, on the other hand, though lovable, is perceived as very eccentric—he can never tell the real story about how Ed gets things done and is thus never taken seriously enough to earn mainstream respect.

4. Francis can fly (in the comic book version of Francis) when necessary; Ed needs to employ the services of a dilapidated air force bomber when he gets the urge to lift off.

5. Ed was much smarter than the mules who played Francis; the horse star performed all his own stunts, with the exception of one shot, where a "stand-in" was required; Arthur Lubin had to work with four different mules in each of his Francis films.

6. To save his human compatriot from murder charges, Francis testifies in court under oath (*Francis Covers the Big Town*); the most Ed can do to get Wilbur out of a Mexican jail in "Ed the Witness" is stomp out correct answers to arithmetic problems to prove he can identify the real culprit's license plate number.

7. Francis talks in pig Latin. Though Ed claims to have mastered Latin before English, the most exotic tongue we hear him utter is French, while reciting a lesson in "Ed Finally Talks": "*Je vois Marie . . .* I see Marie." Rocky Lane is at his rubbery-lipped best in pronouncing the French phrases.

8. Francis is a hard drinker who guzzles whiskey from a bucket while singing "My Bonnie Lies Over the Ocean"; the most potent potable Ed will imbibe is carrot juice on the rocks.

HOOFNOTES
Peer Pressure: Fantastic TV/ Film Animals

Mister Ed did have some film and TV predecessors and follow-ers who, like him, were intelligent, thinking animals. But he topped them all the moment he declared, "How Now Brown Cow."

○ **Topper** (CBS, 1953–55; ABC, Oct. 1955–Mar. 1956; NBC, June–Oct. 1956). Actually the first "fantasy" sitcom, it was based on two stories, "Topper" and "Topper Returns," written by Thorne Smith in the early 1930s. It starred Leo G. Carroll as the banker Cosmo Topper, the only person in the show who could see and hear the ghosts of George and Marion Kirby and their Saint Bernard dog ghost, Neil. This dog liked his brandy, similar to Francis the Talking Mule's hankering for beer, and the Brooks Mister Ed's weakness for bourbon. Edna Skinner (who played Kay Addison on *Mister Ed*) portrayed the Cook on *Topper* from 1953 to 1954.
○ **The People's Choice** (NBC, 1955–58). This McCadden sitcom, also produced by George Burns, took place in New City, California, and starred Jackie Cooper as Socrates "Sock" Miller, city councilman. Sock's basset hound Cleo comments on all human situations, just like Ed, except we hear her thoughts only. Voice of Cleo was played by Mary Jane Croft (*I Love Lucy*). During the closing credits, the dog flips up her ears.
○ **Hoofs and Goofs** (Film, 1957), a Three Stooges movie that features "Tony the Wonder Horse" as Birdie, the Stooges' reincarnated sister. Before Birdie is changed into a talking horse, she's played by Moe Howard in drag. This story is obviously influenced by Universal's Francis the Talking Mule character.

○ **Horsing Around** (Film, 1957) is the sequel to *Hoofs and Goofs* and includes more antics with Tony the Wonder Horse and Birdie.

○ **The Hathaways** (ABC, 1961–62) starred Peggy Cass, Jack Weston and The Marquis Chimps. The hubby thought his wife loved the chimps more than him . . . sound familiar?

○ **Green Acres** (CBS, 1965–71) is the wacky series also produced by Filmways. Arnold, the Ziffel's pig, is indeed a kindred spirit to Ed. Only difference is, and it's significant, we can't understand what Arnold's saying. Only the residents of Hooterville can decipher the piglet, who kept having to be replaced by Filmways because he grew too big. But Arnold watches TV and, like Ed, his romantic interludes are subtitled for our benefit. All in all, Arnold seems to be a good keeper of the intelligent animal torch.

○ **Me and the Chimp** (CBS, 1972) starred Ted Bessell (Don Hollinger on *That Girl*) as a dentist named Mike Reynolds with a wife, two kids and a curious, havoc-wreaking chimp named Buttons.

○ **Mr. Smith** (NBC, 1983) was a short-lived sitcom about a talking orangutan named Mr. Smith (played by C. J., a seasoned film star by this time). Before drinking a mysterious formula which transformed him into a military genius, he was plain old Cha Cha. Executive producer Ed Weinberger played the voice of Mr. Smith.

"People! All They Do Is Talk, Talk, Talk"

MISTER ED'S CAST OF CHARACTERS

CORRALING THE CAST

ALAN YOUNG as WILBUR POST

In 1962, while celebrating Alan Young's newfound career with the *Mister Ed* show, *TV Guide* also noted that his "rapid rise and fall in TV in the early Fifties is still one of the paradoxes of his time." Young was truly a television pioneer, one of the few people to make a successful transition from radio to the brand-new medium in 1950. Others like Fred Allen and *The Great Gildersleeves* had tried and failed. Still, the road has not always been smooth for the delightful comic actor.

Alan Young was born Angus Young on November 18, 1924, in Northumberland, England, to Scottish parents. Press materials report he was born in 1919, but Young says he had to fib about his age because he was so young when he started in show biz. When he was five, his family moved to

Courtesy of Alan Young.
Alan "Angus" Young plays the bagpipes, a skill that came to use several
times on *Mister Ed*, on his own *The Alan Young Show*, circa 1951.

Vancouver, Canada. As is the case with many talented comedians, the family
living room was his first stage, where he entertained family and friends with
comedic impressions of Gracie Fields and Scottish music hall entertainer
Harry Lauder. "As a kid, I'd copy Edward Everett Horton [Bullwinkle's narrator
of *Fractured Fairy Tales*]," Young reveals. "I'd do his walk. You start out
copying, then eventually you make it your own."

By the time he was thirteen, he had starred in every school comedy production and made his first professional appearance—a humorous monologue at his father's lodge hall, the Caledonian Society of Vancouver—for which he was paid the tidy sum of two dollars. At age fifteen, he was already writing and performing his own scripts on local radio, WCJOR out of Vancouver. By the time he was seventeen *The Alan Young Show* had premiered on Canadian network radio from Toronto. Young enlisted in the Canadian Navy during World War II and was honorably discharged in 1945. When he returned to Canada, he continued his comedy career via his radio show on the CBC.

One night in 1945, Hollywood agent Frank Cooper was trying to tune in to the *Duffy's Tavern* radio show (for which *Mister Ed* scripter Larry Rhine wrote). *TV Guide* documented what happened from there: "By accident, he got Young's Canadian station instead. 'He was hilarious,' recalled Cooper.

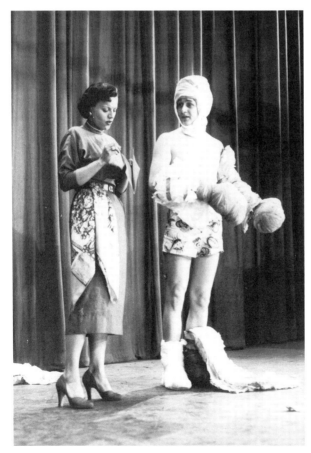

Courtesy of Alan Young.
Guest Kay Starr with Alan Young on The Alan Young Show, circa 1951.

'More than that, he could deliver lines. I sent for him.' " Young Alan Young arrived in New York, and *The Alan Young Show*, sponsored by Bristol Myers, became a summer replacement for Eddie Cantor's popular radio broadcast.

Young's radio show was a hit, and made the transition to television in 1950. He is credited as being the first comedian to receive an Emmy Award, picking up two that year for his live CBS show. But success did not last long.

Courtesy of Alan Young.
**Young communicates with a crow in *Androcles and the Lion*,
a 1952 film.**

"The work was backbreaking," *TV Guide* reported. "In those days a comic did virtually everything himself, up to and including his own choreography. When Young suggested that the network go from live to film, CBS balked and put him on suspension. . . . After CBS cancelled his show, Young made guest appearances for a few years. In 1957, he went to England for two years." He made several films, among them *Androcles and the Lion* (1952), *tom thumb* (1958) and *The Time Machine* (1960).

Fortunately for us, Young had trouble finding work upon his return to America in 1960. If things had been going well, he might never have accepted the role of Wilbur Post, a part which at first did not seem appealing, since it meant sharing the limelight with a horse. Filmways offered Young a piece of the show as an incentive to come on board.

Filmways Chairman Marty Ransohoff recalls his early involvement in casting Young for the lead: "Alan Young was very appealing. He had a marvelous quality. I had a major hand in casting Alan and Connie. Connie had done commercials for me in the fifties. They were a very appealing couple. George Burns and I were in sync in wanting Alan Young to play the lead."

CONNIE HINES as CAROL POST

When young Connie Hines first arrived in Hollywood in 1959, CBS was looking for "an all-American girl who could ski." Before she could blink, the aspiring actress was off to Europe to make a movie for the network's Rheingold Theater. "It was a wonderful love story with two wonderful German actors," Connie recalls. "After the movie, I went to London with the producer and his wife, then I went back to Paris."

When Miss Hines returned to Tinsel Town a few months later with her two letters of introduction, "nobody was here—they were all out of town." That didn't deter the Dedham, Massachusetts-born actress, who hailed from a show business family. She went on numerous casting calls that year, and met executive producer Al Simon when he was casting for his own production, *21 Beacon Street.* She didn't have enough acting credits at the time, but soon landed a role on *Whirlybirds*, a syndicated adventure series. Miss Hines describes the fortuitous way in which she obtained leading-lady status: "I did *Whirlybirds* and they called me back three times to read, to find somebody to play opposite me, and I didn't know that you were supposed to get paid for that. They were so impressed that I didn't ask to be paid they said, 'You know, we're going to take you off minimum and give you the going salary,' and that changed my status. I was now a leading lady. That meant no more walk-ons and no one-liners." The new leading-lady appeared on episodes of *Perry Mason* and *The Untouchables.*

When Filmways began casting for *Mister Ed* in 1960, Connie came in for a screen test. Despite her relatively light list of acting credits, the TV studio awarded Miss Hines the role of Carol Post. Associate producer Herb Browar remembers how excited she was when she heard the good news. The young actress was living in an apartment without a phone at the time and was actually waiting at the corner phone booth for the decision from Filmways. When the auspicious phone call arrived, "you should've heard her scream!" Browar gleefully recounts.

Confessions of a Sitcom Wife

Variety reviews of *Mister Ed* often described Miss Hines as "a captivating lass" and "a delectable miss," but rarely referred to the actress' thespian skills. Yet in spite of the lack of critical acclaim for her performance, she looks back with great fondness on her relationship with Alan Young, who helped her hone her acting technique. When asked what the best part of her *Mister Ed* experience was, Connie replies that it was her opportunity to work with Alan Young. "I learned more from Alan. He would stick up for me—I would get lost in the shuffle. If they were doing close-ups, Alan would be the first to say, 'Wait a minute, you didn't do Connie's close-up,' and they would say, 'Oh, yeah.' He taught me about comedy, listening, reacting, and also, he was my personal friend. He was always there for me."

Did Connie have a say in what her character said or did on the show? She tells a great anecdote about her struggle to put some variety into Carol's dialogue. "It was always very difficult to get me out of the barn. You know, where Wilbur was, and the horse. So it always ended up like, 'Wilbur, lunch is ready,' or 'Dinner's almost ready'—it was always something like that. And so I said to the writers, 'Please, give me something else to say. I'm tired of "Wilbur, lunch is ready!" ' and so they said, 'Okay, sure,' so they gave me another line, something like, 'See you later, honey.' And so I started to leave the barn, and I said, 'See you later, honey,' and Alan said, 'Yeah, go fix lunch!'

© *Orion Television.*
The Post "nuclear family" poses for a publicity photo in 1961. Of course, Carol has no idea that Ed is such a bookworm.

He was always doing something like that!" Connie obviously didn't suffer any complexes from her limited vocabulary, and speaks with the utmost affection about her teasing costar.

Setting the Record Straight

Some television chroniclers claim that Connie Hines considered her role as Carol Post simply "a steady paycheck." This stems from a *TV Guide* article published October 6, 1962, which gave her a bad rap. On the contrary, she felt very fortunate to get a starring role in a sitcom so early in her career, despite concern that she would get typecast (which she did, admittedly). Hines recalls that she ultimately took the role of Wilbur's wife, despite a lot of soul-searching and discussions with her agent, because: *"Mister Ed* had heart, it had a basic honesty about it. It was my feeling that it was a wonderful family situation, which I am very partial to. I knew it would be clean, I knew it would be fun. The producers, the people cared about each other."

She describes the development of her character from the first few episodes, to what we now recognize as Carol Post. "At first, they wanted to make me into a Gracie Allen, but it wouldn't work. I did it as much as I could, but you couldn't have three comics in the show," Connie astutely points out. "Somebody had to be the straight man, and I was the straight man. That's not to denigrate a straight man: If you don't do the straight man right, you don't get the comedy right." Not exactly the words of your run-of-the-mill dizzy dame . . .

EDNA SKINNER as KAY ADDISON, Next-door Neighbor #1

Actress Edna Skinner nearly missed out on the role of Kay Addison. "Constance Miller was set to do Kay," Edna remembers, "but when they did the tests, she and Connie looked like the Bobsey Twins—both were blonde and petite. I wore a mink stole in my test. Larry Keating [Roger Addison] went behind the camera and really supported me. He said, 'I like her.' And so they hired me."

The actress was born in Washington, D.C. She attended the American Academy of Dramatic Arts in New York with some not-too-shabby classmates: Kirk Douglas, Lauren Bacall and Jennifer Jones. Edna had a rich theater background before coming to Hollywood. "Broadway just glistened from 1938 through the 1940s," the actress recalls. In fact, one of the two

**Edna Skinner portrays Kay Addison, who portrays
Queen Isabella in "Ed Discovers America,"
a 1963 holiday episode.**

highlights of her performing career was starring on Broadway as Ado Annie in *Oklahoma*, following Celeste Holm. The other highlight? "Playing Kay Addison on *Mister Ed*," of course. The actress, a prize-winning fisherwoman who now makes her home in Oregon, considers the series "a legend."

During World War II, Edna was a commander in the American Women's Voluntary Services and sold war bonds. She played Maggie the cook in *Topper* from 1953 to 1954 and appeared in the TV version of *The Great Gilder-sleeves*.

LARRY KEATING as ROGER ADDISON, Next-door Neighbor #1

"We considered Larry from the beginning because of his *Burns and Allen* association," claims Herb Browar. Keating played George and Gracie's next-door neighbor, Harry Morton, in *The Burns and Allen Show* from 1953 to 1958 (he was the fourth and final Harry Morton). Al Simon praises the late Keating, who passed away during the start of *Mister Ed*'s third season on CBS, for having "a real comic sense." He was unanimously loved by all the *Mister Ed* cast members, who remember him for his warmth and professionalism.

© *1990 CBS Inc.*
**Larry Keating plays Roger Addision on the verge of
a nervous breakdown in this production still from
"Ed the Emancipator," 1963.**

BARRY KELLY as the Grouchy Father-in-law

Every sitcom needs a curmudgeonly in-law, and Barry Kelly fit the role to a tee. The actor first played Carol's father, Mr. Higgins, during the series' initial season on CBS, in "Horse Wash." Arthur Lubin had worked with Kelly before, in *Francis Goes to the Races.*

© *1990 CBS Inc.*
Barry Kelly as Carol's father, Mr. Higgins, is too exasperated to even look at his son-in-law in "Be Kind to Humans," 1963.

FLORENCE MacMICHAEL as WINNIE KIRKWOOD, Next-door Neighbor #2

The gentle Miss MacMichael began her acting career on Broadway and later performed on radio in New York with Henry Morgan, Phil Silvers and Jackie Gleason. She played the occasional role of Mrs. Florence Pearson, also a neighbor, on *My Three Sons* from 1960 to 1961. Herb Browar still marvels that Florence, who was married to a postman, ever pursued an acting career: "She was too nice a person to be in the business." A 1963 press release cited "reading cookbooks" as Miss MacMichael's hobby. Maybe Herb has a point there . . .

LEON AMES as Col. GORDON KIRKWOOD, Next-door Neighbor #2

Leon Ames went to New York to pursue a stage career as soon as he graduated from high school. He's starred in many plays and feature films, including *The Murders in the Rue Morgue, Meet Me in St. Louis,* with Judy Garland, and *The Absent-minded Professor,* with Fred MacMurray.

Prior to *Mister Ed,* his television credits included the role of Father Day in

© *Orion Television.*
Leon Ames and Florence MacMichael as Gordon and Winnie Kirkwood, the second set of next-door neighbors, 1964.

Life With Father (CBS, 1953–55), and for one season only, he played Stanley Banks, a man who can't get used to his daughter's upcoming wedding, in *Father of the Bride* (CBS, 1961). Ames was one of the founders of the Screen Actors Guild, and served as president in 1958.

GREAT CHARACTER PROFILES

WILBUR POST (ALAN YOUNG) (1961–66)

PROFESSION: Architect (self-employed)
BIRTHDAY: some time between April 20 and May 20 (Taurus)
HOROSCOPE SIGN: Taurus (at least, that's what he says in "Dragon Horse")
MARITAL STATUS: Married in 1958 (he says he's been married for three years in "Stable for Three," a 1961 episode)
ADDRESS: 17230 Valley Spring Lane
PHONE NO.: STate 1-1781 (1961–62); POplar 9-1769 (1963–66)
FAVORITE DISH: Pot roast
SHOE SIZE: 9½ W
HOBBIES: Magic; landscaping

Wilbur Post is, first and foremost, the ultimate straight man to a horse. He's an architect who works out of the barn, a detail which fellow humans find at least slightly strange. "I like working at home, where I have companionship," he explains to his wife. "Someone who cares. Someone who gives me inspiration. Someone who loves me for what I am, not just for the oats and hay he can get out of me." Carol fumes of course when she realizes that Wilbur's not talking about her ("The Horsetronaut").

Wilbur was born in Connecticut and went to school at UCLA. He was practically raised by his Aunt Martha, played by Eleanor Audley, and his nickname as a baby was "Weebie." As a child, he had long blond locks. In one episode, he says that his father never could find work, although we meet his father, a Scottish farmer, also played by Young, courtesy of *Patty Duke*–like trick photography, in episode 56. Wilbur was a member of the wrestling and debating teams in college, and carried water for the football team, under the sorry nickname of "Dippy."

Courtesy of Herb Browar.
Filmways cast and crew celebrate writer Lou Derman's birthday, September 1961. Pictured, left to right: Herb Browar, Alan Young, Connie Hines, Lou Derman doing the honors, Edna Skinner, Al Simon and Larry Keating. Young and Keating sport their caps from "The Hunting Show" episode.

Wilbur tends to get caught up in things. In "Home Sweet Trailer," his assignment from Carol is to regain control of his house from Gordon Kirkwood, who has usurped it with his wife. In the course of his mission, which he better "choose to accept," Gordon insists that Wilbur refer to him by first name, rather than so formally as "Colonel." Wilbur is so tickled by this newfound license to call his former commanding officer "Gordon" (he actually considers it a personal victory) that he completely forgets his initial objectives. Carol's threat to go home to mother helps him to remember quickly, though.

In many ways, the character of Wilbur Post is a country bumpkin, similar to Young's character Aaron Slick in the 1952 film *Aaron Slick From Pumpkin Creek*. Alan Young's gift for slapstick, physical humor, in the tradition of *The Alan Young Show*, is obvious in scenes where Wilbur "scientifically" demonstrates something. In "Wilbur in the Lion's Den," he tries to show Ed how easy it is to put together a kite, but gets stuck with the glue and tears the kite. In "Ed's Cold Tail," he shows Carol and Winnie how to stack food into a refrigerator. This is one of the funniest scenes in the series, with flawless timing and reaction shots between Young, Connie Hines and Florence MacMichael. There is a brilliant contrast between how smart Wilbur *thinks* he is, including condescending remarks like, "*What* do we do with the eggs?" and the foolish things he's actually doing, such as combining orange juice with buttermilk. He's absolutely perfect at playing "Emperor"-type characters (as in "Emperor's New Clothes").

The Doubters

Neighbor #1: ROGER ADDISON (LARRY KEATING) (1961–63)

PROFESSION: Retired businessman
HOBBIES: Investing; raising prize roses and apples; golf

He's a descendant of Paul Revere, known as Sour Puss, Lemon Puss, Doll, Diamond Jim and Mother's Little Financial Genius. He's hopelessly afraid of his moocher brother-in-law, Paul Fenton, and even hides from him in the closet in one show. He has a fetish for his prize roses—his wife Kay wants to sue them for "alienation of affections." He's a sucker for a good poker game, even if it's with card sharks. He makes fun of Ed constantly but gets his just desserts in "Ed the Horse Doctor" when he has to kiss the palomino. He's got a bit of the vaudeville in him—he performs ukulele with Kay occasionally for community theater projects, just like Ethel and Fred Mertz in *I Love Lucy*. He's always trying to make a profit, even if it means fooling Wilbur. Talking animals—horses and cockatoos—call him "a cheapskate." Whenever he's scoring big bucks in some scheme, he sings "Rock-a-bye Baby." He attended State University and was a member of the fraternity Sigma Nu Delta. He was the college bicycle champ—nicknamed "Mr. Wheels"—and head of the debating team. He goes down to Palm Springs whenever he's in need of some R&R.

His business ventures include owning a piece of the Armstrong Circus, owning a piece of a racehorse, Lady Sue, and financing the Addison Towers, which he commissions Wilbur Post to design. He constantly makes fun of his wife's cooking and bemoans her spending habits. He is royal keeper of the "charge-a-plate"—credit card to us modern folk.

Neighbor #2: GORDON KIRKWOOD (LEON AMES) (1963–65)

PROFESSION: Retired air force colonel
ADDRESS: 7138 Valley Spring Road

He's Wilbur's retired commanding officer from "The Great Struggle"—World War II. The air force calls him out of retirement for a short stint to help experiment with chimps as jungle sentries. Unlike George Burns, he is not enamored of his wife Winnie's Gracie Allen–like, nutsy disposition. He's always telling Wilbur to sell Mister Ed. His favorite expression for the architect is: "Pathetic ... a child's mind in a man's body." Whenever Wilbur wreaks havoc in the Kirkwood residence, which is often, Gordon turns on his military demeanor and barks: "At-ten-tion! A-bout face! Hup two three four," as Wilbur obediently exits in automaton fashion. Unlike Addison, who can be rather charming at times, Gordon Kirkwood is only witty at the expense of other people (or horses).

Father-in-law: MR. HIGGINS (BARRY KELLY) (1961–66)

PROFESSION: Retired
RESIDENCE: Somewhere out of town

This guy is so uptight, he doesn't even have a first name. He travels to the Posts by airplane, but from where we never find out. He lives near Carol's aunts and uncles and stays in touch with them. Despite aggravation from Wilbur, he spends his vacations with Carol and her hubby. He's got a wife, but he never travels with or talks about her. He's got enough disposable income to invest in real estate, even if it's through dealings with shysters. He considers himself a very good judge of character, but we learn in "Horse Wash" that this isn't true. He intends to leave his daughter a significant inheritance but threatens Wilbur that he'll "live, and live and live" if Wilbur doesn't stay out of his way. While staying with the Posts, he's put in charge of the Pioneer Day Parade. Mr. Higgins appears in the last five episodes—shows 139 through 143.

The Ladies

The Wife: CAROL POST (CONNIE HINES) (1961–66)

MAIDEN NAME: Higgins
PROFESSION: Housewife (not including brief stint as dance instructor)
ADDRESS: 17230 Valley Spring Lane
PHONE NO.: STate 1-1781 (1961–62); POplar 9-1769 (1963–66)
MEASUREMENTS: 36″, 22″, 36″
WEIGHT: 110 pounds

Her character has "about as much depth as a Saltine cracker," wrote *TV Guide* in 1962, but Connie Hines considers the character she played "cute and adorable. She really represented the kind of female that there was in the fifties. Where you didn't come out and say, 'Look, I'm a partner in this' or 'I'm gonna have a say in this, too.' You know, she was manipulative."

© *Orion Television.*

Deep thinker or not, Carol Post deserves a medal for her willingness to hang in there, in the midst of what must have seemed like sheer lunacy. She was quite a devoted wife to Wilbur. The most spiteful thing she does in the series is serve Wilbur fish, in various forms, three meals a day for several days to make a point about loosening up on the purse strings.

She doesn't take up too many causes in the course of the series. Usually, her extreme actions, such as getting a job teaching the cha-cha, are a result of a fight with Wilbur over money. She does belong to the requisite Ladies Committee, however, and sponsors teas and talent shows.

She really cares for Mister Ed, her competitor, and ultimately sacrifices her own material comforts so that Wilbur and Ed can remain a team.

Neighbor #1: KAY ADDISON (EDNA SKINNER) (1961–63)

MAIDEN NAME: Fenton
PROFESSION: Housewife
MARITAL STATUS: Twenty-plus years, to Roger "Doll" Addison

"Marriage is composed of a team—the worker and the shirker, and you know who the shirker is," Kay preaches to a more naive Carol Post in one show.

Kay is a real "SAP" (sitcom American princess). Cruel and unusual punishment for Kay translates to Roger taking away her "charge-a-plate" for a two-month stint. Even transported back to Plymouth Rock as a Pilgrim ("Ed the Pilgrim"), she takes shillings out of the governor's (Addison's) pocket so she can go to "a sale on spinning wheels." It's great how the scripters keep her character consistent. She even refers to her hubby as "dolleth," an Old English version of the "doll" she normally calls him.

She's a cross between Katharine Hepburn (neither she nor Kate can cook their way out of a paper bag) and Lisa Douglas (Eva Gabor) of *Green Acres*. "I just love the country," Kay exclaims to her husband in one episode. "If they could bring it to the city, I'd live there all my life!" which is *exactly* the sentiment of the *Green Acres* theme song: "The chores . . . the stores/Fresh air . . . Times Square, etc."

When Roger Addison leaves home after a spat, he misses Kay's cooking, which is illogical given Kay's deficiencies in that department. In fact, in another episode, Roger comments that "opening a can" is the height of Kay's culinary skills.

Neighbor #2: WINNIE KIRKWOOD (FLORENCE MacMICHAEL) (1963–65)

PROFESSION: Housewife
ADDRESS: 7138 Valley Spring Road

Originally, Filmways wanted the role of Carol Post to be more like the lovable Gracie Allen. That never really happened. It wasn't until the introduction of Winnie Kirkwood in the fall of 1963 that we got a truly nutty female member of the *Mister Ed* ensemble.

Classic "Winnie moves" include totaling a brand-new sports car, forgetting to mail an insurance payment for her mink stole, and sharpening pencils continuously for her husband in an effort to be more involved in his hobbies. She unconditionally accepts the grouchiness of her husband, who, it turns out, married her for her money. When Winnie and Carol go to a crackpot gypsy to have their palms read, Madame Zenda tells Winnie that her husband treats her like a doormat. She complains to Carol that this is absolutely untrue. "No?" Carol begs to differ. "You have 'Welcome' written all over your face" ("Ed Visits a Gypsy").

WINNIE'S MOST CHARACTERISTIC LINES

○ "For a moment, I thought it was a camel upside down." ("Old Swayback")

○ On Ed's wearing sneakers: "You're lucky Mister Ed isn't a filly, he'd be running in high heels." ("Ed the Race Horse")

○ To spatting Wilbur and Gordon: "Now you two kiss and make up, or do whatever it is that men do." ("Ed the Pilot")

WINNIE'S MOST UNCHARACTERISTIC LINE

○ "I think I know how to get that Japanese beetle [new secretary] out of my husband's garden." ("Ed in the Peace Corps")

It's way too calculating and mean-spirited a remark to have come from Winnie's gentle soul.

The Desperate Music Producer: PAUL FENTON (JACK ALBERTSON) (1961–63)

CONNECTION: Brother to Kay Addison
PROFESSION: President of the Paul Fenton Record Company; music producer; part-time loafer
BUSINESS ADDRESS: 1040 North Sunset Blvd.
ARCHENEMY: Brother-in-law Roger Addison

"When he's not talking on the telephone, he's in the refrigerator. He's wearing my clothes, he's eating my food, he's destroying my house—he's not a brother-in-law, he's a 200-pound termite," Roger Addison laments about Paul Fenton in "Mister Ed's Blues." Addison will never forgive Fenton for being the first one to kiss Kay at their wedding.

Fenton produces Ed's two musical megahits, "Pretty Little Filly" and "Empty Feedbag Blues." Both songs revive the producer's career.

He's the master of catchphrases and buzzwords ("The blues are coming back bigger than ever"), calling Wilbur names like Chickie Baby, Wilbur Baby and Kid and encouraging him with pugilistic pep talks: "Keep in there, keep sluggin', keep pitchin', you'll be great, atta boy!" He's absolutely pitiful as the ingratiating, groveling, financially desperate music producer. Both songwriting episodes, "Ed the Songwriter" and "Mister Ed's Blues," do a good job of highlighting the comic ability of Jack Albertson.

If Paul Fenton were living today, he might possibly be producing Richard Simmons' exercise videotapes or investing in truffle pigs.

GUEST STARS ON *MISTER ED*

Mister Ed, like many sitcoms of the day, featured star turns by several film and television personalities, which helped to boost ratings and garner press attention. As director of *Mister Ed,* Arthur Lubin got to handpick the guest stars and featured character actors. He recalls that some of the celebrities, such as Zsa Zsa Gabor, didn't command as hefty a fee as others. Jack Albertson really helped the show a lot with his "big name," according to the director.

HOOFNOTES

MISTER ED'S SPECIAL GUEST STARS

○ Jack Albertson (Broadway star; *Burns and Allen*)
○ Elvia Allman (*Burns and Allen*)
○ Eleanor Audley (who went on to *Green Acres*, playing Oliver's mother)
○ Jack Bailey (M.C. of *Queen for a Day*)
○ Raymond Bailey (*The Many Loves of Dobie Gillis, My Sister Eileen, The Beverly Hillbillies*)
○ Jacqueline Beer (*Burns and Allen, 77 Sunset Strip*)
○ William Bendix (*The Life of Riley*)
○ Oscar Beregi
○ Bobby Buntrock (Harold Baxter a.k.a. Sport on *Hazel*)
○ George Burns as himself
○ Spring Byington (Broadway star; *December Bride, Laramie*)
○ Sebastian Cabot (*Suspense, Checkmate*, later on *Family Affair*)
○ Hans Conreid (*The Danny Thomas Show*)
○ Nancy Culp (*Beverly Hillbillies*)
○ Johnny Crawford (*The Rifleman*)
○ Willie Davis as himself (Los Angeles Dodgers)
○ Richard Deacon (*Burns and Allen, The Dick Van Dyke Show*, later on *The Mothers-in-law*)
○ Donna Douglas (Elly May on *The Beverly Hillbillies*)
○ Leo Durocher as himself (manager, Los Angeles Dodgers)
○ Clint Eastwood as himself (*Rawhide*)
○ Victor French (*Get Smart*)
○ Leo Fuchs
○ Zsa Zsa Gabor as herself
○ Thomas Gomez (Broadway star)
○ Alan Hale, Jr. (*Gilligan's Island*)
○ Barry Kelly (*Francis Goes to the Races*)
○ Sandy Koufax as himself (Los Angeles Dodgers)
○ Jack Kruschen (*Hong Kong*)

○ Jack LaLanne as himself
○ Charles Lane (*Dear Phoebe, The Lucy Show, Petticoat Junction*)
○ Marc Lawrence
○ Mike Mazurki (later on *It's About Time*)
○ Jon Provost (*Lassie*)
○ Hayden Rorke (*Mr. Adams and Eve, No Time for Sergeants*, later as Dr. Bellows on *I Dream of Jeannie*)
○ Johnny Roseboro as himself (Los Angeles Dodgers)
○ Benny Rubin
○ Irene Ryan (*The Beverly Hillbillies*)
○ Vin Scully—voice-over as himself (TV announcer for Los Angeles Dodgers)
○ Moose Skowran as himself (Los Angeles Dodgers)
○ Ricky Starr (a midwestern college wrestling champion with a unique comedy gimmick combining ballet with wrestling)
○ Sharon Tate
○ The Great Blackstone as himself
○ Miyoshi Umeki (MGM's *Tea House of the August Moon; The Courtship of Eddie's Father*)
○ Abigail Van Buren as herself
○ Mae West as herself

Alan Young with guest stars
Jack Albertson and Zsa Zsa
Gabor in "Zsa Zsa," 1961.

Courtesy of Alan Young.
Abigail Van Buren advises Ed
on his love life in "Ed Writes
Dear Abby," 1963.

Guest star Irene Ryan poses
as a wax figure along with
Mister Ed and Alan Young
in this publicity still from
"Love and the Single
Horse," 1965.

MISTER ED'S REGULARLY FEATURED PLAYERS

- ○ Hazel Shermet
- ○ James Flavin (*Man With a Camera, Burns and Allen, The Roaring Twenties*)
- ○ Olan Soule (*My Three Sons*)
- ○ Robert Carson
- ○ Neil Hamilton (went on to play Commissioner Gordon on *Batman*)
- ○ Frank Wilcox (*Burns and Allen, The Beverly Hillbillies*)
- ○ Henry Corden (succeeded Alan Reed as the voice of Fred Flintstone)
- ○ Nick "Nick-o-Demus" Stewart (*The Alan Young Show, Amos 'n' Andy*)
- ○ John Qualen
- ○ Richard Reeves (*Date With the Angels*)
- ○ Ben Welden (generic thug on *Superman*)
- ○ Kathleen Freeman (*Topper*)
- ○ Barbara Morrison
- ○ Rolfe Sedan (the mailman in *Burns and Allen*)
- ○ George Neise (*Witchita Town*)
- ○ Joe Conley
- ○ Lee Goodman
- ○ Percy Helton (went on to *The Beverly Hillbillies*)
- ○ Henry Norell (*Oh, Those Bells*)
- ○ Sandra Gould (Gladys Kravitz in *Bewitched*)
- ○ Harold Gould
- ○ Les Tremayne (*The Adventures of Ellery Queen*)
- ○ Lou Krugman
- ○ George O'Haulon
- ○ Hank Patterson (*Gunsmoke;* later, Fred Ziffel on *Green Acres*)
- ○ Connie Hines' Australian silky terrier, Tiger

"Wilbur, Isn't It Amazing What You Can Teach an Animal to Do?"

•••

ALL ABOUT ED, PUNKIN, ROCKY AND LES

A behind-the-scenes look at *Mister Ed* reveals what you might expect from a show whose star was an animal: unique production challenges and situations not common to run-of-the-mill sitcoms. First and foremost, trainer Les Hilton was responsible for Ed's choreography. Did Ed *really* know that he was talking on the phone? Maybe not, but once you combined the gesture with Rocky Lane's gravelly wisecracking, who wouldn't be convinced that Ed was calling the saddle shop to order himself a nice gift?

Hilton was the liaison between the animal world and the human world, who carefully protected his star pupil. Adjustments in schedule were an everyday occurrence—the humans had to wait for Les to teach Ed his scene (luckily, the horse was very adept) before they could rehearse. Setting Ed up to talk was also time-consuming, so Arthur Lubin waited until the end of the day to do the horse's talking scenes. Teaching Alan Young how to ride and give commands to Ed (the actor had never been on a horse before *Mister Ed*) took extra sessions on the weekends. Yet no one seemed to mind, except maybe Ed, who rushed off the set at the end of a day's work so he could go home and chow down. During the shooting season, Ed maintained a busy schedule, reporting to the set at General Service Studios about four days a week.

Mister Ed's Ancestry

Did you ever wonder what Mister Ed was like before he became a TV star? Fortunately for *Mister Ed* fans, a woman named Janie Nicolaides, who knew Mister Ed in his earliest days, when he was still called Bamboo Harvester, wrote up the history of Ed's life in 1979. Janie is married to John Nicolaides, who was the financial vice-president of Filmways TV Productions. Her father, Red Foster, was a horse trader in the San Fernando Valley at the time of Ed's birth. Here, from her illuminating history of Mister Ed's life, is an excerpt which describes the star's "roots":

Courtesy of Alan Young.
Ed flanked by his trainer, Les Hilton, and Alan Young, circa 1961.

Mister Ed was foaled in 1949 in El Monte, California. His dam was an Arabian by the name of Zetna. . . . His sire was Chief Tonganozie, a half Arabian who was by The Harvester. . . . [Ed] grew up to be a beautiful stallion and was ridden many times in the Rose Parade, as his Grandsire The Harvester had been.

Zetna and Chief must have been mighty proud of their son as they watched him on the TV set each week, though puzzled at his Hoosier accent.

Behind Every Great Horse Is a Great Trainer: Lester Hilton

Les Hilton was a remarkable trainer of horses. He had a solid background training animals and was well respected in the industry. He'd served his apprenticeship under Will Rogers and got his professional training working with the mules on the Francis films for Universal. The first trainer assigned to Francis was fired because he hit the animal all the time, Arthur Lubin remembers. So Les came on during the second Francis film that Lubin made, and it was to be the start of a fifteen-year association between the two men.

Hilton was extremely modest, never even asking to be named in the *Mister Ed* credits. Arthur Lubin and Al Simon agree that if he had asked for the credit, he would've received it without hesitation. Physically, he was a small man, about 5'9", with a weathered face. "He was like Charlie Chaplin, always kicking the ground," Herb Browar describes. "Very shy. He really knew horses. Usually these guys don't get attached to horses, but Les kept saying he'd never met a horse like Ed. He kept that horse immaculate."

A Star's Treatment

Les was insistent that he be Ed's primary caretaker, dispensing both food and affection. He did not allow anyone else to feed Ed carrots, unless the script dictated that Alan Young share a carrot with his horse. The trainer's insistence was not a mere case of overprotectiveness. If the horse was to master all the skills that were required of him on the show, it was essential that Ed develop a primary bond to his trainer.

"Les said, 'I do not want everybody to come up to Ed and caress him

Les Hilton instructs Ed for a time change promo done by CBS in 1962, to announce the show's schedule change.

because I give him his food, I give him his love, I give him everything, and I don't want anybody else to interfere with me,' " Al Simon explains. "That's why Ed would try so hard to do something. When there was a question of learning something for the show, he worked so hard, you could see he strained to do it, and he was doing it for Les."

How much did a hardworking horse like Ed consume each day? Orion Television reports that Mister Ed ate twenty pounds of hay and drank more than a gallon of sweet tea each day. On the show, his character complains that hay tastes terrible. He only drinks water, carrot juice on the rocks, hot carrot juice (when he's feeling under the weather) and his own beverage concoction, Wilburini, named for his loving owner.

Ed had his own "star's stall" at the back of the soundstage. "There was a row of dressing rooms for the actors and at the end was a scene dock, with an area there that was big enough for us to build him a stall," Herb Browar recounts. "And over the top we had a roof for him. The wrangler who worked with Les made sure there was enough hay, and we had this big gold star that we tacked up on the top of the stall, and we had a place for his blanket, and he was treated like a star. He got fed at the end of the day."

TV Guide downplayed the real Ed's pampering (we know Wilbur spoiled Ed silly on the show) in June 1962: "For Mister Ed, there's no lush diet or aristocratic stable. When he performs he gets no sugar lumps or other tidbits, just a friendly pat or an encouraging word. If he doesn't come through he may even receive a not-so-friendly spank on the rump."

"Les would never strike him," Alan Young explains. "He would just take a long whip and he used to hold it across Ed's forelegs so Ed wouldn't talk. . . . And now and again when Ed just got a little fed up, like a child, Ed would

Hilton works with Ed on the set with special guest star Mae West in 1964.

say, 'Oh, I've had enough of this, I'm bored,' [and] Les would slap him on the hooves. And it used to upset him so much, he'd come over to me. And he'd put his muzzle right by my neck." Ed does this a lot on the show anyway, in the closing scenes when he's standing by Wilbur at his desk.

Mister Master

"Anything we wanted him to do, he'd do. When you're setting up a scene, there's a lot of people moving around, adjusting the lights, doing things, and Ed would just be standing there," marvels Herb Browar. "It was kind of incongruous—everyone was running around and he was just standing there."

The horse got so good at his job that he sometimes performed scenes flawlessly. Alan Young jokes that scenes usually had to be repeated for *his* benefit, not for Ed's. "Ed did a master scene once with his trainer," scripter Ben Starr remembers with awe. "Arthur Lubin would tell Les Hilton what Ed should do. I watched that horse open that stall door. He took the blanket off Wilbur, who was sleeping. Then he went over and covered Addison with Wilbur's blanket. Then the horse walked back into his stall. It was a master scene" (from "The Bashful Clipper").

Alan Young describes another scene, performed perfectly, palomino style: "There's one show where Ed had to walk into my office, go over to the filing cabinet, open a drawer, take out carrots ('C' for carrots) and then close the drawer, and then go over and drop them on the desk. He did that in one take, and when he finished, the whole crew burst into applause." No, Ed didn't take a bow, though his character was quite the ham.

"Ed did some remarkable things," Al Simon recalls. In a couple of episodes, "The Horsetronaut" and "Ed the Sentry," Les Hilton really gets to showcase Ed's smarts. The horse proves to be so intelligent during military psychological exams, for example, giving the doctors their stethoscopes and handkerchiefs, unplugging electric currents attached to carrots and throwing a basket of peppered apples out the window, that the testers are afraid Ed will steal *their* jobs! "Horses are supposed to be dumb," reminds Simon. "Of course Ed himself would argue against that." And, of course, he does.

Who Says You Can't Teach an Old Horse New Tricks?

Ed was not a trick horse, which meant that Les Hilton had to *unteach* him every time he taught him something. For example, if there was a scene where Ed had to come in, pick up the phone and answer it, the next time Ed walked in, he'd head for the phone and pick it up. So Hilton had to unteach him. Alan Young recalls that Hilton would tell his star pupil, 'It's a whole new scene, you do what I tell you.' So Ed would come in the door and look around, 'What do I do now?' " At that point, the set would be turned over to Les so that he could teach Ed whatever it was he had to do. And because Ed was so bright, he learned his scene in fifteen minutes. "And he would do things in one take," boasts Young.

Ed was better versed in film production than most graduate film students. He finally caught on that the only time a scene was actually being filmed was when clapsticks were used at the beginning to sync up sound. Consequently, if Ed didn't hear clapsticks during rehearsal, he wouldn't perform! The joke on the set was that they had to use clapsticks all the time, even in rehearsal, to convince Ed to give it his all.

Ed could answer commands of twenty to twenty-five words from Les, but he also got to know what "That's a wrap!" meant, which of course was spoken for the benefit of the humans on the set. And when Arthur Lubin made such an announcement at the end of a day's shooting, Ed would be the first one to bolt for the door. He didn't even wait for Les Hilton. "Nothing stood in his way," Herb Browar remarks of the horse's "type A" behavior. "Les owned a horse trailer, and at the end of the day, he'd put Ed's blanket on him, get him ready to go, and then he'd go do some paperwork in the front with one of the wranglers. And while he was there, Ed would start kicking the front of the trailer. He wanted to go home and eat, and in traffic if the light was too long, he'd start kicking the trailer. We had to replace that metal a couple of times."

Ed the Dancing Fool

One way that Mister Ed's writers let us know just how hep this horse is, is by making him a hipster, literally. Trouble is, how many steps can a horse do? No matter how badly a palomino wants to pirouette, a horse still has two left feet. However, Ed did master one key dance routine, performed exclusively by his hind quarters. It's very simple: step left, together; step right, together. And repeat. Camera medium close-up on Ed's rear.

I call it the "all-purpose" dance because it's used to represent every dance step known to mankind, according to the demands of the particular script. You can tell what step Ed is supposed to be doing by his costume. If a story takes place in Hawaii, Ed wears a grass skirt, we hear canned Hawaiian music, and we see "Horse Hula"! If on the other hand, he's glued to the TV set watching Jack LaLanne, and he begins to shake his booty, Ed's dance is "Calisthenics" (what we moderns call aerobics). And if there's any type of contemporary theme dealing with rock-and-roll, and Ed happens to be wearing a long wig, well, naturally, he's doing the Twist, the then-current dance sensation. Trainer Les Hilton boasted to *TV Guide* in 1962 about the horse's dancing acumen: "Why, it would take even a brilliant horse a couple of days to learn the Cooch, which is what they called the Twist several generations ago. Ed learned it in 20 minutes." Perhaps it was so easy because Ed had already mastered the "Dance of the Islands."

Ed is not the only character who lets it all hang out. In one episode, "Ed-a-Go-Go," the teen next door, played by guest star Johnny Crawford (Mark McCain on *The Rifleman*), demonstrates the newest dance steps to Wilbur Post, who wishes he wasn't so square. Johnny and his friends perform the Froog, the Monkey, the Swim and the Mule (no relation to Francis). The episode finale features everybody twisting to Wilbur's authentic bagpipe playing. Ed wisely chose not to do the Highland fling in this scene. Dance numbers for the humans were choreographed by Wally Green.

MISTER ED'S
ALL-PURPOSE
Dance

RIGHT
LEFT
LEFT
RIGHT
LEFT
RIGHT

USED TO REPRESENT EVERY DANCE STEP KNOWN TO MANKIND. ADD GRASS SKIRT AND DON HO MUSIC FOR "HORSE HULA", BLACK WIG AND GUITAR FOR "THE TWIST".

James Spegman.

"You Never Heard of a Talking Horse?!" The Real Inside Story

The moment you've all been waiting for—*how they made Ed talk.*

Sorry, mum's the word. To this day, *Mister Ed*'s producers will not reveal how they made the horse appear to speak so convincingly. It wasn't until 1970 that the producers would even reveal the man behind the voice of Mister Ed, veteran western star Allan "Rocky" Lane. But as to how they made him talk ... forget it!

Mister Ed's creators believe that to reveal how Ed talked would only spoil the show's timeless magic. Perhaps they've got a point. On August 29, 1965, the *New York Sunday News* said of director Arthur Lubin's top secrecy concerning "the behind-the-scenes wizardry": "He remained as close-mouthed about the whole affair as though it were H-bomb plans he was protecting."

Although there are no verifiable or authorized explanations of how Ed talked, there are several theories. Which of the following hypotheses seems closest to the truth? You be the judge ...

I. The Skippy Theory

This theory is the most colorful and funny of them all, and is currently cited by *Mister Ed*'s star, Alan Young. It goes like this: A harmless, peanut-butter-like substance was mixed with soft nylon and shoved up under Ed's lip. The horse would move his lips to dislodge it, just the way a person tries to get peanut butter off the roof of his mouth. The only trouble was, Ed would talk whether or not it was his turn to, which you will see every once in a while on the shows. At these moments, Les would use his riding crop to tap Ed on the hooves, signaling him to stop talking.

II. The Marionette Theory

Several parties attribute Ed's talking ability to a system resembling that of a puppeteer and marionette. A former photographer on the *Mister Ed* set describes the system as follows: A nylon string was held across Ed's gums and pulled by a man (presumably Lester Hilton) who stood by Ed's hind quarters, out of camera view. The harder the string was pulled, the wider Ed would open his mouth, but once the horse realized that the trainer wanted him to open his mouth, the string could be tugged very gently. The horse was never in any discomfort at all. Like a marionette, Ed could move his lips at varying degrees, according to the angle at which the strings were pulled. So there could be a noticeable difference between Ed's singing in the shower, for example, and his mundane conversations with Wilbur. *Mister Ed*'s syndicators, Orion Television, support this theory in their press release: "To create the look of Ed talking, Hilton employed a nylon bit to painlessly make Ed's lips move."

As a result of Orion's printed statement, other television chroniclers have published this theory as fact, but it hasn't been verified by the show's producers. It's true that there are some scenes where a nylon (monofilament) bit of some sort is in use, but it's never clear that it's causing Ed's lips to move, and conceivably may have been used to direct him through a scene. When asked about the nylon string visibly tugging at Ed's bridle in certain episodes, Alan Young explained: "When Les was too far off camera, he used a piece of nylon to get Ed started. On the loop in his bridle or his eyeglasses."

III. The Costume Party Theory

There is reason to suspect that the age-old "man in a horse suit" gag forms the underlying explanation of how the horse could talk. The show's producers even hinted at this in "Don't Laugh at Horses," an episode that features Jack Albertson and Alan Young sharing a horse suit while performing a dance number.

Basically, if you support this theory, you are among those who believe Ed was actually not a horse, but a horse *suit,* navigated by two men. Ironically, the son of *Mister Ed* writer Larry Rhine explained Ed's talking this way himself as a young boy. When his father asked him if Mister Ed talked to him at the season-opener ice cream party in 1964, Robert Rhine replied with a negative: "The man wasn't inside."

Courtesy of Larry Rhine.
Scripter Larry Rhine, his wife, character actress Hazel Shermet, and their
children Vicki and Robert greet Ed at the show's fifth season-opener
party, fall 1964.

Fellow *Mister Ed* scripter Ben Starr concurs with the Costume Party Theory:
"I would talk to that horse. I'd go up to him and say, 'Hi, Mister Ed, this is
your old friend Ben. You can talk to me. I know there's really a man in there."

IV. The Charlie McCarthy Theory

If you cast your vote for this technique, you think that Wilbur Post was a ventriloquist, practicing his cabaret act out in the barn with his horse Ed, over the course of six years. It was a *very long* rehearsal. The producers also hint at this theory in the second episode, appropriately titled, "The Ventriloquist."

V. The Horsepower Theory

The widespread rumor that Ed talked via electric shock treatments is by far the flimsiest, most absurd theory of all. Mister Ed was simply loved too much to ever have been subjected to electric voltage. Alan Young admits that "we've heard wires and electric shocks. We had the SPCA on the set the first day of shooting. After that, the SPCA never came around, because everyone knew Lester Hilton, and I've seen many times where Ed was asked to do something, and Les just said, 'No, I won't allow this.'" The biggest "jolt" that Ed ever received was from the electric blanket that Wilbur gave him at the end of "Don't Skin That Bear."

VI. The "Polly Want a Theory?" Theory

Mister Ed director/producer Arthur Lubin tells cynics: "A parrot talks. Why can't a horse?"

VII. The "Same Way That Francis the Mule Talked" Theory

"Les Hilton is really the one who figured out how to make Francis talk," Arthur Lubin revealed. "We tried chewing gum, that didn't work. Then we tried chewing tobacco. That made the animal sick and we had to postpone shooting. Then finally Les came up with a way that worked very well." Al Simon confirms that the same method was used to make both Francis and Ed talk. "Arthur came up with the way Ed talked, from his Francis pictures.

People thought the movement of the mouth could be animated. Animation would be terrible, the whole thing might as well be animated. Many times Ed's mouth was not in sync with what he was saying. We thought that would bother people, but we discovered it didn't."

Incidentally, in 1942 a film short was made called "Cow Cow Boogie" which starred real cows with animated mouths, singing an Andrew Sisters–type melody. Al Simon's right—you can't look at something like that for too long. The joke wears pretty thin, pretty quickly.

VIII. The "He Really Can Talk!" Theory

This theory is by far the most appealing, because it relies solely on the power of imagination, increasingly rare today. Journalist Leslie Raddatz (with tongue firmly in cheek) wrote in *TV Guide* in the December 18, 1964, issue: "In the make-believe world of television, where Lassie is really a boy and Flipper is really a girl, it is refreshing to know that Ed does his own talking.... If everybody [on the set] hadn't been so darned nice to me, I might have thought they were purposely arranging it so that I couldn't see Mister Ed talk." Nick at Nite, present-day home to *Mister Ed,* says Ed really talks too. How else could Ed exist in "TV land"? the cable network maintains.

Mister Ed Lets the Cat out of the Bag!

Surely you must be wondering, weren't there *any* situations in *Mister Ed* where Ed spoke to other people besides Wilbur? Not counting his cleverly concealed wisecracking remarks to heels and swindlers (they don't know it's him who's talking), there are actually *two* instances in the series in which Ed speaks *directly* to other people. In both cases, he addresses little boys, ensuring a lack of credibility should the tykes squeal.

○ "Kiddy Park"—Ed converses with the little boy on his back at the kiddy park pony rides. He tells the kid, played by Bobby Buntrock (Harold "Sport" Baxter on *Hazel*), that Encinada is in Mexico.
○ "Ed the Zebra"—Ed goes incognito as a zebra, courtesy of a freshly painted black fence, and joins the other zebras at the zoo. He has just listened to a scoutmaster's lecture about zebras being smarter than horses, and tells one of the young stragglers not to believe a word of it.

Besides talking to kids whenever the mood fits, there are countless times when Ed gets pressure from Wilbur to go public. Usually it's for some monetary reason—for example, to win $25,000 in George Burns' novelty act competition. In that episode, Wilbur literally gets down on his knees and begs Ed to talk, but no dice. To Ed, silence is golden.

The Arthur Lubin Legacy: From Mule to Horse

When it comes to acknowledging the talent behind *Mister Ed,* most people are apt to cite the contributions of Ed's trainer, Les Hilton, head writer, Lou Derman, and series star, Alan Young, and deservedly so. But what about the man behind the lens, Arthur Lubin, who was by this time a veteran at filming extraordinary animals? In December 1964 *Variety* praised the director for his role in the show: "Arthur Lubin, who has directed mules, fish and cats, duals as producer-director. [He is] one of the show's main props and certainly a factor in its long success." Lubin did not direct the very first two *Mister Ed* episodes, "The First Meeting" and "The Ventriloquist" in 1960, because he was busy in Italy making a Hercules movie. Rod Amateau, producer/director of *The Burns and Allen Show* from 1956 to 1958, covered for him, but Lubin was irreplaceable when it came to directing talking animals. When he returned from the Continent, he reshot some of the scenes with Ed talking.

Lubin recalls that the *Mister Ed* writers had to be extremely selective about what Mister Ed said or did. "I always warned them in writing each script, 'Don't give the horse too much to say, and whatever he says should be a laugh, but you can't laugh every moment or you wear the audience out.' I learned that from the Francis pictures. If you give the animal too much to say, you get bored with him and his mouth will be tired. The dialogue ought to be simple and easy." Humor and succinctness, to put it succinctly.

Like all hardworking groups, the show's writers were known to get punchy every so often. And the sign of a good director is one who knows how to handle his troops in just such moments. "We used to have fun with Arthur," chuckles scriptwriter Larry Rhine. "We'd put in a direction, 'Ed curls his lower lip, snaps his fingers, crosses himself,' and Lubin would say, 'Boys, you're being naughty.' " Les Hilton did a pretty good job of getting Ed to approximate all those things anyway.

Allan "Rocky" Lane: A Study in Gruff Artistry

It was lucky circumstance—an actor's pride and discretion—that resulted in publicity for *Mister Ed* above and beyond what was expected. Allan "Rocky" Lane had been a proud Hollywood actor. He did not want the American public to know that he had been "reduced" to playing the voice of a horse. "He still had the lovely actor's ego," explains Alan Young. He would play the voice of Mister Ed, because he needed work, but only on the condition that he not be named in the credits. Filmways agreed. "Mister Ed ... Himself" read the credit line at the end of every show. Incidentally, use of "Himself" in TV and movie credits is now a cult tradition that can be traced back to *Mister Ed.* "Himself" was used in the 1988 movie, *Hot to Trot,* to identify the voice of Don the Talking Horse. And the following year, the Oscar-nominated film *Field of Dreams* credited the haunting mystical voice as "Voice ... Himself." Pretty spooky, huh?

Rocky's embarrassment about working on *Mister Ed* was the best thing that could have happened for the show from a publicity standpoint. It wasn't long before Filmways—and later CBS—were flooded with fan mail from kids (and adults) who really believed Mister Ed was doing his own talking. To have seen credits like "Voice of Mister Ed ... Allan 'Rocky' Lane" would have spoiled the illusion. And Rocky was unquestionably terrific at playing Ed's voice. He brought a "horse sense" to the role that few could have imagined possible.

Lane would arrive on the *Mister Ed* set wearing a big white cowboy hat. "Rocky always wore off-white, an impressive-looking man," recalls Herb Browar. Already sixtyish years old by the time he worked on *Mister Ed* (he was born sometime between 1901 and 1907), Lane's years as a rugged western star were behind him. Yet he was still extremely dignified, and apparently camera-shy during this period of his life. Combing through the *Mister Ed* photo archives at CBS, one is hard-pressed to find a photo of Lane at work. His anonymity was, of course, contractual. "He was a very shy man," Browar adds. The only way to catch a glimpse of Lane is to talk with the people who worked with him on *Mister Ed* (there are no living relatives): "He was his own worst enemy," some cast members say. But everyone agrees there are few people who could have fit the bill so perfectly as the voice of Mister Ed.

Most surprising is Rocky Lane's having recorded Ed's lines right on the stage while the show was being filmed. The actor stood off to the side, behind a triptych with a window in the middle panel, on a special stand that was built for him. Through the window, he could watch Ed's lip movements and make sure the lines were in sync. He spoke his lines into a special microphone that improved the sound. There was a constant coordination between Rocky and Ed's trainer. "Rocky would watch the horse," Herb Browar explains. "He and Les worked hand in hand. Les had to anticipate the lines, he had to practically have a script in his mind, and after rehearsing the scene a couple of times, they would get it down pat." Having Rocky record the lines right there, syncing them to Ed's mouth movements, was the best way to achieve authenticity. Alan Young agrees that this system actually helped him to believe Ed was talking to him. "I'd talk to him, and the voice came back."

In the dubbing phase of postproduction, when all the audio elements (dialogue and sound effects) were put together onto one track, additional reverb was added to Ed's voice to give it that infamous echo quality. And some of Rocky's lines and extra sounds like yawns and mumbles had to be added at the dubbing session, but the bulk of the script was recorded right there on the stage, at the end of each shooting day.

Rocky's unique role was accompanied by equally unusual shooting hours. "Rocky had only one complaint," Lubin remembers with a grin. "I always shot the horse last, the moving of the mouth. I got rid of the rest of the cast. And the reason I did that was because the leading lady, or the two girls we had, if we kept them after four o'clock, with the heat, they started to fade. So I always shot the scenes which featured Ed alone last, that was Rocky's only complaint. He had to wait until everyone else was gone."

One of the most remarkable qualities about Rocky was his knack for truly horselike ad-libs. "Rocky would stand as close as he could without the horse looking over at him," Alan Young notes. This proximity allowed for opportune ad-libbing. For example, when playing Pin the Tail on the Donkey in "Horse Party," the horse drops the marker, and Rocky says, "Oops, dropped my tail." "If the ad-lib was worthwhile, they would leave it in," remembers Al Simon. "There were times that Rocky recommended an idea, or one of the cameramen had an idea, and we would use it." The veteran actor would also add some finishing touches in postproduction, like "yawning" when the horse stretched, "groaning" when the horse strained to stand up, and would even intentionally slur or flub some lines to make them sound as though a horse were saying them. "He knew more about the voice of the horse than anyone, to such a point that he became the horse," Al Simon explains. And Rocky truly loved horses. He used to get up early in the morning and go down to the racetrack to watch them.

Naturally, the former movie star wanted credit for his performance once *Mister Ed* became a success, but the show's producers held him to his contract, aware that the identity of Ed's voice had become as much a built-in puzzle as how they made him talk. To show their appreciation for Rocky's extraordinary work, however, Filmways gave him a nice raise, which he accepted gladly.

In the course of the series, Rocky learned that there could be a downside to being *too* good at his job: "His character merged so much with the horse," Connie Hines recalls of Lane, still with a sense of awe some thirty years later.

"Do you know, they forgot to give him a dressing room, they forgot to give him a parking place, when there was a party, they forgot to invite him. Of course, it was always corrected. He was so great at his job. He became one with that horse." Can you imagine the role reversal that must have been going on? Ed getting hay and caviar while Rocky can't even find a spot to park his Studebaker! No wonder Ed is crabby so much of the time . . . his alter ego is mad! Herb Browar rightly points out that Rocky Lane *couldn't* attend parties with members of the media community, because he was bound by his contract to remain anonymous. And by the way, Rocky's parking space was across the street from Filmways, in the Eastman Kodak parking lot.

"I'm Fine, but My Voice Is a Little Horse . . ."

Because Rocky provided the voice for Ed, the horse always had *two* health reports at any given time: his scripted health status and Rocky's actual health condition. For instance, in episode 49, "Bald Horse," Ed is in perfect health (though Addison pulls a scam to convince Wilbur that the horse is losing his hair), yet he sounds nasal, with no reference to it by Wilbur, because Rocky Lane obviously had a cold during that week's shooting. In shows where Ed is scripted to be sick, as in "Ed's Bed," Rocky is fine, yet the actor exaggerates the voice of someone with a cold to give Ed's lines horse proportion.

Mister Ed's producers tried to find a backup for Rocky Lane, in case the actor should ever come down with the flu or be otherwise indisposed. Herb Browar recalls taking a folk singer down to Todd A-O soundstage to record some lines one afternoon, but he was never actually used in any of the shows.

The Career of Allan "Rocky" Lane

Maybe it was because in his movie "hayday" Allan "Rocky" Lane was never far from the side of his stallion, Black Jack, that the man who played Mister Ed's voice truly believed he knew what a horse would sound like if he could talk. In his Hollywood peak, every one of Rocky's movie posters referred to the stars of the picture as: "Allan 'Rocky' Lane and his stallion 'Black Jack,' " who incidentally could perform tricks on command.

Allan Lane was born Harry Albershart on September 22 in Mishawaka, Indiana, in either 1901, 1904 or 1907, depending on what you read. He was an athlete at Notre Dame at South Bend, and was discovered by Fox Film Corporation movie agents in the late twenties. His first film role was in a part-talkie, *Not Quite Decent,* in 1929. He got his break in 1936, when he appeared in *Stowaway* with Shirley Temple. Other films that followed include *Charlie Chan at the Olympics* (perhaps no coincidence that Ed yearns to catch a Charlie Chan flick in one episode?), *Big Business* and *Laughing at Trouble.*

He starred in his first western in 1939 under RKO, *Law West of Tombstone,* but it wasn't until signing with Republic Pictures in 1940 that his career as a B-western star took off. His only hiatus from westerns occurred during World War II, when there was a shortage of good-looking leading men in

Courtesy of Herb Browar.
The *only* known photo of Rocky Lane from the *Mister Ed* years, snapped for a Treasury Department newsletter. In February 1964, cast and crew received honors for their film short, ''Wilbur Gets the Message About Payroll Savings.'' Proudly holding their citations, standing left to right: Rocky Lane, Herb Browar, Al Simon. Seated left to right: Jacob Mogelever, Savings Bond promotion manager, Connie Hines, Alan Young, Arthur Lubin, guest star George O'Hanlon and Lou Derman. Camera shy: Mister Ed.

Hollywood. When Wild Bill Elliott, Republic's Red Ryder, was promoted to A westerns, Rocky took his place in the long string of popular B flicks. The last Rocky Lane (and his stallion Black Jack) western was produced in 1953. Two years later he made a Red Ryder TV pilot called "Gun Trouble Valley." He also appeared in several TV series: *Gunsmoke, Colt 45, Bonanza, Alfred Hitchcock, Walt Disney* and *Cheyenne*. By the late 1950s, B westerns were a thing of the past, and Rocky's starring days were through.

Rocky's career got a second life, ironically, when it was reincarnated as the voice of a horse, and very few people knew about his involvement until after the show was canceled.

Punkin, Ed's Stand-in Double, Singles

Yes, Mister Ed did have an understudy, named Punkin, who was owned by Les Hilton, but you'll be pleased to know that Ed's look-alike pretty much goldbricked for six seasons. That's because horses, far smarter than mules, don't flub their lines that often. Arthur Lubin can attest to the vast difference in I.Q. between Ed and his celluloid predecessor, Francis: "With Francis, we had three mules. They weren't a very bright animal. If we were able to get one mule to do one trick, we were fortunate."

The director explains why they needed an understudy for Ed, despite his remarkable acuity: "For our protection, not only did we have Mister Ed, we had an understudy which the trainer rehearsed all the time in case anything should happen to the number one Mister Ed. . . . The understudy's name was Punkin. He was in training all the time. It was like a leading man in a two-hour show. You had to have a big physical examination to make sure you weren't going to lose him in the middle of the picture. The same thing happened with Mister Ed. We wanted to be sure that if anything should happen to him, the series would still go on with an understudy, but that no one would know."

Punkin was used only once in the series, by Alan Young when he guest-directed "TV or Not TV" in 1965. Young wanted a shot of the horse's back, sitting and facing Wilbur, who was lying in a hammock. Punkin was younger and stronger than Mister Ed, and was used for this particular pear-shaped shot. According to Janie Nicolaides, who knew Ed through his entire life, Punkin also helped out during tech rehearsals: "He would stand under the lights and in camera position so the lighting director and cinematographer could lay out their shots and then Ed would do the dress rehearsal and, of course, be in all the actual filming."

In a much earlier episode, "Ed the Hero," Punkin has an extremely minor walk-on role. Ed mocks Punkin, calling him "a phony pony." The understudy *literally* plays a look-alike for Ed, who refuses to participate in the parade on Catalina Island. Since Ed is expected at the festivities, the Posts have no choice but to hire a stand-in.

Handle With Care

Despite Ed's image as a devil-may-care horse of adventure, Alan Young claims that, in reality, the actor Ed "was guarded like a little angel." The valuable palomino was meticulously pampered and protected by his trainer, Les Hilton. In at least three shows, special horseshoes were dummied in order to protect him. In "Taller Than She," a blacksmith makes Ed a special pair of elevator horseshoes so he can win the affections of his tall girlfriend. The shot of Ed wearing the five-layer horseshoes had to be dummied so that Ed wouldn't be endangered. In "Horse Wash," Les Hilton would not allow Ed to walk through the car wash wearing ordinary shoes. Special rubberized ones were created to prevent the horse from slipping. "If you could have seen the expression on Ed's face as he went through the soap, water and wind!" director of photography Arch Dalzell recalls of that day at Cahuenga Car Wash. While posing for publicity photos in his regal "Sheriff's Parade" costume ("Tunnel to Freedom"), Ed also wore special skidproof horseshoes. Alan Young remembers that the ornate costume, valued at over $50,000, was lent to Ed by one of the show's admirers, who simply wanted to see the horse modeling it.

Aside from his responsibilities as a TV actor, Ed was asked to participate in a lot of outside publicity stunts, however Hilton's protectiveness precluded some of the more risky events. Director Lubin recalls that "the only thing that Les would not let the horse do was be in the Hollywood parade, feeling that the people yelling at him 'Mister Ed!' would frighten the horse, and he might jump off the float. And he never would agree to be in the Thanksgiving parade." Imagine Ed trotting by Macy's in Herald Square on Turkey Day. Come to think of it, Ed would have made a more charming parade host than Willard Scott. At least someone *wrote* his jokes.

Sayonara, Tokyo!

Concern for Mister Ed's well-being kept him on U.S. soil. Although Ed refers to himself as a "gay international playboy," the horse never actually got to leave his native land. He came close in April of 1963 when the show's producers received an invitation to fly to Japan to do some shows. (By this time, the show was a very big hit there, dubbed in Japanese, of course.) "We were sponsored by the Matsuhitso Company," Alan Young explains, "and they wanted to fly us over there to do a few shows. Everything was set until the Japanese government informed us of their quarantine on animals. So Ed wouldn't have been allowed in for six weeks." Weren't there any exceptions for the famous palomino? "Well, our producer called up the consulate and they cut it down to two weeks. Then we found out the airlines have the final say on the disposition of the animal should it become obstreperous, and we didn't want anybody putting shots or needles into Ed." Of course Ed's character was petrified of vaccinations, too.

Ultimately, the closest anybody got to seeing Ed in Japan was a scene from "Ed the Musician," in which the horse tells Wilbur about his nightmare: He's in Japan with Wilbur, and they're both taking a bath in a big tub. Ed's smitten with the little filly named Fujiyama who's scrubbing his back. Why is it a nightmare? Wilbur tells Ed that the two can never be one: "She's East and you're West." Perhaps no coincidence, this episode was scripted around the time of the purported trip to Japan.

Cleanliness Is Next to Ed-liness

Typical of all sitcoms prior to *All in the Family,* there are no references to bathrooms on *Mister Ed,* for humans or for horses. Which of course does lead one to wonder how this activity was dealt with *off* the screen, when the star of the show was an animal.

"Our stage was the sweetest-smelling stage you could imagine," recalls Alan Young. Hard to believe? Well, one of the many signs that Ed was smarter than the average horse was how he handled the whole bathroom situation. All agree that the palomino excelled in personal hygiene.

When production on the series first commenced in the fall of 1960, the horse would relieve himself whenever the need arose. It could be right in the middle of a scene with his human colleagues, which really did happen in the shooting of "The Bashful Clipper." While Ed was rehearsing a scene with Larry Keating in which the horse had to walk over to Keating's cot and give

Courtesy of Alan Young.
Ed poses in regal costume, including protective shoes, for the Sheriff's
Parade in "Tunnel to Freedom," 1964.

him Wilbur's blanket, nature prevailed. Ed's trainer, Lester Hilton, told Larry Keating to "freeze" until Ed was finished, to avoid any further showering. Ed was so sensitive he began to notice the negative reactions he was getting from his coworkers. So he stopped!

From then on, Ed would modestly wait until the day's shooting was over, until he actually got home to the ranch, to let nature prevail. In case of an accident, there was always a utility man on the set who would clean up after any of the animals if the need arose (*Mister Ed* episodes were filled with lots of creatures besides horses, such as elephants, lions, goats, birds and bears). But Ed was rarely a problem.

"We had to do some location work on the *Gunsmoke* stage," Alan Young explains to illustrate Ed's fastidiousness. "And when you've had horses on a stage for two, three, four years, you can never get the smell out. And so I was amazed, our stage smelled so clean. Ed never did anything onstage. I said, 'Lester, why doesn't he go?' Les said, 'He doesn't want to, he wants to get outside.' You could always tell when Ed had to go, his eyes rolled. 'I gotta go!' And Lester would take him outside, into the hay, and there he would relieve himself." Knowing this about Ed, it makes sense that his character was written to be bashful about bathrooms. It's true he does stow away in a ship cabin's bathroom en route to Hawaii with the Posts, but later in the series, in "The Horse and the Pussycat," he is reluctant to hide in the hospital room john while visiting Wilbur. "I can't go in there," Ed tells his laid-up owner. "It doesn't say 'Horses' on the door." Sheesh, formalities!

"Holler but Don't Hit"

....

TYPICAL **MISTER ED** DYNAMICS

You'd be hard-pressed to find any episode of *Mister Ed* that doesn't contain five basic ingredients, or dynamics, that contribute to the show's special alchemy.

ED-IPUS COMPLEX ... THE LOVE TRIANGLE

When one person loves two people (or two people love the same person) in any story or play, you get a love triangle, a classic device for the stuff of romance and chaos. *Mister Ed* follows this surefire format, but twists it a tad, ensuring a permanent place in the annals of wacky TV-dom. Let's call it the Palominomian Theorem: *When one architect has two love interests—one human, the other nonhuman—there follow riotous scenes of domestic dissonance, all of which are resolvable within a twenty-seven-minute time span.*

Mister Ed's

Love Triangle

WILBUR:
THE MAN

ED:
THE HORSE

CAROL:
THE WIFE

James Spegman.

Wilbur's a married man, but he's as devoted to his horse as to his wife. Does this leave you just slightly confused? Ahh, if only Ed could fit inside the Studebaker station wagon with the Posts, then we'd be sure they were a nuclear family, but his horse trailer, with that tail flapping in the breeze, is a dead giveaway that something's amiss. Yet it's the rivalry between Ed and Carol, and the ensuing confusion and zany cover-ups, that keep us watching. Occasionally, *Mister Ed* would disguise itself as *The Donna Reed Show,* with seeming order and harmony among the family members, but that was only a device to get us in and out of the episodes. As soon as we got our first glimpse of Ed out in the barn, we discovered that he was up to something positively outrageous, and we knew we were in store for a half hour of antics.

Unsolvable Query #1

If Wilbur loves Carol and Ed, and Carol and Ed love Wilbur, do Ed and Carol love each other, by the **law of transitivity**?

Some "Ed-ipus" One-liners

WILBUR: Try to put yourself in his place.
CAROL: I wish I could, I'd be better off.

WILBUR [to Carol]: He's an only horse—it's not as if we were blessed with two.

CAROL: He's your horse, not your son.
WILBUR: A mere accident of birth.

WILBUR [to Carol]: I'm glad I'm not Ed's father. Because then he wouldn't have a very understanding mother.

ED [to Wilbur]: If your mother were a horse, we'd be brothers.

CAROL: It's not enough to take your wife on a second honeymoon. You have to take your horse along!

ED [to Wilbur]: Why did we take her along on our honeymoon?

Ethics 101

Carol Post was born to be an ethics professor. She often poses moral dilemmas to Wilbur, of a stature that would do Plato proud, in which he has to choose between her and Mister Ed. Of course these situations are only dilemmatic to Wilbur. Most men married to a blond bombshell wouldn't dilly-dally in their responses the way Wilbur does. In "Ed the Sentry," Carol sets up the following dialogue with worldly finesse:

CAROL: If you were on a desert, with Mister Ed and me, and there was just enough water for two of us, who would get the water?
WILBUR: You and Ed, of course.
CAROL: If there was just enough water for one of us, who would get it?
WILBUR: Well, uh—
CAROL: Why is it taking you so long to answer?
WILBUR: You, you'd get the water, naturally.
CAROL: Well, that's better.
WILBUR: Unless you'd care to give yours to Ed, I mean, I gave my water to you.
CAROL: You'd give all of the water to Mister Ed!
WILBUR: Don't be ridiculous. I'd have only one choice, of course.
CAROL: Of course—Who?
WILBUR: Who?
CAROL: While you're choosing between us, I could be fainting on that desert.
WILBUR: So could Ed faint, and he'd be a lot heavier to drag back into town.

My Little Pony . . .

Mister Ed was the only sitcom of its time involving a married couple that didn't have kids. Even *I Love Lucy* and *Burns and Allen* eventually wrote offspring into their scripts. Hence, Ed as an 800-pound bundle of joy. Was there ever a possibility of incorporating actual Post children into the story line? "There was some talk about it," Connie Hines recalls. "But it would've taken away from Ed. Wilbur's relationship with Ed was the most important thing. I don't think it would have been too good."

The closest the Posts ever get to having a baby occurs in "Ed Gets the Mumps," in which Carol watches her friend's baby, Madeline, for a few days. Ed is so jealous of the infant, he concocts a case of phony mumps: "I gotta find some sickness that'll bring Wilbur running back to me. Nothing fatal, just sympathetic." Ed reacts like a neglected son: "Go ahead, if a stranger is more important than your own flesh and blood," when Wilbur leaves him to go baby-sit. Wilbur is so infatuated with his horse that he takes for granted that Ed *is* a member of the family. He's the perfect counterpart for Ed: The horse is melodramatic, and Wilbur is gullible and softhearted, a prime consumer for Ed's soapbox speeches.

Not surprisingly, the pranksterish palomino acts like a small child in scary situations. (In most episodes, he's just seven or eight years old.) In "The Prowler," there's a burglar at large who's frightening everyone, including Ed. He tells Wilbur that he's not going to sleep alone in the barn:

WILBUR: You mean you're going to sleep in my room?
ED: Yup—right between you and Carol.

This sounds outrageous but of course Ed's referring to the space *between* Carol and Wilbur's "sweetheart beds," not actually sharing a bed with them.

In another episode, "The Disappearing Horse," Ed is a model of Freudian anxiety. During a magic act, he doesn't pull the lever as rehearsed. Wilbur is the laughingstock of the auditorium, especially painful since he dreams of being the next Harry Houdini:

WILBUR: Ed, what are you doing to me?!
ED: What if I disappear forever—I'll never see you again!

Freud writes (without the slightest clue that talking horses would one day prosper): "The first phobias of situations in children concern darkness and loneliness. . . . Common to both is the desire for the absent attendant" (Lecture 25, "Anxiety," *A General Introduction to Psychoanalysis*). Just substitute "Wilbur" for "absent attendant," and you've got an explanation for Ed's fears in these episodes, among many others.

These father-son feelings are definitely a two-way bridle path in *Mister Ed.* When Ed gets his first job, Wilbur recites an emotional speech on his horse's rite of passage, accompanied by sappy violin music (a real *Mister Ed* touch). Alan Young is a natural at exaggerating emotions in these melodramatic scenes:

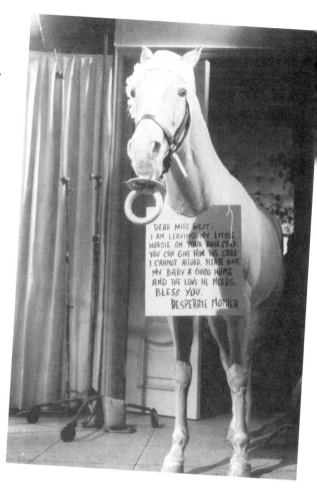

**Photo: Gene Trindl.
Ed parks himself on
Mae West's doorstep,
dressed as an
abandoned baby,
in "Mae West Meets
Mister Ed," 1964.**

WILBUR: Just think, tomorrow's Ed's first day on the job. Life's funny, you know. You get a young horse like Ed, you coddle him, you play with him, you spoil him a little bit, you hope he doesn't grow up. First thing you know, he's punching a timeclock.

CAROL (*sarcastic*): It's tough.

WILBUR: Good for him, though. Work's good, builds character. I wouldn't want him drifting through life like Kay's brother. A horse has got to learn to stand on his own four feet.

CAROL: Go to sleep, honey.

WILBUR: I think I'll make him a nice lunch tomorrow. Something that'll give him energy. What should I make for him, Carol?

CAROL: How about a triple-decker hay sandwich?

—*"Unemployment Show"*

Like raising any child, Wilbur must endure Ed through his various stages. During the horse's carousing, James Dean phase, Wilbur is known to use the expression (on more than one occasion) "His hay hasn't been slept in." And then there's the time that Ed wants his own bachelor pad, so he makes Wilbur write a letter to "Dear Abby" for advice. In "The Heavy Rider," Wilbur's complaint about Ed sounds like a typical generation-gap struggle: "When I was a kid, horses had more respect for their elders." He laments about the gap again in "Ed's Juice Stand": "This new generation of horses. What are they coming to?" And what about the episode where Ed runs off to find his "little green corner of the West"? Wilbur certainly has his hands full, between rescue missions and CARE packages for his four-legged teen rebel.

In the third *Mister Ed* show, "Busy Wife," Ed begins the transformation from salty old nag ("People ... all they do is talk, talk, talk") to spoiled brat, and remains one for the rest of the series (we're talking 140 more shows!). To mark his premiere as a mischievous tyke in that episode, Ed butts in on the Posts' party line (with a mock-Chinese accent: "Solly, long numbah"), and whinnies in protest when locked in his stall. Clearly the writers believed Ed's babylike relationship to Wilbur had more "legs" than the original setup, in which the horse is virtually his *owner's* guardian. Ed still refers to the architect as "a fine lad" in the thirteenth episode, not the way you'd expect a kid to refer to his pappy, but don't fret: Ed's uncanny knack for manipulating Wilbur's heartstrings is in full bloom by then. A good example of this occurs in "Ed the Godfather," in which Ed croons a maudlin song, entitled "In My Mother's Arms," as soon as Wilbur asks Ed's stable guest, an expectant filly, to leave. Ed's tactics prove successful. Not only does pregnant Gina get to stay but Wilbur joins Ed in the song! Ed and Wilbur's musical duets, more like barbershop quartets with two legs missing, are always a highlight of the series.

Love Rectangle?!

In "Ed in the Peace Corps," Ed admits that the show actually *needs* the format of a love triangle. When a newcomer arrives, Ed takes action: "The eternal rectangle. A man, his wife, his secretary, and his horse. One of us has got to go, and it won't be me." Even Wilbur alludes to the importance of the dynamic trio: "I have one wife and one horse, and I'm not breaking up the set." There you have it. A balance predicated on imbalance. A prize formula for this sitcom of the fantastic variety.

"I Am a Bad Horse"

Ed never received any corporal, "horselike" punishment from Wilbur, which would have been inconsistent with the premise that Ed was something more than Wilbur's beast of burden. There were only the occasional jerks who got pleasure from slapping Ed on the rump (that's actually how the writers told you they were jerks! Ed told us he'd get "cauliflower tail" from such abuse).

Wilbur would use psychological tactics to discipline his horse—for example, making him sit in a corner while wearing a dunce cap or write on a blackboard one hundred times, "I am a bad horse" (an identical scene can be found in *Bill and Coo,* a 1947 all-bird movie produced by Ken Murray, whose variety show alternated with *The Alan Young Show* on CBS).

Wilbur actually puts a muzzle on Ed twice, so that he can finish up his architectural plans in peace, but even that's done in the cartoon spirit, with Ed *mugging* to camera (even he knew how to flirt with the audience).

THE FAR SIDE   By GARY LARSON

As a young colt, Mr. Ed was often sent to the hall for speaking out of turn.

"MAKE LIKE A HORSE"

Ed is a horse.
Horses don't talk.
Therefore, Ed doesn't talk.

Uhh . . . let's try another angle, shall we?

Wilbur is Mister Ed's owner.
Owners tell their horses what to do.
Therefore, Wilbur tells Ed what to do.

Oops! Don't expect to brush up on your logic by watching *Mister Ed*. As you can see, the show does not lend itself to deductive reasoning. The show's delightful lack of sense, however, brings us to the next absolutely essential dynamic for any bona fide episode of *Mister Ed*: Everybody's identity is topsy-turvy, which isn't so nutty when you think about it, given the show's basic premise—that there exists a horse who can talk. "In it, everyone gets confused as to who he or she really is," wrote *TV Guide* in 1962 while describing a scene between Wilbur and Ed at the bridle path. "The horse forgets that, being partly human, the power to move forward rests with him. Wilbur forgets that, being wholly human, he is supposed to tell the horse what to do. The audience forgets that Mister Ed is a horse at all."

Ed slips in and out of his horse identity quicker than he guzzles down a bucket of his homemade "Wilburini" juice (for recipe, see Chapter 8). "It was such a nice day, I thought I'd go down to the stables, rent me a man and go riding," Ed tells his owner in "Be Kind to Humans." This is whimsical outrageous stuff! Yet Rocky Lane's delivery of Ed's voice is so convincing that we don't doubt the palomino for a second.

More Mixed-up Conversations

ED: What do you say we go out riding and pick up a couple of fillies?
WILBUR: I'm not a horse, remember?
ED: Too bad, we could have a ball double dating.

—"Ed's Juice Stand"

WILBUR [to Dr. Ed, noted brain surgeon]: You are a doctor first, and a horse second.

—*"Doctor Ed"*

ED: You should never have told me horses sleep standing up. It gave me a mental block.

—*"Ed the Chauffeur"*

ED: How come whenever you start talking about vacation, I'm a horse again?

—*"Pine Lake Lodge"*

ED: Can't a guy have a little fun?
WILBUR: You're not a guy, you're a horse, and sometimes I wish you'd act like one.

—*"Wilbur the Good Samaritan"*

ED [to Wilbur]: I don't expect you to be perfect like me. You're only human.

—*"Saddles and Gowns"*

These bits of dialogue are a great way for the writers to emphasize the "You're more than a horse, you're a real human being" confusion in *Mister Ed,* and at the same time poke fun at some of the most common clichés in the English language.

"It's Some Horse Nuttin' Around" . . .

Or is it some nut *horsing* around?! Human identity is not the only kind that trickster Ed adopts in order to achieve his objectives. In "Dragon Horse," a frightened Ed *sneaks* into the house and sleeps on the living room floor. (Scenes in which the horse goes into the living room are among the zaniest; the film is sped up to convey his hurry, but it looks velvety, like he's walking through honey.) Wilbur wanders downstairs for a late-night snack and sees Ed on the floor:

WILBUR: Oh no! (*Ed awakes*)
ED: If you had a dog, you'd let *him* sleep in the house.
WILBUR: A dog is different. A dog is a household pet.
ED: Call me 'Rover' and wake me at eight.

In this exchange, Ed sounds a lot like Bert Lahr's compromising Cowardly Lion from Oz.

Ed obviously has an edge over ordinary animals (though he'll never betray them), and he frequently enlists their services to prove a point. In "Don't Skin That Bear," directed by Alan Young, Ed brings a real bear home from the zoo to educate Wilbur on the immorality of bearskin rugs. The palomino instructs the bear to: "Plop down on the floor and make like a rug." In this scene, there is an implied universality of animal language. The bear has no trouble understanding Ed, who's talking a mixture of "horse" (we know that from the "neighing" sound effects) and "human," mostly "human" for our benefit.

Parallel Plots and Subplots

A typical episode of *Mister Ed* usually contains plots and subplots which parallel the human and animal worlds. Wilbur's trouble with Carol is often mirrored by Ed's difficulty with a fickle filly. Horse and owner are equally sentimental and superstitious. Wilbur saves Ed's horseshoes while Ed holds on to Wilbur's riding boots. The horse even plays "shoe toss" and nails the architect's shoe over his barn door for good luck. A great example of "like owner, like horse" is a shot of Wilbur reading *Principles of Animal Psychology,* followed by a shot of Ed studying *Principles of Human Psychology.* They're plotting to "outpsych" each other in this one.

There are even larger thematic parallels. For example, in "Ed's Cold Tail," *cold* is the theme: Ed wants a heating system in his stall; Carol wants a bigger refrigerator. In "Ed the Chauffeur," the theme is *driving:* Winnie Kirkwood totals her husband's new car; Ed rents a milk truck and drives wildly. The focus is on *fatherhood* in "What Kind of Foal Am I?" The upcoming visit of Wilbur's father-in-law triggers a desire in Ed to search for his longlost father.

ED: I want my daddy right now!
WILBUR: Ed, I want you to consider me your two-legged father.
ED: A horse is entitled to a father with hooves and a tail. . . . When I was a little kid, I used to go around singing "What Kind of Foal Am I?"

Mister Ed is infamous for his many references to pop culture (discussed in Chapter 7), as in the above pun on the then-popular Anthony Newley tune.

"LIE DOWN ON THE COUCH, MR. POST"

In a typical episode of *Mister Ed*, where would you be most likely to find Wilbur Post?

a. Out in the barn, conversing with his palomino

b. On top of a roof, trying to convince his horse that the doctor's needle won't really hurt *that* much

c. In a psychiatrist's office, undergoing psychological evaluation

If you answered "a," congratulations! You're obviously an astute TV viewer. If you chose "b," you're probably one of the few fans who remembers that episode involving Ed and a vaccination and a ladder and something about the horse *shimmying* up a tree (which we never actually see). And if you answered "c," in a shrink's office, you'd be *almost* right. That's the *second most likely* place to find Wilbur.

Hollywood sitcoms of this time were having a field day with themes of sanity and insanity, a pre–Woody Allen fixation on neurosis. And *Mister Ed* was no exception—no other show was as well designed for such diversions. In fact, insanity in *Mister Ed* is not a diversion at all, but actually another of the show's staple dynamics. What other sitcom in 1961 could boast a premise so surreal, a story line crying out so loudly for psychiatric intervention? To be sure, *Mister Ed* inspired similar lunacy in future sitcoms like *My Favorite Martian, My Mother the Car, Bewitched* and two other Filmways productions—*Green Acres* and *The Addams Family.*

Richard Deacon as the stock psychiatrist character.

Interestingly, *Mister Ed*'s scenarios involving shrinks, played by great character actors like Richard Deacon (who is most recognized for his role as Mel Cooley on *The Dick Van Dyke Show*), in effect spoof the whole psychiatry business. Wilbur's doctors inevitably end up getting so carried away by his overwrought confessions that they become completely unprofessional, breaking every rule in the book. They forget who they are, why Wilbur's there; they even lie back on the couch themselves . . . you get the (Rorschach) picture.

More than the love triangle, more than the confusion over who's human and who's animal, Wilbur's foolish, erratic behavior seems to be the most memorable *Mister Ed* feature. In his attempts to cover up for Ed's mischief, or by simply being his own boyish and innocent self, Wilbur winds up in silly, strange situations. If you had to pick the show's "famous last words," ironically, they would be Wilbur's pleading remark to Mister Ed: "If you'd just concentrate on being a normal talking horse, everything would be okay." You can even picture them etched on Ed's or Wilbur's tombstone someday.

The architect's shenanigans make total sense to *us,* who are in on the secret, but to the other characters who lack that key piece of information— that Mister Ed can talk—Wilbur remains a "kook."

Wilbur's frequent run-ins with stock psychiatrists are amusing in a predictable sort of way. You know, a cop finds Wilbur in the park playing hide-and-seek with his horse, so he "brings him in" for psychological testing. A good half of his visits to doctors are ordered by some arm of the law, but just as often, and this is where *it really gets interesting,* Wilbur initiates the sessions himself, in order to role-play Ed's hang-ups. This is a very sophisticated idea when you think about it. Ed comes down with some phobia or temporary mental disorder, and Wilbur pretends to have the symptoms himself so he can learn how to cure Ed. In "Psychoanalyst Show," Wilbur goes to a psychiatrist (Richard Deacon) to learn how to cure Mister Ed's fear of heights. In "Ed Gets Amnesia," Wilbur feigns loss of memory, pretending to be the great pianist Vladimir Rabinsky so he can figure out how to unmix his mixed-up horse. In keeping with the confusion theme, Ed not only loses his memory in this show but thinks he's a man and Wilbur's a horse. In "The Price of Apples," Wilbur actually takes Ed to an animal psychiatrist (very prophetic, given today's animal behaviorists), to cure his horse's addiction to Roger Addison's apples. Wilbur takes the whole thing literally, telling Dr. Griffith, again played by Richard Deacon: "I hope he's not too big for your couch." It was still possible in those days of TV innocence to laugh about themes of substance addiction. Ed even uses terms like "taper off" to describe his obsession with Roger's apples, and the doctor accuses Wilbur of having "one too many."

HOOFNOTES
Shrinks, Vets and Medical Skeptics

(A compendium of medical personnel who plague the *Mister Ed* series. Here's your very own directory, which you may want to post on your refrigerator door for reference.)

CHARACTER	GUEST STAR	EPISODE
Dr. Stekel (shrink)	Richard Deacon	"Ed the Musician" (#87)
Dr. Griffith (animal shrink)	Richard Deacon	"The Price of Apples" (#76)
Dr. Sam Jones (vet)	Richard Deacon	"The Blessed Event" (#69)
Dr. Bruce Gordon (shrink)	Richard Deacon	"Psychoanalyst Show" (#17)
Dr. Baker (vet)	Richard Deacon	"Ed Gets Amnesia" (#54)
Captain Vernon (military shrink)	Irwin Charone	"Ed's Dentist" (#97)
Dr. Howard (vet)	Tom B. Henry	"Ed's Dentist" (#97)
Dr. Jay Pearson (dentist)	George Neise	"Ed's Dentist" (#97)
J. P. Hoxie (shrink)	Harold Gould	"Ed the Pilot" (#114)
Dr. Brink (shrink)	Les Tremayne	"Ed the Bridegroom" (#139)
Dr. Cathcart (internist)	Lindsay Workman	"Ed Gets Amnesia" (#54)

Dr. Chadkin (obstetrician)	Frank Wilcox	"Ed the Godfather" (#123)
Doc Evans (vet)	Hank Patterson	"Ed the Horse Doctor" (#42)
Dr. Evans (vet)	Percy Helton	"Bald Horse" (#48)
Dr. Connors (vet)	William Fawcett	"Pageant Show" (#9)
Generic vet	Cliff Hall	"Cherokee Ed" (#142)
Herbert Fosdick, Jr. (optometrist)	Roy Stuart	"Ed's Contact Lenses" (#124)
Herbert Fosdick, Sr. (optometrist)	Howard Wendell	"Ed's Contact Lenses" (#124)
Dr. Gruber (shrink)	Lou Krugman	"Don't Skin That Bear" (#140)
Dr. Reynolds (internist)	Lee Goodman	"Ed the Beneficiary" (#39)
Dr. Robbins (internist)	Rolfe Sedan	"The Horse and the Pussycat" (#138)

The Next-door Neighbors

Besides medical skeptics, *Mister Ed* employs the standard device of next-door neighbors as straight men, or "foils," to Wilbur. Neighbor Roger Addison, played by Larry Keating, is always the first to laugh at Wilbur's inevitably foolish predicaments. He's known to make such remarks as "Wilbur, you're beautiful!" to denote a warped appreciation for the architect's eccentricities. *Beautiful* meaning *crazy* was a popular TV-ism at that time. Other TV men who remark on each other's "beauty" from time to time include *Mister Ed*'s second next-door neighbor, Gordon Kirkwood, Mister Ed himself, Ricky Ricardo and Fred Mertz and of course Ralph Cramden.

By far, Larry Keating was the best-loved cast member. Audiences knew him well from his work in *Burns and Allen* between 1953 and 1958, playing Harry Morton, also a neighbor. Alan Young recalls that Keating told him he too should play a neighbor in his next TV role. According to Keating, a neighbor's role was easier than the star's because it didn't involve as much travel and promotion. Young apparently took this piece of advice to heart, because in his next sitcom role, arriving twenty-two years later on *Coming of Age* (CBS, 1988–89), he played a next-door neighbor named Ed, ironically.

Keating's craft as a TV veteran was a major contribution to *Mister Ed*. "He was without a doubt a very, very important element in the success of the stories," recalls director/producer Arthur Lubin. "What a dear man," Connie Hines adds, who at the time was still a relatively unseasoned performer. "Larry saved my fanny so many times. He would show me tricks. When Edna Skinner would upstage me (she was so tall, and I was so short), he would tell me to stand a certain way."

Early in 1963, Larry learned that he was terminally ill with leukemia. For the last six months of his life, he continued to play Roger Addison. He died on August 26, 1963, at the age of sixty-four. The last episode Keating appeared in was #80, "Patter of Little Hooves." Alan Young remembers that during the shooting of "Leo Durocher Meets Mister Ed" (#81), Keating was fooling around on the base paths at Dodger Stadium, where much of the show was filmed. He asked Alan Young to assist him getting up, and reported gravely to his friend, "This is the last time you'll pick me up." Larry did not appear in this episode, and he died just six days later.

While the show's producers were busy trying to fill the Addisons' void, since neighbors were an essential part of the *Mister Ed* mix, the character of Kay Addison (Edna Skinner) remained for the transition and was highlighted in fantasy sequences and musical duets with Jack Albertson, who played her brother, Paul Fenton. Skinner appeared in nine episodes without Keating and was ultimately replaced by new neighbors, Winnie and Gordon Kirkwood.

Gordon and Winnie
take over the
Post domicile in
"Home Sweet Trailer,"
the 1963 episode
which marked their
debut on the series.

The second set of next-door neighbors continues the tradition of doubting Wilbur's sanity, picking up right where Roger Addison left off. "I wonder if they have get-well cards for his kind of sickness," Gordon Kirkwood muses. And if you thought that Roger Addison was a tad rough-edged, Gordon Kirkwood is absolutely sandpaperish. After all, he is a retired air force colonel. "Well, you know, the colonel was not very lovable," Connie Hines recalls of the switch in neighbors. "Larry Keating, even though he was very firm with Wilbur, was very loving. My character was more warm to Larry than to the colonel." Case in point, Connie Hines dances up a storm with Keating in two episodes, once as a cha-cha instructor and another time as a hula girl. During these instances, it's Kay Addison and Wilbur who look on the two swingers as if they're loony. This is another example of just how relative (and delicate) sanity is in *Mister Ed.*

A good situation where the writers thwart our expectations about who's sane/who's insane happens in "Ed's Dentist." In this episode, Gordon Kirkwood is the crazy one. He's bent on exposing Wilbur as deranged, so he follows the man-horse pair around town in order to photograph their wild escapades. He takes a picture of Mister Ed in the dentist's office (the horse is there for a new crown), but is in such a hurry, he doesn't notice that his camera is turned backward. When he rushes home to show Winnie and Carol the photo, it's a self-portrait. Very silly stuff. The photograph we see was obviously taken at arm's length and is perfectly in focus.

The Grumpy Father-in-law

Mister Ed has the obligatory father-in-law character, Mr. Higgins, to play off Wilbur's eccentricities. The architect has a no-win relationship with Carol's dad, a sourpuss par excellence played by Barry Kelly. As far as Mr. Higgins is concerned, Wilbur is a certified "kook." His visits to 17230 Valley Spring Lane burst with sight gags and bits of physical comedy at which Alan Young is so adept. Here's a classic example of a "familial faux pas": In "What Kind of Foal Am I?" Ed is obsessed with finding his long-lost "Pa-pa." Just as Wilbur is offering his father-in-law a brand-new box of chocolates (his "favorites, chocolate and cream centers"), Ed flashes a sign to his boss, "Going to Mom." Ed's announcement startles Wilbur, causing him to stumble with the box, catapulting melted chocolates all over Mr. Higgins' shirt. True to the pattern, Ed's "crazy causes" are responsible for Wilbur's mishaps.

"Never Ride Horses" features yet another visit from Carol's dad. (He appeared in several shows during the 1965 season.) This show is overflowing with "Wilburisms," one awkward move after another. While eating salad at the dinner table, the architect is distracted by Ed's "pro-social" message, painted on the window shade. Not concentrating on his dinner, he squirts lemon at Mr. Higgins. This scene is wonderfully directed by Lubin. Wilbur's fumbling builds until Carol's father is absolutely suffering. To end these scenes, Mr. Higgins usually implores his daughter, "Carol, please come home, we've left your bedroom just the way it was." Carol tries to defend her man: "Wilbur only does silly things in front of you," but usually digs a deeper hole for her hubby.

You'd never believe it, but Barry Kelly was an extremely sweet man, Alan Young recalls. He used to take his wife's homemade fudge down to the Filmways set. Kelly's grouchy character reminded Young of the roles played by Ed Begley, Sr., whom he worked with on radio in the 1940s. Begley played the father of Young's girlfriend on the program and made similar "squinty-eyed" facial expressions of malcontent while reading his lines.

HOW TO RESOLVE ANYTHING
IN 27 MINUTES

A page from Carol Post's diary might read as follows:

> Tuesday I found Mister Ed sleeping in our <u>bed</u> during our second honeymoon...
>
> Thursday Mister Ed wore all my new lingerie in a magic act— and <u>took a bow</u>, no less!...
>
> Yesterday I found a bill from the feed store. Wilbur spends <u>fifteen cents an apple</u> on that horse...

(To get a sense of what Carol's complaining about, if you factor in the rate of inflation, fifteen cents is probably equivalent to what you'd pay nowadays for one of those mammoth apples at a Korean deli in New York City.)

Courtesy of
Connie Hines.

The fourth typical *Mister Ed* dynamic shapes up as follows: No matter how outraged or shocked by her husband's behavior, no matter how often she is made to feel like second fiddle to a horse, Carol Post winds up forgiving and loving Wilbur, in spite of his equine fixation. Carol's unconditional love for Wilbur is a key dynamic to resolving family harmony at the end of each episode. To use Carol's own words, "Mister Ed should be my worst competitor." In other words, life's a bit wacky with a husband who's crazy about his horse, but at least Carol isn't sharing Wilbur with another *woman*. In fact, some of the silliest moments in *Mister Ed* occur when Ed telephones Wilbur in the middle of the night, and Carol overhears things like, "Of course I love you too. Now go back to sleep." Wilbur usually explains the call as "just a wrong number," but Connie Hines is great at being the perpetually frustrated, confused wife. She gets better with each season.

How does Carol Post handle being mad at her husband? Now and then, she does "go home to Mother" (an entire book could be devoted to sitcom wives who go home to Mother, probing questions like, "What do they do when they get there?" and "Aren't they bored?"). However, we never actually meet Mrs. Higgins, and Carol always ends up coming back, very forgiving.

Carol is also one of the many 1950s/60s sitcom wives who enroll their husbands in the "Frequent Sofa Program" (or FSP). During a spat, she tells Wilbur to sleep out in the "barnsy warnsy," or to go off to "couchy-bye" downstairs. But we know she loves him, despite her control of the bedroom. "Arthur Lubin used to say to me, 'Don't forget to bubble,'" Connie Hines says, reflecting on her years playing the ultimately optimistic Carol. "And that was it. I was supposed to be a loving wife whose husband could do no wrong. He was a little nutsy, but she loved him, she accepted him, with all his warts. And that's the way it was then."

Some of the episodes that showcase Carol's loyalty are surprisingly dramatic (at least, as dramatic as this show gets), and hinge on keeping/selling Mister Ed. Carol's love for Ed is actually a "love for *Wilbur's love of Ed.*" In "Ed Agrees to Talk," Carol's devotion is clear. She tells Mrs. Adams, an SPCA inspector, "We would never mistreat our horse.... Oh, Wilbur, I'm sorry I started the whole thing [hitching Ed to a wagon to prove a point]. You don't have to buy me a new car. Ohhh!!" (And she exits, in tears.)

In "Zsa Zsa," Carol wants a mink coat. These episodes have a similar pattern: (1) Carol wants something; (2) Wilbur tells her they can't afford it; (3) conflict ensues; (4) conflict is resolved, and all is well. A then-peaceable and youthful Zsa Zsa Gabor guest-stars in this episode. Arthur Lubin remembers that the glamorous Hungarian was very happy to have the opportunity to appear in *Mister Ed.* In this episode, Carol and Mister Ed both make sacrifices for each other, almost like an equine version of O'Henry's "The Gift of the Magi." "Mister Eddie" leaves Wilbur for Zsa Zsa, and Carol gives up the chance to own a mink coat. When push comes to shove, it's Carol's devotion to Wilbur that restores family harmony (and the love triangle). She tells him: "A mink coat doesn't mean that much to me. Not as much as losing Mister Ed means to you. I'm going to send this check right back."

If you're thinking of going back and watching the *Mister Ed* episodes with renewed vigor, be on the lookout for Carol's most common gesture. It may be a clue to either a spat in progress or a conflict on the verge of resolution. You can always find Carol *shrugging her shoulders and shaking her head.* Ahh, but look a little closer. If she's smiling, the gesture means: "Gee, isn't Wilbur silly, but I do love him so." But if she's frowning, the gesture implies: "Oooh, you and that horse, you can sleep in the barn tonight." And that's exactly what he does, as noted earlier. In "Ed's Mother," Carol Post herself best sums up *Mister Ed's* dynamic of unconditional love: "Okay, honey, I don't mind if you're an animal lover. As long as you don't stop being a wife lover." And that's the bottom line.

"I'M JUST A DUMB ANIMAL, WHAT'S YOUR EXCUSE?"

Ever notice how in every episode of *Mister Ed,* as soon as Wilbur leaves the barn, Ed faces the camera and confides in *us,* the audience? During these moments, he reveals his motives behind a scheme (as in theatrical asides), or he comments on silly human behavior (the "quintessence of human futility" for all you lit majors). Or he admits his fears or is omniscient, a device perfected earlier by George Burns in *Burns and Allen* and continued in *Wendy and Me.* Like George, Ed steps out of the scene, *breaks the fourth wall* and shares with us whatever's on his mind. His soliloquies or monologues to the camera are a regular feature of every episode. "If you really analyze it, Ed is doing everything for the benefit of the audience," observes Al Simon, so it works when Ed winks to the camera, for example. Incidentally, besides financing the pilot, George Burns staged the first three months of *Mister Ed.* Alan Young remembers that George was very concerned that the show be "put on properly" in its early stages, and director Lubin recalls that George "got bored" after directing a few episodes.

The fifth and final dynamic in *Mister Ed* is as follows: Ed's character *appears* to be a dumb animal, literally *dumb* to all the characters but Wilbur, but actually, he's very street-smart and savvy. This contradiction makes Ed the "wise fool" in the classical sense, and as the fool, he has ultimate control over situations. He talks to Wilbur and confides in the audience, but it's always on his terms. If he wants to avoid accountability, no problem. He just turns into a horse again. Wilbur picks up on this in "Ed's Cold Tail," when Ed uses his crackerjack excuse for not having to talk—faking laryngitis. "Ed, you've lost your voice," Wilbur blurts out. "You're back to being a *dumb* animal again." Besides lots of horse puns, the writers have a good time with the double meaning of "dumb." And in "The Good Samaritan," Ed registers a complaint about the paperboy under Wilbur's name, causing the kid to get fired. When Wilbur asks him why he did it, Ed replies innocently, "How do I know? I'm only a horse." Of course he's much more than a horse. Throughout the series, you get the feeling that Ed might have invented the incandescent bulb if Thomas Edison hadn't beaten him to it.

The best part of Ed's soliloquies is that, occasionally, when he's in rare form, he lets us in on the larger "gag" of *Mister Ed.* We get a sense that *Mister Ed* is every bit as self-conscious about itself as a sitcom as we are. These are the moments where we, along with the writers and producers, get to laugh at the *show,* not the story itself. Arthur Lubin claims that the audience loves "inside" lines which make reference to him as the director. For example, in "Robin Hood Ed," while the horse is directing Wilbur in a screen test, Ed turns to the camera and says, "I wonder if Arthur Lubin has all this trouble."

Candid Camera: Ed, on Ed

Here is a sampling of Ed's hilariously insightful speeches to the camera:

○ You can fool all the horses part of the time; and part of the horses all the time; but you can't fool this horse *anytime.*
○ We gotta be kind to humans—people need all the help they can get.
○ Wilbur is a simple man. Sometimes you gotta frighten him into things.
○ People should skin each other and leave us animals alone.
○ I think I'll become a Robin Hood and dedicate my life to helping the poor. Only it's gonna be rough finding them in this fancy neighborhood.
○ People—they sure can get a horse into a lot of trouble.
○ I'm gonna take from the rich and give to the poor. And it won't be easy—after taxes, who can tell the difference?
○ Time and Ed wait for no man.
○ There's more than one way to skin a Wilbur!
○ Boy, isn't nature wonderful! To think, we had all this before people came around and spoiled it!

The Ed Commandments

Despite the fact that a talking horse breaks every rule in the book, there were actually guidelines for developing Ed's character. Sure, the writers could give him any old line to say and manipulate the laugh tracks to respond obediently. But to really develop Ed as an individual with (almost always) predictable behaviors, his words had to follow a characteristic pattern. Here are the six unspoken "Ed Commandments" which were used, perhaps unconsciously, to shape Ed's remarks, and make him the TV icon that he is today.

1. Mister Ed applies "horse sense" to people situations and "people sense" to horse situations:

WILBUR: Ed, when did you learn to hula?
ED: When a grasshopper got into my tail.

ED: Some days it just doesn't pay to get out of the hay.

2. Mister Ed has the experience of an elder but the mettle of an infant:

ED: My first solo—my four legs are shakin' like they were the Wright Brothers.

3. Mister Ed is a walking "Ed-itorial"—he's got an opinion about absolutely everything:

ED: He's got fat in places where you're not even supposed to have places.

4. Mister Ed is always, always honest to the camera (to us, the audience):

ED: It's tough to be a horse when your heart isn't in it.

5. Mister Ed takes for granted that he is a member of the Post family and expects all the benefits that a Post child would receive:

ED: Oh, Wilbur, I don't know how much you plan to leave me [in your will], but remember one thing, that cat got $50,000.

6. Mister Ed will never seriously jeopardize Wilbur Post's happiness and will sacrifice his own life with the Posts in order to preserve Carol and Wilbur's marriage:

ED: No one's sending me home [from the Posts' Hawaii honeymoon] like excess baggage. I'm gonna live here, and become a beachcomber.

STRAIN THE BRAIN

"Strain the Brain," hosted by Happy Hannegan, was the name of the radio trivia contest which Ed played and won in "TV or Not TV" (episode 137).
1. If Ed and Carol were both drowning, who would Wilbur save first?
2a. What is the "Law of the Jungle," according to Wilbur?
2b. What is the "Law of the Jungle," according to Mister Ed?
3. What special kind of bank account does Carol have?
4. What does Carol sarcastically suggest that Wilbur get bronzed?
5. What muscular condition does Ed get from delivering so much mail?
6. Why does Mister Ed go off to become an army sentry?
7. When Addison overhears Ed talking in episode 2, how does Wilbur explain the phenomenon?
8. What does Ed give Carol for her birthday?
9. What gift does Wilbur give Ed for their fifth anniversary?
10. What Shakespearean role does Gordon Kirkwood find Wilbur playing in a scene with Ed?
11. What kind of a name is Ed for a horse?
12. What are the contents of the CARE package that Wilbur makes up for Ed as he's leaving home in "Mister Ed Writes Dear Abby"?

ANSWERS

1. "That's a silly question" . . . Ed's a good swimmer.
2a. Wives before horses.
2b. A smear campaign spread by humans to give animals a bad name.
3. A joint husband account, with a horse.
4. The horseshoes Ed wore when he was biting his nails.
5. A charley person. People get charley horses, so horses get charley people.
6. He thinks Carol is allergic to him.
7. Ventriloquism.
8. A singing telephone-gram.
9. A camera and tripod.
10. Juliet, in the balcony scene. Of course Ed plays Romeo: "What balcony can hold a horse?!"
11. What kind of a name is Wilbur for a man?
12. A giant toothbrush and comb, shower cap, sunglasses, comic books.

5

"A Man Toils From Sun to Sun, but a Horse's Work Is Never Done"

···

CREATING A **MISTER ED** EPISODE

A STABLE OF TALENT

The *Mister Ed* creative team was extremely well credentialed, having worked previously on such shows as *I Love Lucy, Burns and Allen* and *Red Skelton.* Quite naturally, they brought with them a "golden age of television" discipline. How, then, could a show propelled by staff so well versed in TV comedy be anything but funny?

Ed's Writers: Putting Words in the Horse's Mouth

Mister Ed was fortunate to have many top-notch comedy writers on its roster, in varying capacities. **Willy Burns,** George Burns' brother, and **Norman Paul,** had been the writers for *Burns and Allen.* The two went on to serve as script consultants throughout the entire *Mister Ed* series. Alan Young knew Norman Paul from his own radio days. "He was my first writer on radio when I came to America [circa 1946]. I brought him out to Hollywood."

Mister Ed head writer **Lou Derman** had a long, successful background in radio, including *Life With Luigi,* before moving over to television. Before *Mister Ed,* he wrote for the sitcom *December Bride* (CBS, 1954–61), as well as material for Ed Wynn, Milton Berle, Eddie Cantor and Jim Backus.

Mister Ed scripter, **Ben Starr,** who wrote for the series during the first and third years, had written for Bob Hope and *I Married Joan* before joining the Filmways team. During *Mister Ed*'s run, Starr also wrote for *My Favorite Martian,* another popular fantasy sitcom for CBS.

Larry Rhine joined Lou Derman in 1963, and together, they wrote some of the funniest *Mister Ed* episodes. Rhine actually moonlighted on *Mister Ed* while retaining his full-time job as writer for Red Skelton, whose show was a television mainstay for twenty years.

Collaboration Was King: The Writing Process

Though he was not officially listed in the show's credits, George Burns had a real interest in *Mister Ed*'s story development. It was more than just George's owning a piece of the show. General Service Studios was like one big happy family. "I think the reason *Mister Ed* worked so well was that so many good people contributed to it; there were a lot of people who liked the project," Al Simon recalls about the earliest days of the series. "I think George Burns set up this system of collaborative writing which worked so well for him on *Burns and Allen.*"

Everyone involved with the show remembers the role that George Burns played in *Mister Ed*'s creative development. Even CEO of Filmways TV, Marty Ransohoff, recalls that "George was very involved. He was at every final writer's session."

At the beginning of the series, there are a few episodes in which Ed has an unusually minor role, strange since the show is named after him. Scripter Ben Starr, who wrote the first year's episodes with Lou Derman, offered an explanation: "When we started the show, we had about seven scripts not shot yet. One day, George said, 'I'm tired of that horse, he keeps talking, I'm sick of it.' So we did a show that focused on the people ["The Missing Statue"]. But when the show actually got on, and we saw that people loved the horse, George said, 'Put the horse back in!' "

Script Meetings With George Burns

As you can imagine, working with George Burns could be very colorful at times. "They had a little writers' office," Herb Browar remembers. "Norman Paul wrote all the George and Gracie shows. He liked to lie down on the couch and that's how he'd write. There was a guy named Tommy Clap, he could type as fast as you could talk."

"Lou and I would get a story," Ben Starr says as he describes the script development. "Then we would go to George Burns' office," the same office he had for years at General Service Studios. "We would pitch to George and his brother Willie, and Norman Paul. We'd have a blast. He'd give me a cigar. I'd immediately start to cry because as soon as I got in, George would start singing."

Alan Young laughingly admits, "I put a damper on things when I came into the writers' room because I didn't smoke, I didn't drink, and they'd quiet things down for me." Alan Young adds that George Burns was the best editor there ever was.

"Everyone would throw in ideas," Al Simon adds. "Then the shows were finished up. Right before production, George might add a few more things."

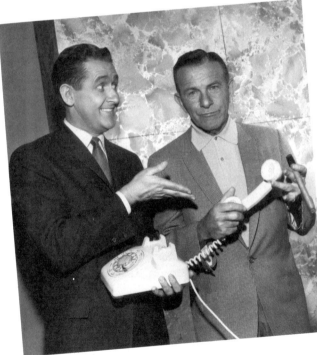

© *1990 CBS Inc.*
George Burns makes a cameo in "Ed Finally Talks," 1961.

Interview With George Burns

On July 19, 1990, the author was lucky enough to spend twenty minutes with show biz legend George Burns, then ninety-four years young. When I arrived at George's modest Hollywood office, the room was filled with the scent of cigar . . . I knew I was in the right place. He was dressed casually, wearing tweed slacks, a sports jacket and fishing cap. The walls were adorned with many photos, including several of the beautiful Gracie Allen, and one of Jack Benny, George's best friend, looking not quite as beautiful dressed in drag.

GEORGE BURNS: The most important thing about *Mister Ed* is that there's a man who everyone thinks is crazy because the horse can only talk to him.

NN: What interested you about the project when Arthur Lubin first came to you in 1958?

GB: He had done Francis the Talking Mule pictures, and they were successful, so I said, "Sure, let's do it."

NN: Why does Ed only talk to Wilbur?

GB: He should only talk to one person, the man, who everyone thinks is nuts. The horse isn't the star of the show, the man is.

NN: I heard a story that you were casting for the lead of the show, and all these actors' names were brought up as possibilities, and you finally said, "Get Alan Young. He looks like the kind of guy that a horse would talk to."

GB: That sounds good, you can use it.

NN: Did you want Willy [Burns] and Norman Paul, the writers from *Burns and Allen,* to work on *Mister Ed?*

GB: Yes, because *Mister Ed* was very important to me. I owned a piece of the show, and I wanted it to do well. But the show was taken over by another writer, Lou Derman. They even had the horse driving once ["Ed the Chauffeur," episode 99]. I nearly died when I heard that!
    The horse is a horse. The horse can do anything a horse can do. Any horse can do what this horse can do. But there's

only one thing that this horse can do that none of the horses can do. He can talk. Outside of that, he picks up his tail when he goes to the bathroom just like any horse. And you don't have to worry when you got Mister Ed. You don't have to give him a star's dressing room. Just give him a little hay. You don't have to worry about billing for the horse, no problem with bathrooms. Well, you got a problem with the bathroom because he does it on the stage.

NN: I heard that *Mister Ed* was Jack Benny's favorite show.

GB: It had to be his favorite show because I was his favorite friend, and if it wasn't his favorite show, I'd hit him!

NN: Did you try to shape the character of Carol Post after Gracie's character?

GB: No. Maybe the writer of the show tried. When Gracie was a hit, everybody had a dizzy dame. They were all dumb, but Gracie didn't think she was. Gracie thought she was smart. And she was smart.

NN: What kinds of things in the show did you get involved with creatively?

GB: Once Arthur Lubin shot the horse a little bit wrong for me. He shot under the horse's belly. So I called him into the office and said, "Arthur, don't shoot the horse under the horse's stomach. Shoot above that because under there, you see the horse's privates, we don't want to see that."

NN: I heard that you had a great time with the writers. That they'd work on a story and then come into your office.

GB: That's right. We'd talk in the office and smoke cigars, and we'd sing and enjoy ourselves. I very rarely had anybody put anything on paper. We all made it up, in the office. So the writers, when they went home at night, if they wanted to go out with their wives, they could do that. They didn't have to sit home and write, and then bring in the paper. We'd sit in the room, we'd think of a story, and we'd develop it right there and then. If the story was good, we would use it. And if it wasn't good, I'd get another writer. The nice thing about being a boss, nobody can fire you.

NN: Do you have a favorite *Mister Ed* story?

GB (*Pause*): I made money. I got paid every week.

"Joke Comedy With Juvenile Whimsy"

Variety on October 6, 1964, in reviewing the season premiere, "Hi-Fi Horse," wrote: "What the writers, Lou Derman and Larry Rhine, put together each week for Young, Connie Hines, Leon Ames and Florence MacMichael is joke comedy with juvenile whimsy. Most of the one-liners are Ed's, as it should be, and this is what gives the show its strong tug with the sub-teeners."

Ben Starr, who cowrote the first season with Lou Derman, explains how they got the show to appeal to both kids and adults: "We wrote it on two levels: We wrote it so children would enjoy it, which was pretty easy to do since we had a horse doing things; but we wrote it mainly for adults. If you take a look at the shows, they were very strongly plotted. We dealt with adult themes. We always treated Ed as if he was a young boy. We never played him like a truly precocious kid. He was very fundamental. He was street-smart, but very basic. If he ate the vegetables in the garden, it was simply because he was hungry."

"Everytime that horse opens his mouth, it has to come out funny," Lou Derman told *TV Guide* in 1962. Writer Larry Rhine, who scripted episodes with Lou Derman starting in the third season, relished the opportunity to write stories for *Mister Ed.* "I loved the show," Larry said recently. "This was situation comedy. So we came up with legitimate premises for Mister Ed." The veteran writer was used to the sketch-comedy format from his *Red Skelton* work. "I'd leave Skelton and make a right to Lou's place to work on Ed." It was Esther Derman's chicken dinners that convinced Larry to join the *Mister Ed* team in 1963, if truth be told.

Head Writer Lou Derman

"Lou Derman was one of the most beautiful people in the business," Rhine recalls. "He was responsible, in my judgment, for the success of the show in many ways." The head writer developed two premises that really defined *Mister Ed.*

THE TWO PREMISES OF LOU DERMAN

1. Ed is a teenager.
2. The phone connects him to the outside world.

© *1990 CBS Inc.*
**Ed poses with
the man who
made him funny—
head scripter
Lou Derman—
in 1961.**

The first rule of thumb was to treat Ed as a teenager. "The minute you said that, it opened up all the premises," Rhine explains, "because Wilbur was the father and Ed was the recalcitrant teenager kicking over the traces literally and figuratively. So this gave us our premises. He wanted a pad of his own. And he wanted to be 'Taller Than She' [episode 83]. And he wanted to play the guitar, and this was the sixties and he wanted his mane to grow long. So it gave us our stories.

"It is a little tricky to realize how important the second premise was. Lou had the idea of a telephone in the barn that would stretch over to Ed's stall. The importance of this was that it connected Ed with the outside world. And Ed couldn't be connected otherwise because he couldn't talk to anybody but Wilbur. Here he could talk to everybody because they didn't know it was a horse. So when Ed got in his stall after misbehaving, Wilbur would say, 'You're a bad horsie and you're going to stay there,' and he'd slam the door shut, and we'd always take good care to leave the phone there. And Ed would pick up the phone and say, 'Hello, Locksmith, this is an irate citizen. A poor innocent horse is locked in his stall,' and he'd get out, and he'd leave a note, 'I've run away, don't try to find me at Pier 7 at nine o'clock.' "

Rhine believes that these premises of Lou Derman really contributed to the charm of *Mister Ed.* "You know, people like to personify animals," the writer explains. "Look at Disney. He had all the animals talking, and people accepted that. All the way back to Krazy Kat and Mickey Mouse. But this show had a few conceits that the average talking-animal show didn't have. The fact that Ed could only talk to Wilbur. See, if the horse talked to everybody, you wouldn't have a show. But here was a great source of embarrassment for Wilbur."

Lou Derman was almost as versatile as Mister Ed, the character he created. All right, Lou couldn't skateboard. But listen to this: "Lou Derman was a very interesting character," Rhine points out. "He had an undertaker's face . . . you'd never figure that anything funny would come out of that. He was an excellent writer. He was an excellent photographer. He was a marksman with pistols. He went out and competed with the police and the marines. He appeared at the Magic Castle Friday nights and did comedy magic. He innovated comedy magic. They never had that before. Magic itself is very limited. You find the card, you link the rings, and everyone tries to figure out how you do it. But Lou always had a comedy twist. He built a room in his home to create these illusions. And while we were writing, he'd be working on these things. He wrote for a magazine called *The Linking Rings.* He had a column there and he got letters from people all over the world."

Lou Derman threw much of himself into *Mister Ed* episodes. Besides being an L.A. Dodger fanatic, Alan Young remembers that Lou loved Mexico, perhaps explaining why an early episode takes place south of the border, in "Ed the Witness." Lou and his partner would write one show a week. "We did the last two shows in one week, just to see if we could do it," boasts Ben Starr with youthful enthusiasm.

"This Has Been a Filmways Presentation"

Does that sign-off message sound familiar? It was spoken at the end of every *Mister Ed* episode (by either Larry Keating or Allan "Rocky" Lane), and later, on *Green Acres* (by Eva Gabor, with a little "dahling" added), to identify the shows as Filmways productions. Al Simon and Marty Ransohoff thought up the line in the earliest days of their TV company. "Companies don't take advantage of their trademark enough," Simon points out. No other TV production company of the 1960s used such an attention-getting technique for identifying themselves.

PRODUCTION GEMS

As if putting on a show each week about a talking horse weren't enough, the producers of *Mister Ed* made sure that they infused the episodes with lots of whimsical touches, clever little devices of fancy rarely seen in TV shows today. Like dressing Ed up as his devilish alter ego, or putting Wilbur in a king's robe to represent Carol's daydream. Making certain scenes more like live-action Looney Tunes might have been for the benefit of *Mister Ed*'s kids in the audience, but it's hard to imagine that the adult viewers refrained from chuckling too, even if it was just out of a sheer "I can't believe they're actually doing this" reaction.

When looking at these playful scenes, you get the feeling that the whole production team was very much in sync creatively. "Sometimes these ideas like Ed's devil would come out of a writing session," explains Herb Browar. The creative group's understanding of the workings of comedy, and the traditions of vaudeville, slapstick and burlesque, was clearly sophisticated.

Honest-to-goodness Special Effects

Mister Ed is so founded in fantasy and "suspension of disbelief," relying heavily on cinematic tricks and stunts (thank goodness!), that it would've been impossible to film the show "in front of a live studio audience," as is the case with many of today's sitcoms. Imagine how it might have been, though: Right in the middle of a pivotal *Mister Ed* scene, the producers suddenly have to dismiss the studio audience for an hour lunch break so that Ed can perfect his answering of the telephone. That never would have cut it. Hence, the device of laugh track was heartily employed.

Granted, the show will not go down in communications history as "seamless" television. It's full of rough edges and quirks, even an occasional mistake or two. Certainly the majority of its special effects are positively preposterous. Yet it is the lack of sophistication and realism—what we are seeing in *Mister Ed* is clearly unbelievable—that makes the show so appealing. Nearly every episode has that characteristically honest, homespun look. And compared to more polished contemporary sitcoms like *The Dick Van Dyke Show* and *Hazel,* TV audiences must have found *Mister Ed* to be a refreshing departure.

Nowadays, TV and movie fans are caught up in special effects *ennui,* a "What have you done for me lately?" mentality. Still, *Mister Ed* fans continue to enjoy the show for its relative technical innocence, and its heavy reliance on the old-fashioned power of imagination. Those of us who were very young kids during *Mister Ed*'s original run never noticed the lack of sophistication. Little did we know that we'd actually come to *celebrate* it some thirty years later. And we certainly didn't see the mistakes. As a reference point, we were also the ones who thought *Batman* was a serious crime-action series, not realizing it was deluxe camp until years later when it went into syndication.

Mister Ed's far-fetched special effects are neither inconsistent nor annoying. In fact, by watching and enjoying the show, you implicitly agree to accept them at face-value . . . and they "make sense" in the context of the ridiculous whole. Case in point: Precisely the way Mister Ed looks balancing on a surfboard, wearing fan-blown scarves, while pasted against surfing footage, is as important to the show as the fact that he is soaking up local culture. The effect has as much to do with enhancing the silly mood and charm of the episode as anything the characters might say or do.

Associate producer Herb Browar still praises the ingenuity of the late Larry Chapman, special-effects man on *Mister Ed*. "It was mind boggling, the way he had to work things out, and he had to build things too." Herb is still very touched by the memory that Larry made his son a bicycle from spare parts which the boy could ride whenever he visited the *Mister Ed* set.

Unsolvable Query #2

If Ed only has access to an *extension* phone, how does he manage to telephone Wilbur in the living room and the bedroom from out in the barn?

© *1990 CBS Inc.*

Favorable Faux Pas

Mister Ed is chock full of production inconsistencies, bloopers if you will. And we wouldn't have it any other way.

○ *Nighty night?*: Ed gets up from sleep, and Wilbur takes off his striped night cap (yes, with a pom-pom); Ed goes back down to sleep and *still* has his night cap on. Either the same footage is used, or else Ed is the quickest hoof in the West.

○ *Give us a hand!*: A classic faux pas occurs in episode 41, "The Wrestler," in which Les Hilton's hand is visible in the barn mirror, directing Ed. Think about it: Which scene would you enjoy more—a tidier one without the disembodied hand in the wall mirror, or the existing scene *with* the hand? C'mon . . . fess up. It's a lot more fun seeing the hand.

○ *Mr. . . . Father-in-law*: What's Carol Post's real maiden name, anyway? Don't look to the credits for an answer. Her grumpy papa, Mr. Higgins, is credited three different ways throughout the series, although in the scripts themselves, he's always referred to as "Mr. Higgins." At various times he's listed in the credits as "Mr. Carlysle" ("Horse Wash"), "Mr. Hergeshiemer" ("Never Ride Horses") and "Mr. Higgins" (the law of odds required that they get it right *some* of the time).

○ *Postal puzzle*: In "Pageant Show," the address for the Posts' house is 17340 Valley Boulevard, not the 17230 Valley Spring Lane in the rest of the episodes.

○ *"Now you see it, now you don't!"*: In "Ed-a-Go-Go," the Kerrigans' door has "7138" printed on it in one shot. (By the way, this was the Kirkwoods' address when they were still regulars on the show.) In the very next shot, the door has no address on it!

○ *Person-to-person*: In "Horse Sense," Wilbur gets a phone call from a gentleman who admired the writing style of his Letter to the Editor (ghost-written by Ed, of course). He tells Wilbur that he'd like him to write a book on animals for a spring release, but *never identifies himself.* Seconds later, Wilbur is addressing the caller as *Mr. Boyd, the publisher.*

A Bit o' the Vaudeville

We've got sight gags galore: bananas flying across the room and landing in the mouth of an African mask; a cork from a champagne bottle shooting into Roger Addison's mouth; Ed tossing a bucket which lands perfectly on a monkey's head. And of course Alan Young was a talented physical comedian, having mastered the art of the pratfall on his own TV show which ran from 1950 to 1953. (*Mister Ed* is rife with scenes showing Wilbur wrestling, being flipped, falling and tripping.) Even in the very first show, we get a hint of the antics to come, when Carol steps on a rake in the backyard, causing it to stand up and smack Wilbur in the face. And there are countless pies and cakes being thrown into faces (faces of grouches, of course).

Fun With Film

Mister Ed deals with real animals so often that the film is played with in postproduction to make the otherwise impossible, TV possible. When the producers want to show a racehorse, Lady Linda, listless from a broken heart, they slow down both the film of her galloping and the trumpet music to a full stop. Or when Ed stages a massive sit-down at Tally Ho Stables, we are actually seeing film of horses getting up, run backward, to simulate horses sitting down. The same technique is used when Clint Eastwood guest-stars. To illustrate how resistant Ed is to carrying Clint, the palomino sits down with the young star on board, but in reality, it's reversed film of Ed standing up. Alan Young points out that it's extraordinarily difficult for a horse to sit down while carrying a passenger.

Devil Horse

At some point, it was decided that a talking horse acting of his own volition might have been a tad dull, and Ed's devil alter ego, a very cartoonish feature, was introduced. In "My Horse the Ranger" and "Saddles and Gowns," Ed and even Wilbur come face-to-face with their fun-loving parts, their devils, dressed in the stereotypical garb. Note Ed's darkened eyebrows. "The devil's advocate" is how *Variety* referred to the horse star in these 1964 episodes.

When Ed naively says to his mischievous side, "You're a devil!" the fiend replies, "I didn't get these horns at the five-and-ten!"

© *Orion Television. Reprinted with permission.*
Ed with his devil alter ego in "My Horse the Ranger," 1965.

Tall Tunes

Music is used playfully to exaggerate or counterpoint what we're seeing in *Mister Ed*. When Ed decides to take up a life of hard labor, i.e., pulling a wagon (unheard-of for this Hollywood horse), in "Ed's Ancestors," we hear *Exodus*-like music, evoking labor on a tragic scale, followed by camera cuts of Ed lamenting, "Oh, my achin' back!" with a relieved laugh track.

Sappy violin music is used in Ed's romantic interludes, and to express the maudlin dedication of a blacksmith to his noble calling. In both instances, the cliché "restaurant" violin music makes the audience aware of the self-conscious, deliberate drive for humor.

Theme Song Particulars

The lyrics to the *Mister Ed* theme song were introduced in episode 7, "Little Boy."

○ *Episode 1*: Music only. Ed can't say hello; it would spoil the surprise.
○ *Episodes 2–6*: "Hello, I'm Mister Ed" followed by music only.
○ *Episodes 7–143*: "Hello, I'm Mister Ed" followed by music and lyrics.

Some of Ed's (Mouth-Painted) Signs

Ed was always communicating with Wilbur, even when he wasn't physically there in the barn. He'd leave his classic "running away from home" notes, or better yet, a freshly painted sign, with marvelous, not-too-sloppy, not-too-neat hoofwriting. Here are just a few of the signs that he hung on his stall door, held in his mouth or wore as sandwich boards over the course of the series:

Laryngitis
Went to Cahuenga Car Wash. Bring Money.
Do Not Disturb—This Means You, Wilbur
Ed-a-Go-Go—Minors Only
Old Fogies Must a Go-Go
Out to Lunch
Pony Express. Have Saddle Will Travel.
Quarantined! Horse Mumps.
Smile
Be Modern—Drive a Car
Beware of Dog
Ride a Taxi
Don't Ride Horses
Gone Home to Mother

All Choked Up

When the story called for Ed not to talk, the writers came up with two interesting devices to restrain him: (1) fitting him with a muzzle (twice, so Wilbur can get his work done), and (2) giving the horse a bad case of laryngitis, so even if his heart is in the right place and he agrees to talk to help Wilbur, his vocal cords can't comply. And of course there's the occasional situation where Ed simply *pretends* to have laryngitis, bundling himself up in blankets, towels and hot water bottles.

Miscellaneous Production Gems

○ *Put up or shut up*: Ed is infamous for being able to shut his stall shutters with his teeth, really fast. The film is sped up, and he does this whenever (a) he wants to avoid blame for some bit of mischief that he's committed, and (b) as a form of protest against whoever's in the barn, usually Addison.

○ *Face-to-face*: In "Horsetronaut," Wilbur misses Ed so much, he imagines Ed's face superimposed on the face of his secretary, Miss Culbertson (played by Hazel Shermet). She's chewing gum; Ed is munching on apples, making the similarity between the two more striking. Wilbur reaches out to stroke Ed's face, and his secretary shrieks. The architect claims that she had a fly on her nose.

○ *Animation*: In "Never Ride Horses," Ed hires a plane to skywrite "Don't ride horses," and the effect is created through animation (looking a lot like "Surrender Dorothy" in *The Wizard of Oz*). Also, in "Ed the Counterspy," while Ed is doing "horse code," we see an animated flickering light from the window, used to represent the dots and dashes.

○ *Sounds like*: There are many situations where sound effects are really exaggerated or not consistent with the visual—for example, when the producers want to convey Ed making a racket in his stall, they add canned kicking and neighing. We get the idea—Ed wants to get out so he can make a phone call, or Ed wants to sneak a peek at the model undressing. Or when we hear the baby Madeline crying in "Ed Gets the Mumps," we see her perfectly calm face!

Did You Ever See a Barn Dance?

In several episodes, Ed's barn works like a mobile home, picking itself up by its wood beams and moving to far more exotic locales. Well, not really, but did you ever take a good look at Mr. Manaloa's stables in the Hawaii episode? If you examine the set closely, it's one and the same as Ed's, but for the removal of a panel, brighter lighting and the use of a different camera

Mister Ed's DIGS

PHOTOS OF ED'S RELATIVES

ED'S BLANKET HANGS HERE

EXTERIOR FEED BIN

CORRAL

INFAMOUS SHUTTER DOORS THROUGH WHICH ED GREETS US: "HELLO, I'M MR. ED"

CEILING BEAMS— HIDING SPARE PADLOCK KEYS AND AMNESIA- INDUCING BUCKETS

SLEEPING HAY

BACK DOOR TO STABLE— ENTRANCE FOR ROBBERS AND SCOUNDRELS

FEED BIN— HOLDS HAY AND HIDDEN CIRCUS PROGRAMS

ED'S STABLE

DOORWAY TO WILBUR'S OFFICE

WILBUR'S BUILDING SKETCHES

SHUTTER DOORS LEADING FROM STABLE TO OFFICE

TELEPHONE TABLE, AN ESSENTIAL

ED'S BUREAU: MIRROR ON WALL, PLAYHORSE CALENDAR, SHOWER CAP, COMB

WILBUR'S DRAFTING TABLE/CHAIR

SET OF BARN DOORS FOR LARGE ANIMAL GUESTS, LIKE BONGO, THE ELEPHANT

INK BOTTLES THAT ED INEVITABLY SPILLS ON WILBUR'S BLUEPRINTS

WILBUR'S OFFICE

TYPEWRITER TABLE— FOR ED'S LETTERS TO THE EDITOR", ETC.

SOFA

HOME TO HOBOS AND HUSBANDS DURING MARITAL SPATS

FILE CABINETS— ED'S FAVORITE DRAWER? "C" FOR CARROTS.

WALL WITH TWO AFRICAN MASKS

WINDOWS— FOR SPYING ON WILBUR'S ANTICS

James Spegman.

angle. Or did you ever notice that Ed's lodgings at Pine Lake Lodge, with the addition of a painted backdrop of mountains and lake, look strangely familiar? The same goes for the country barn in the episode "Wilbur's Father." And when Ed runs away from home to do hard labor in "Ed's Ancestors," he telephones Wilbur for help from his own barn! No wonder Ed complains of boredom so much of the time . . . he never gets to leave his own backyard. And for one episode only, "Ed's Dentist," the paddock behind the barn is covered by a wide roof, which Ed can conveniently perch upon to hide from the needle-wielding vet.

"20-20" Quiz

When did Ed first discover that he needed eyeglasses for reading?

Answer: The day after associate producer Herb Browar found a pair of gigantic eyeglasses in a novelty shop, while strolling along Hollywood Boulevard one evening. When he brought the gag specs in to work the next day, someone had the bright idea to try them on Ed . . . and a four-eyed, four-legged legend was born. Later variations included shades for sunbathing and beachcombing, as well as "fashion frames."

Should a Horse Be Allowed to Fly?: *Mister Ed's* Philosophy of Special Effects

Everyone involved in the creation of *Mister Ed* really believed that Ed could talk—it would've been difficult to develop the stories otherwise. But when it came to involving the horse in elaborate environments, driving a truck for example, or flying a bomber plane, the creative team was firmly divided into two camps of opinion. Some said it was perfectly okay to have the horse doing all those things, and others said it was absolutely unacceptable. Both above-mentioned scenarios with Ed did get produced, so the argument that ensued among the Filmways staff was purely philosophical.

One group maintained that because Ed was a horse, you couldn't have him do anything that a horse couldn't physically do. "I can see Ed doing something with an elephant because he can stand, but you can't put him in a plane," Al Simon contends. "It just doesn't feel right." Still there are others who think, "What the heck? If Ed can talk, then why can't he navigate a plane too? It's all imagination." If your sympathies are with the second camp, then you advocate the zaniest, silliest, most wacky and contrived premises for *Mister Ed*. If you agree with the first group, you believe certain creative limits should be established.

The Making of "Leo Durocher Meets Mister Ed"

Those of you who love the episode in which Ed gets to play his debut game with the Los Angeles Dodgers might be wondering how they got Ed to slide home so convincingly. "We had a fake horse, a stuffed horse from one of the prop houses," Herb Browar reveals. "And the special-effects man rigged the horse up with some bungee rubber. It was anchored at home plate and he stretched it up the third base line and anchored it there."

For the dramatic finish in which Wilbur yells "Slide, Ed, slide," the associate producer explains that they "set the camera up and we cut the bungee rubber, and the horse, with all the dust because of the tension of the rubber, was pulled right over home plate. And we did an insert, a close-up of the horse's leg on home plate. And then the Dodgers' catcher, Johnny Roseboro, climbed the batting cage [so as not to be trampled] for a great reaction shot—that was his own idea."

How did Filmways ever get the opportunity to sign Ed on with the Dodgers for a day, anyway? Larry Rhine recalls that *Mister Ed*'s producers approached manager Leo Durocher in 1963. Durocher invited Larry, Lou Derman and Arthur Lubin down to the stadium to watch a game one night, with plans to talk between innings. Lou Derman and his wife, Esther, were die-hard Dodger fans, which might explain why the episode was thought up in the first place. Durocher suggested that Filmways pay the players $100 each to appear in the *Mister Ed* episode. (That nominal fee is indicative of the vast salary difference between what players were making then, and what they're making now, not including multimillion-dollar endorsement deals.)

What a surefire, winning idea Filmways had—combining two pop-cultural institutions, Mister Ed and the Los Angeles Dodgers, in one episode. It might have been great for the fans to see their favorite horse trotting around the bases, but to the Dodgers' business manager it was another story. "Dodger Stadium was very new then," recounts Alan Young. "And Leo Durocher was tickled pink about us being there and so were the players. And Ed hits a home run and he goes around the bases. When he gets on the grassy part:

cha-poom, each time, *cha-poom.* All of a sudden, this guy comes running out. He's been sitting in the office, watching. He comes running out, yelling, 'You're ruining the grass!' We said, 'You're ruining the take! C'mon.' So we reshoot it, and Ed runs around again: *flump, flump, flump, pum.* 'I never would have allowed this if I knew my grass would be ruined,' the business manager said." Well, it turned out that a little wear and tear to the grass didn't matter in the final analysis—Filmways had a winning episode to begin their new season, and the Dodgers got some very nice publicity.

**Pitcher Sandy Koufax autographs a baseball for
Alan Young . . . or is it for Mister Ed?, who nuzzles up
to the guest star in a publicity shot from
"Leo Durocher Meets Mister Ed," 1963.**

"Ed the Chauffeur"

Why the episode is called "Ed the Chauffeur" we'll never know. The only one he tools around with is himself, barely. "We got a dilapidated milk truck from Arden Farms on La Cienega near Olympic," Browar explains. "I took one of the mechanics over there with me, and he got the thing to run. We had a fake leg that we used when Ed had to signal a turn."

"Ed the Stowaway"

Making Ed surf in Hawaii is a perfect example of an activity that met with some objections by the Filmways staff. "In my business, you always get objections," Larry Rhine points out. "And the writer tries to overcome the objections. I wanted to get Ed to ride a surfboard. And immediately, everybody said, 'How are we gonna get Ed on a surfboard?' And I said, 'There you said it, we're gonna do it,' and we did it!" Director of photography Arch Dalzell remembers how he got involved in this episode: "I had to reach back in my head to figure out how I was going to put Mister Ed on a surfboard and show him surfing. So with rear-projection process, and with Ed's patience

© *Orion Television.*

and trust in me, I had Les get him a big surfboard and had special effects splash a lot of water on him." Predictably, some of the series' best "stunts" were the ones initially considered to be the craziest.

"Ed and the Elephant"

There were times when General Service Studios must have resembled Noah's ark, especially when Filmways was simultaneously producing *Mister Ed* and *Green Acres.* One of the givens was that Ed had to deal with lots of different species in the shows. And horses don't naturally take to other big animals, especially elephants. But in two different episodes, "Ed and the Elephant" and "Wilbur and Ed in Show Biz," Ed does scenework with a pachyderm. The first time he met a baby elephant, Ed was very frightened. He started to rear up, and you could see the veins in his throat bulge. But no sooner did the elephant's trainer tell the animal to "be nice" to Ed than the chubby tyke went up to Ed and ran her trunk down his mane, just like a person would. Ed immediately relaxed, and the rehearsal began.

"Ed the Pool Player"

How does Ed manage to get sweet revenge from a pool shark, Chicago Chubby, who comes to town and takes the neighbor for $430? "We got a real pool player, a good one, and we shot his moves, and then we cut back to Ed with the cue stick in his mouth," Larry Rhine confesses. And all this time it seemed apparent that Ed was the perfect candidate to play opposite Paul Newman in *The Color of Money.*

Footage With Mileage

There are at least four instances in *Mister Ed* where a piece of footage was used in more than one show. It was not done to save a buck, as you might at first think. It was actually done to save a *yuk,* as associate producer Herb Browar explains: "It was entirely possible that if a bit got a big laugh, we would reuse it another time if it worked, but it would've been on very rare occasions." The table below outlines which bits were "recycled" for humor economy.

_____ FOOTAGE WITH MILEAGE _____

The Bit of Business	Episodes Where It Appears
Ed "aerobicizing" to Jack LaLanne	"Psychoanalyst Show" (#17) "Doctor Ed" (#77)
Ed pretending to be a cow at a loading dock	"Lie Detector" (#52) "Ed's Juice Stand" (#118)
Ed scuba diving in the nearby lake	"Ol' Rockin' Chair" (#70) "Dragon Horse" (#119)
Ed peeking out of his stall door into the yard	Opening titles (#1–#143) "Ed Agrees to Talk" (#19)

Swing It, Jack!

One of the best examples of reused footage is that of Mister Ed exercising with Jack LaLanne, who's on the TV set in his stall. Ed works on a lovelier neck ("That's for me!"), and when Jack asks the "ladies" at home to start toning their hips, he's suddenly speaking Ed's language. Ed replies by doing his "all-purpose" dance, exclaiming happily, "Swing it, Jack!"

Cow for a Day

This very funny scene involving Ed and two dockworkers, Charlie and Joe, was one of head writer Lou Derman's favorites, according to fellow scripter Larry Rhine. Both times it's used, Ed has run away from home. The two men are loading cows onto a boat, and Ed moos to prove he's a cow so he can get on board with the rest of the girls. The two men accuse each other of drinking when each says he heard Ed moo. Charlie and Joe are played by Richard Reeves and Ben Weldon respectively. Weldon was a regular crook on the _Superman_ series.

Frog Horse

In this recycled scene, Wilbur and Ed go down to the lake late at night to recover some object that Ed has thrown at the water's bottom. In "Ol Rockin' Chair," it's a monstrous variation of a rocker that Wilbur made from Ed's old horseshoes. Ed threw the creation below because it became an object of greed for Roger Addison. In a later show, "Dragon Horse," Ed has submerged a merry-go-round statue that he's afraid of, calling it a "fink jinx." After an unsuccessful scuba attempt to retrieve the object, Wilbur passes his air tank to Ed and lets the first "frog horse" handle the job. Incidentally, the rocking chair made of horseshoes was actually sent to the *Mister Ed* producers by a fan of the show. When they got this unusual gift, Al Simon said, "What are we going to do with this?" and head scripter Lou Derman replied, "I'll write a script around it," which is just what he did.

The zany bit of business in the living room where Wilbur gets all tangled up in the rocking chair was actually a restaging of a "stuck in chair" gag that Alan Young had performed earlier in his career. In this scene, Carol Post imagines her husband dressed as a king, a la Imperial margarine commercials, while he tries to sit comfortably on "Old Ironside."

A Shot at the Title

In "Ed Agrees to Talk," Mrs. Adams from the SPCA looks out into the Posts' backyard and sees Ed peering from his stall door. This is actually the shot from *Mister Ed*'s opening, Ed nodding his head a bit, sans titles.

HOOFNOTES
Ed Effects ("Ed-fx" for all you production buffs)

We love Ed for the sheer versatility of his prowess. He can cook, clean, paint . . . what *can't* he do? And the way he throws himself into things, no matter what his familiarity with the subject matter or level of expertise, is to be envied. Come to think of it, there isn't anything half-assed about Ed, even if he is descended from Francis. If only we had a fraction of his gumption. And nothing seems too complicated for him, either. The writers would dream up some horsebrained activity for the equine, and if Ed's trainer couldn't figure out a way to make it happen, the special-effects man always would. What follows is a shopping list of the many everyday, run-of-the-mill activities Ed performs during the series, courtesy of brains and brawn—Ed's brains and the producers' brawn.
Note: Film footage of Ed performing a simple motion, like holding a pool cue in his mouth while nodding his head, or lifting a "barbell," was repeated and run backward and forward to represent Ed beating a pool shark like Chicago Chubby or lifting weights to get in shape.

ED-FX

all-purpose dance—used to represent hula, go-go, horse
   "aerobics"
aviating
barnside Ping-Pong with Wilbur
beating laundry dry with his tail
billiards
bowling
catching softballs in his tail glove
chess

crying
delivering the mail
delivering the morning newspapers
driving a milk truck
filing for Wilbur, or getting carrots from the "C" file
freezing his tail stiff with dry ice
hitting an "inside-the-parker" at Dodger Stadium
jumping rope
making telephone calls
opening and closing the stall shutter doors, sped up
operating a shortwave radio
painting fences
painting with oils on canvas (y'know, *art*)
parachuting
playing instruments as a one-horse band
playing tetherball
reading the paper
roasting carrots on an open fire
running a printing press
scuba diving
singing in the shower
skateboarding
standing on the barn roof
sunbathing
surfing
tapping off the alarm clock with his hoof
turning out his stall light bulb
typing a letter
vacuuming the barn
watching TV
weight lifting
winking (slo-mo in the McCadden pilot)
writing on a blackboard

© 1990 CBS Inc.

Unsolvable Query #3

What color is Mister Ed's blanket?

Such enigmatic issues as the color of Mister Ed's blanket do come up when you're dealing with a black-and-white TV series. Surely Ed's favorite prop wasn't shaded in tones of gray! Informed sources have sworn that Mister Ed's adorable, spiffy blanket (pictured here) was green with reversible plaid. We all know, though, that the plaid side was never revealed. And not to forget the best part, his name was appliquéd in white lettering.

HOOF-MAGIC!

THE TOP TEN SNAZZIEST THINGS MISTER ED DOES WITH HIS HOOVES

10. He signals a left turn with his hoof while driving a milk truck ("Ed the Chauffeur").

9. He's locked up in stocks with fake front hooves ("Ed the Pilgrim").

8. He plays the drums with his hoof ("Ed the Musician").

7. He stomps out his own beatnik chant ("Ed the Beachcomber").

6. He makes a hoofprint on the first copy of "Love and the Single Horse."

5. He kicks the stall door with his hoof, shouting "Oh, begorra" when Wilbur offends him by dressing up in a horse costume.

4. He taps off his alarm clock with his hoof at high noon ("The Heavy Rider").

3. He crosses his hooves whenever he's telling a white lie.

2. He scrubs his saddle in a steel wash bucket with his hoof, singing, "Oh, this is the way we wash our clothes, wash our clothes, wash our clothes . . ."

(drumroll . . .)

1. And most of all, he slides into home plate (*safe*) with that darned hoof!

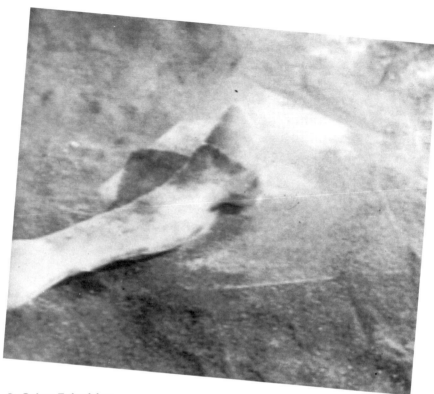

© *Orion Television.*
Ed's momentous slide from third . . . and he's *safe!*

Jack Pierce: The Horse's Mouth in Makeup

Filmways TV Productions could pride themselves on consistently hiring the best in the business—from the top down. But when it came to makeup, they really scored a coup when they hired Jack Pierce, the Hollywood master. Pierce had been responsible for creating the look of the Frankenstein monster, Igor, and the Wolfman in the great horror films of the 1930s. It almost makes you wish there were more *Mister Ed* episodes that called for monster makeup, so we could have seen Pierce do his stuff. "I considered it an honor to be made up by him every day," recalls Edna Skinner. Alan Young, naturally a blond, remembers that in the beginning, Pierce applied black coloring to

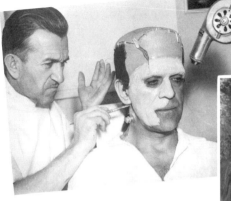

Makeup master Jack Pierce transforms Boris Karloff into The Monster for *The Son of Frankenstein* (Universal, 1939).

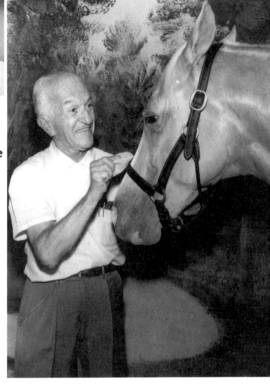

© *1990 CBS Inc.*
Over twenty years later, Jack Pierce transforms Ed from horse to superstar in this behind-the-scenes photograph from 1963.

his hair by melting down graphite, which did a heck of a job ruining his pillowcases at home. Eventually, Pierce switched to modern hair dyes. Why darken Alan Young's hair? "So I wouldn't blend in with the horse, who was also blond."

"Fashions by Ohrbach's"

A lot of TV shows back then had clothing sponsors, but what exactly did that mean? Edna Skinner explains. The former Broadway actress just loved having the opportunity to play a glamorous personality like Kay Addison. And true to the character, Edna would go shopping every Friday at Ohrbach's for the following week's wardrobe. She would go on these costume jaunts with

Connie Hines and Myrtle Logan, head of wardrobe. There were never clothes hanging around on the set; everything was handpicked by the actresses themselves at the store.

HOOFNOTES
Mister Ed Production Credits

Director/Producer: Arthur Lubin
Executive Producer: Al Simon
Associate Producer: Herbert W. Browar
Director of Photography: Maury Gertsman (1961); Arch R. Dalzell (1961–66)
Script Consultants: Norman Paul, Willie Burns
Assistant to the Director: Ira Stewart
Film Editor: Douglas Hines
Format Developed by: Sonia Chernus
Music Coordinator: Raoul Kraushaar (first season)
Music Supervisor: Dave Kahn (1961–66)
Art Director: Archie Bacon; Stan Jolley
Hairstylist: Esperanza Corona a.k.a. "Wispy"
Special Effects: Larry Chapman
Sound Editor: George Eppich
Sound Recorder: Don Bassman
Sound Mixer: Earl Spicer
Wardrobe Supervisor: Myrtle Logan
Set Decorator: Armor Goetten; Ruby Levitt
Casting: Kerwin Coughlin
Script Supervisor: Maggie Lawrence
Makeup: Jack Pierce (1961–64); Norman Pringle (1964–66)
Soundstage: Todd-AO
Fashions: Ohrbach's
Automobiles furnished by: Studebaker (1961–63); Ford (1964–66)

Courtesy of Alan Young.
Alan Young and Ed pose in their matching duds designed by knitting
expert and columnist Ursula Dubois, 1965. Ed wears the first "leg
warmers" in recorded history.

"A Carrot for Your Thoughts, Buddy Boy"

••

ED AND WILBUR, THE TEAM

WILBUR: I'd rather have you than 25,000 dollars.
ED: I'd rather have you than 25,000 *carrots*.
                              —*"Ed Finally Talks"*

The comedy team translated well from radio to TV. Ricky & Lucy, Abbott & Costello, Burns & Allen, Ralph & Norton, Fred & Barney—all set good examples of how TV teams could be a winning formula. And then came Ed & Wilbur. *Mister Ed* not only adopted the team model but improvised on it, giving us one of TV's funniest, nuttiest, most unique couples ever. There have been other human-animal duos on television—for example, Timmy & Lassie and Bud & Flipper. But these relationships always seem to exist within sentimental, moralistic, family adventure series formats, great for battling the forces of evil, but pretty limited in comic appeal. They lack that key piece of magic—real communication between the teammates. Sure, Flipper can get up and dance to let Bud know that the man in the boat is recklessly killing plankton, but can he pick up the phone and call the cops himself?!

Buddy Boys

> They ambled around Westchester stopping now and then for beer
> or to talk or take a nap under a tree and it settled down into a nice
> friendship.
>
> *—from "Ed Shoots It Out," by Walter Brooks*

The TV Ed we know and love isn't exactly the guy Walter Brooks had in mind (for starters, our Ed doesn't drink white *or* brown goods), but one thing's the same. He and Wilbur have an understanding that is unparalleled by any other TV duo. These buddy boys, an "odd couple" of the stable set, have a special bond that transcends species. Alone, they are nothing exceptional. Wilbur Post is a mild-mannered, well-meaning, average architect who fantasizes about being a great magician, but who is rather awkward. Mister Ed is a somewhat chubby, lazy palomino who, without his gift for gab, would go through life unappreciated. Yet together, they are irrepressible. And in moments of danger, you might even say they're invincible. "Partners in crime" is how a fan aptly describes the two. When in danger, Ed's motto is: "Two frightened heads are better than one." And he's known to speak generously of his boss: "If I gotta go, there's no one I'd rather take with me!" Now, that's loyalty!

Alan Young was exceptional at playing the role of Wilbur, especially in maintaining the crucial suspension of disbelief. "Alan doesn't get enough credit, to this day," explains associate producer Herb Browar. "If you take a close look at the episodes, it really seems as if he's relating to that horse. It's completely believable."

Young himself, in a characteristically down-to-earth, modest manner, describes the experience of working with Ed as having been nearly identical to working with other human actors: "After the first six months, I had finished a day's work with Ed," Young offers, "and I said, 'Gosh, I'm tired today.' And they said, 'Sure, look at the work you've done.' And I said, 'It was just scenes, the two of us.' And they said, 'No, it's been a monologue. There was no two actors there, it was just you and the horse.' And I had never realized that. To me, it was two actors, doing dialogue. And I guess that's why it worked so well. I never thought of Rocky Lane off camera." And the critics noticed. "Young ranks with Donald O'Connor as an all-time great in the art of conversing with animals," praised *Variety* in October 1962. "He makes what must be a difficult task look easy, and extracts a maximum of fun from his chore."

Mister Ed Episodes Directed by Alan Young

During the end of the 1965–66 season, Arthur Lubin was out of town directing feature films. Because Alan Young was so familiar with what Ed could and couldn't do, he was a natural to substitute-direct the episodes. Although Young considers himself more of a writer than a director, he directed five consecutive shows, some of the funniest in the bunch:

"TV or Not TV" (#137)
"The Horse and the Pussycat" (#138), codirected by Ira Stewart
"Ed the Bridegroom" (#139)
"Don't Skin That Bear" (#140)
"Ed and the Motorcycle" (#141)

Alan Young, script in lap, "directs" Mister Ed for "TV or Not TV," 1965.

No Horse Is an Island

Why does Mister Ed only talk to Wilbur? Maybe it's because Wilbur is the only one who's innocent enough to *believe* Ed talks. He's a perfect example of the "man-child," the perpetual adolescent. Other TV characters who are wonderfully naive and simple, in spite of whatever grown-up occupations or trappings they may have, include: Maynard G. Krebs (*The Life and Loves of Dobie Gillis*), who has a goatee, wears footsie pajamas and sees Santa Claus on Christmas Eve; Eb Dawson (*Green Acres*), who just *doesn't get it;* Jethro Bodine (*The Beverly Hillbillies*), who couldn't be an adult no matter how much money he had; and Herman Munster (*The Munsters*). For these characters, days will never be nine to five. Life will always be filled with childish wonder, chaos and at times embarrassment.

Ed recognizes this quality in Wilbur, and thus, a relationship worth making into a series is born. In the five-year course of the show, Mister Ed gives his owner various explanations for why he has selected him as the exclusive "other half" of his dialogue.

HOOFNOTES

WHY ED TALKS ONLY TO WILBUR POST

1. "Because, inside, you're all horse."
2. "Because you love animals. Because you trust them."
3. "I got tired of talking to parrots, and you were the next step up."
4. "Because you're the only one I liked well enough to talk to, Wilbur."
5. "I only talk to you and dumb animals."
6. "I hate skeptics" (implying Wilbur *isn't* one).

Ed and Wilbur's Very First Conversation

How did this "bee-you-ti-ful" interspecies friendship begin? Reprinted now for your reading pleasure is the *very first* exchange between Wilbur and Mister Ed, out in the barn, Hollywood, circa January 1961. (Note: Later in the series, Ed tells us that his and Wilbur's anniversary is *April 12*).

WILBUR *(wistfully to himself)*: It's been a long time since I was a little boy.

ED: It's been a long time since I was a pony.

WILBUR: Who said that?! No, that's impossible. Did you say that?! No, how could you?!

ED: Did you say it?

WILBUR: No, I didn't hear it! How could I? But I did! Oh, this is impossible. I don't believe it. Now, while I'm looking right at you, say something!

ED: Like what?

WILBUR: Anything, anything!

ED: HOW NOW BROWN COW.

—"The First Meeting"

I Now Pronounce You Man and Horse

ED: Oh, the things a horse has to do to keep his man.

—"The Horse and the Pussycat"

"Man and Horse" is *the* major relationship in *Mister Ed*. You might even say that this sitcom is really a western gone awry. Roy Rogers and Trigger were certainly no closer than Wilbur and Ed. Could you imagine Roy giving his horse a close shave? With a cordless electric, no less? Or having the following conversation?

WILBUR: Ed, do you still want me to only ride you bareback?

ED: You can ride me bareback, piggyback, anyback, just so it's your back on my back!

—"Ed and the Motorcycle"

In *Mister Ed* the bullets have been replaced by bowling, the shooting done away with for shopping. The Indians have left the prairie to make way for burglars and Communist spies. Even the bar brawls have been transformed into arguments with neighbors over damaged (or eaten) property. Yet the

THE FAR SIDE

By GARY LARSON

...and then I see Wilbur go around to the back of the barn carrying this shovel and he's got this wild look in his eyes and he's like real nervous and then I notice he's trying to bury this big plastic bag which at first I figure is just full of manure but then I start to wonder what the hey is going on and then...

Mr. Ed spills his guts.

union between man and horse was never more focal to a TV show's premise than in *Mister Ed.*

The almost chemical bond between Ed and Wilbur extended off camera as well. "Lester Hilton would drive down the freeway in the morning," Alan Young recalls. "I'd come on the freeway here, and I would drive behind the trailer. I could tell how Ed was going to be that day, because if he felt great and ready, his tail was outside, in the breeze. But if he just felt, 'Oh, I'm not quite awake yet,' his tail was tucked in. And you could tell when he pulled up, if you heard him kicking the stall, he was saying, 'Hey, let's get going, let's get going!' If he just stood there, it meant 'I'm not quite ready to work yet.'"

At Their Buddiest . . .

Here are some moments from *Mister Ed* where Ed and Wilbur's bond is delightfully obvious:

○ Wilbur gets caught in the rain, thanks to a practical joke by Ed. When the architect arrives home soaking wet and sneezing, Ed carries over to Wilbur his personalized "Mister Ed" blanket in his mouth. Rocky Lane's voice has just the right "talking with your mouth full" quality. "Here, buddy boy, wrap this around you." Seconds later, Ed begins to sneeze. On *Mister Ed,* if an animal catches a cold from a human, it's perfectly reasonable. Wilbur covers Ed with part of the blanket. "I'm glad I have your bug," Ed quips while snuggling up with his owner. "That's togetherness." ("Ed and the Bicycle")

© *1990 CBS Inc.*
Wilbur and Ed share a blanket and a sneeze in "Ed and the Bicycle," 1962.

© *CBS Photos.*

○ Ed tries to teach "horse talk" to Wilbur so he can understand Lady Sue, a troubled racehorse. "It's based on short neighs and long neighs," Ed informs his owner. Wilbur asks Ed to show him "d." "Certainly," Ed replies, and clears his throat with the civility of a chess champion in an international tournament. ("Horse Talk")

○ Wilbur gives Ed away so he can be with his love, Princess Helen. While Wilbur is pining away over a photo of Ed and himself, the horse returns home with the announcement "Helen and I are no longer an item." The duo cry with joy and relief. "We're just a pair of sentimental old slobs," Ed admits. "Get my nose." So Wilbur puts a handkerchief to Ed's muzzle, and we hear a great sound effect of a blowing nose. ("Wilbur Sells Ed")

It's clear that besides hankies, the two share a real sensibility. Even if they begin at opposite camps of opinion, by the end of an episode, Mister Ed usually succeeds in converting Wilbur to his view of things.

Existential Ed

Ed and Wilbur spend an awful lot of time gabbing about mundane stuff like hay, oats and next-door neighbor Addison's prize apples. But sometimes their dialogue lapses into almost Star Trekkian commentary on the state of human affairs. And that's what's so ultimately funny about their repartee. To hear a horse sound off on justice, divorce, patriotism and equality, and what's more, to have a human take him seriously, is always at least slightly amusing.

ED: I'm a thinking horse.
WILBUR: What's my thinking horse thinkin' about?
ED: Life, Faith, the reason for existence, deep stuff—you wouldn't understand.
WILBUR: C'mon, Ed, tell me. If it is over my head, I'll get another horse to explain it to me.
ED: I don't know, Wilbur. There must be more to life than just eatin' hay and brushin' flies off your back.

—"Ed the Artist"

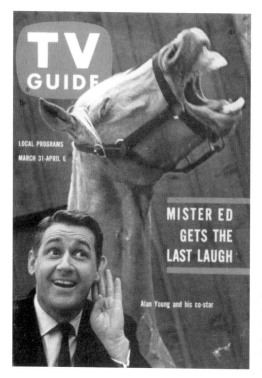

© *NewsAmerica Publications.* **Reprinted with permission from** *TV Guide*®**magazine.** © **1962 by NewsAmerica Publications Inc., Radnor, PA. All rights reserved. Photograph by Richard R. Hewitt. Alan Young and Mister Ed make the cover of** *TV Guide,* **March 31, 1962.**

The literally down-to-earth surroundings of the barn make their lofty discussions seem less stuffy, actually very palatable food for thought. Wilbur and Ed's "positions" on subjects are never predictable, either. Often, Ed is the curmudgeonly grouch who's been around the bridle path enough times to know better than to weaken to romance. But just as often, he's smitten with some new filly and hopelessly irrational. The perpetual yin-yang relationship of "hoss" and "boss" is one of the nicer surprises *Mister Ed* has to offer.

Hocus-pocus: The Would-be Magicians

Mister Ed head writer Lou Derman vicariously endowed the character of Wilbur Post with an interest near and dear to his own heart: magic. Consequently, if Wilbur had his druthers, he'd be reincarnated as The Great Blackstone. Wilbur frequently employs Ed in his magic acts to sensationalize them (he needs all the help he can get). And he's not far off base—which would *you* rather see? A rabbit being pulled out of a hat or a palomino that levitates? Ironically, whenever Ed does get into the act, his cowardly antics turn Wilbur's "magic" into outright burlesque. Instead of the long-awaited "ooohs" and "ahhhs" of the crowd, Wilbur gets met with snickers and guffaws. His inability to perform illusions successfully is just one more way he reaffirms his lot in life as a lovable schlemiel. Occasionally, Carol helps out as the requisite "attractive assistant," clad in a top hat and rhinestone teddy.

THE "MAGIC SHOW" EPISODES

1. *"Little Boy"*—Wilbur performs as "The Great Wilburini" at a kids' party.
2. *"Ed the Shishkebab"*—features a cameo by magician Harry Blackstone and a brief screen appearance by Lou Derman (he assists Blackstone).
3. *"Ed and the Elephant"*—Wilbur learns the Art of Elephant Levitation from "The Great Mordini" (Henry Corden), in exchange for elephant-sitting Bongo.
4. *"Disappearing Horse"*—Wilbur performs this illusion for the community theater project.
5. *"Ed the Musician"*—Wilbur performs a magic act for Carol's club.

My Little Pilgrim

In one of *Mister Ed*'s delightful "holiday fantasy" sequences (there are three of them—see Chapter 8 for full details), Ed and Wilbur are transported back to seventeenth-century New England. Even though they undergo superficial character transformations, they remain buddy boys. Wilbur is a clutzy Indian named "Chicken Heart," and Ed is an astute steed who helps the Pilgrims with their first Thanksgiving. True to the timeless *Mister Ed* premise, Wilbur's character is the only one who knows Ed can talk, and the duo team up to do great things.

This dialogue excerpt from "Ed the Pilgrim" between Chicken Heart and "horse" is like a "Who's on First?" routine. It's silly and frustrating, filled with "Indian Speak" all the way. Hollywood meets Borscht Belt meets Plymouth Rock...

ED   (*from behind trees*): Don't be chicken, Chicken Heart.
WILBUR: Who speak?
ED: Me, Chicken.
WILBUR: Who you? Where you?
ED: Here, chick, chick, chick.
WILBUR: You talk, horse?
ED: Go to head of teepee.
WILBUR: How can horse talk?
ED: Night school.
WILBUR: Night school?!
ED: Ask foolish question, get foolish answer.
WILBUR: Horse talk to all men?
ED: *No. Only to you. I like you, Chicken Heart.*
WILBUR: I like you, too, horse that talk like man.

Riding High

It's never clear how often Wilbur and Ed ride together. Wilbur alludes to their moonlight rides on Saturday nights and their weekly romps on Sundays; Ed always seems to have a rendezvous in the park with some filly on Sundays (not a "day of rest" for our equine Romeo). In the original *Mister Ed* stories, Walter Brooks writes: "Mr. Pope had bought [Ed] so he could ride Saturdays and Sundays when Mrs. Pope was giving cocktail parties." How about impromptu rides any old day of the week? Whenever Wilbur suggests they go for one, the horse complains that he's got flat feet, fallen arches or some other hoof malady.

Eccentricity Loves Company

If "misery loves company," then so does eccentricity, and Wilbur's got a heap of both, caused by his unique predicament. If Wilbur is destined to be a nut (and he is), there's no one he'd rather be a nut with than Ed. When push comes to shove, the duo must admit that they derive a certain pleasure from knowing they're crazier than most. In "Ed's Dentist," Wilbur must submit to yet *another* mental interrogation.

ED: Did you pass that psychiatric exam?
WILBUR: Yeah.
ED: You're a bit eccentric. What man talks to a horse?
WILBUR: What horse talks to a man?
ED (*chuckles*): I guess we're just a couple of kooks.

In the scuba lesson which occurs in two different episodes, "Dragon Horse" and "Ol' Rockin' Chair," Wilbur cautions Ed so he won't yank suddenly on the cables: "Now remember, when I tug, I want a nice, long pull. No jerks." "Except the two of us," Ed retorts, without missing a beat.

In "Ed Gets the Mumps," the attention-starved horse combs through the medical encyclopedia in search of a disease to adopt. When he comes across "dementia precox," he dismisses it instantly. "No, I'd have to act screwy, and Wilbur'd never know the difference."

We learn that as a young boy, Wilbur already showed signs of a peculiar, St. Francis of Assisi disposition toward his furry and feathered friends. To the architect's dismay, his Aunt Martha, played by Eleanor Audley, reveals the truth about his childhood in "Animal Jury": "He was always terribly fond of animals," Martha boasts. "Why, he'd sit and talk to them by the hour, and do you know, he'd look at them as though he really expected them to talk back. Well, of course it never happened." "Oh, yes it did," Wilbur replies musingly.

Even though the man-horse twosome seems to be equally off balance, occasionally Wilbur outright accuses Ed of being insane. In one episode, he tells Ed he's just "a screwball horse who has no right to be talking in the first place," actually reiterating the show's nutty premise. In "Be Kind to Humans," Wilbur is so shocked that Ed took in three hobos, he asks Ed: "Did you fall off a carousel when you were a child?" There are a couple of merry-go-round gags in the series. In "Home Sweet Trailer," Ed actually hides between two merry-go-round horses to elude Gordon Kirkwood, who's working him to the bone. We don't get to see Ed doing this, but it sure is funny to imagine.

HOOFNOTES

"WAIT, CAN YOU BLINDFOLD ME?": ED AND WILBUR, THE GAMESTERS

○ *Charades (from "Ed's Cold Tail")*

Situation: Ed pretends to be sick with laryngitis so Wilbur will buy him a stall heating system. Wilbur enters the barn, and Ed "can't talk."

WILBUR: Well, I got it! We'll play Charades, O.K.?
ED: *(Nods "Yes")*
WILBUR: Now, how many words is it?
ED: *(Stomps his front right hoof three times)*
[After a dozen more lines have been exchanged:]
WILBUR: *Sounds like* eat.
ED: *(Nods "Yes")*
WILBUR: HEAT?
ED: *(Nods "Yes")*
WILBUR: I NEED HEAT. Is that what you're trying to say, Ed?
ED: *(Nods "Yes")*
WILBUR: HA, HA, HA ... FORGET IT!

○ *Ed's Card Trick (from "Ed's New Neighbors")*
1. Pick a card.
2. Tear it in half.
3. Now tear it again in quarters.
4. Now throw the pieces up in the air.
5. "HAPPY NEW YEAR!!!"

○ *Palomino Solitaire (from "Ed's Ancestors")*: Simple: Ed cheats!

○ *Pin the Tail on the Donkey (from "Horse Party")*: Ed and his five horse friends play this traditional birthday game at Ed's ninth-birthday party.

○ *Bobbing for Apples:* Another game played at Ed's party. Only trouble is, the guests keep *eating* the apples instead of bobbing for them.

○ *Assorted Barnside Games:* bowling (Ed cheats, stomping his hoof to knock down the last standing pin), Ping-Pong, tetherball, billiards, chess.

○ *The Contests:* These competitions are inevitably won by Ed's brain and Wilbur's brawn":

○ *"Giant Jackpot Show":* a radio trivia contest with a grand prize of $5,000. Ed becomes a finalist and trains Wilbur for the match, but forfeits the grand prize to an elderly couple. He's a sucker for a sob story. ("The Contest")

○ *"Identify the Flower":* In this newspaper contest Ed and Wilbur have to put together a puzzle and guess the flower. They win the twenty-first prize, a miniature horse named Pequito. ("Patter of Little Hooves")

○ *"Strain the Brain":* a phone-in radio contest hosted by Happy Hannegan (played by George Neise). Ed wins a color TV set. ("TV or Not TV")

STRAIN THE BRAIN

See if you can answer these questions about the man-horse bond in *Mister Ed.*

1. Imagine that you're standing in your den. If you don't have a den, use your barn. A horse is standing outside the window, coaching you on the fine art of being a horse. He asks you to *turn your ears out.* Now, how in the world do you do that?!
2. Why does a horse have a tail, according to Ed?
3. What trivia question does Ed answer correctly to become eligible for a $5,000 grand prize on the "Giant Jackpot" radio show ("The Contest")? Hint: The category is "Geography."
4. What trivia question does Ed answer correctly in ten seconds to win the color TV set on "Strain the Brain" ("TV or Not TV")? Hint: The category is "Sports."
5. When Ed dresses up like a gypsy in "Ed Visits a Gypsy" (he's the spitting image of Yasir Arafat), what does he "predict" that Wilbur will buy his horse for his birthday?
6. In "Mister Ed's Blues," what gift does Ed tell Wilbur he wants for his birthday?
7. In which episode do Wilbur and Ed reminisce about their first meeting, including a flashback to the first show, and what's the occasion?
8. What does Wilbur dub himself while performing magic for the kids in "The Little Boy"?

ANSWERS

1. First, you "tighten up your forehead. Then you suck in your cheeks. Next, you scrunch up your nose. Now, you let your ears flop down. And most important of all, you've finally got to 'think horse'!" (From episode 79, "Wilbur Post, Honorary Horse")
2. For balance.
3. "What is the capital of Iceland?" (Reykjavik)
4. "Who were the qualifiers in the interzonal chess tournament in Amsterdam in 1965?"
5. A sterling-silver saddle, an imported cashmere blanket and platinum horseshoes.
6. Two pairs of bowling shoes.
7. In "The Bank Robbery," the two are celebrating their fifth anniversary together.
8. "The Great Wilburini," the same name Ed uses for his soft-drink concoction in "Ed's Juice Stand."

"Don't Take Away My TV Set—That's Cruelty to Animals"

ED THE PREMIER MEMBER OF THE TV GENERATION

Mister Ed is the quintessential TV horse. Not only is he the ultimate TV creation, but his character goes absolutely gaga for the medium. Ed is a member of the "TV generation," the segment of the baby boom demographic born after 1950, that never knew life without television. Our early (and not so early) recreational lives focused around the tube, and as kids, Sunday night meant gathering around the family TV set to see what "really big shoe" Ed Sullivan had cooking up (after *Mister Ed* was over, of course). Mister Ed is usually portrayed as a seven- or eight-year-old, depending on the particular script, making him a perfect candidate for the TV generation. (He would have been born after 1950, despite the fact that Bamboo Harvester, the real Ed, was born in 1949. No doubt they needed a mature horse who could handle the diversity of Ed's role.)

Ed the Stall Potato

Like his human peers, Ed is an absolute TV junkie. He's America's first *stall potato;* so much so, that if he were living today, the Nielsen company would want to measure his very American TV-viewing habits.

Ed is representative of the fairly innocent American TV viewer of his time, thoroughly enchanted by the tube, not yet tainted by years of trash. He's gullible, getting caught up in the fantastic, escapist plots. He's loyal to the characters, he looks forward to watching them every week and he considers barring of his TV privileges to be cruel and unusual punishment. In one episode, Wilbur tells Ed that his punishment for telling a lie will be no television for two weeks, no comic books and no rides in the park. We're talking harsh here.

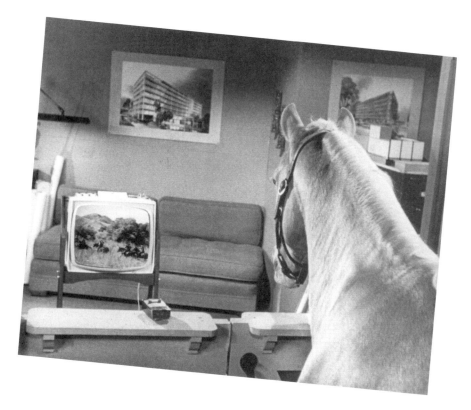

© *1990 CBS Inc.*
Mister Ed—America's first stall potato, 1961. Note Wilbur's sketches on wall.

Color TV or Bust

Throughout the series, Ed covets many objects and life-styles, but more than anything else, in one early episode, Ed pines for a color TV set. Not surprising when you think about it. In 1961 wasn't that the typical American aspiration? While munching on chips and watching the news with Wilbur in the barn one evening, Ed self-consciously comments on their activity: "Typical American scene—a man and his horse, watching TV" ("Ed Sniffs out a Cold Clue").

There's such an excitement about color television all through the series. Ed eavesdrops on a Kirkwood marital spat and exclaims, "It's so beautiful, it should be in color." When he does finally win a color TV set on a trivia game show, his initial preoccupation is with discovering whether or not Skelton's *eyes* are red too, not with how good the reception is.

Stall Aerobics

Ed was even ahead of his time in realizing that too many bonbons in front of too many late-late shows resulted in too many inches (he's 36"-49"-54" and the next saddle size up from his is "stylish stout"). "I gotta cut down on those alfalfa snacks when I'm watching TV," Ed tells himself in one episode. And in another show, he asks Wilbur to buy him some "low cal" hay. These were the days when new diet products were revolutionizing the marketplace ("One Calorie Diet Pepsi Is Here"), sweetened with saccharin and sorbitol (yuk! remember those?).

Given Ed's TV obsession, the writers came up with the perfect solution for the horse's on-again, off-again flab-reduction campaign: His name was Jack LaLanne, the TV fitness guru. And he made more than one guest appearance on *Mister Ed*'s stall TV set, giving Ed the excuse to perform his all-purpose dance. Rocky Lane is excellent as the horse straining to do exercises designed for the human anatomy—for example, leg lifts while lying on one's side.

Mister Fad

TV brings with it the instantaneous transmission of fashion and fads. Commercials create needs that Americans, horses no exception, never knew they had. Ed is the American marketer's dream. He's the ultimate litmus test for pop culture. If it's hot, Ed's doing it. If it's out, Ed's pooh-poohing it. Correcting one's vision, for example. Eyeglasses just won't do in 1965. Contact lenses are the thing. Ed's rationale: "Fillies don't make passes at horses who wear glasses." Only try convincing an optometrist to fit a horse with contacts. In "Ed's Juice Stand," Ed has such beautiful teeth, Wilbur tells his horse he could star in a toothpaste commercial. Ed agrees, since he's got 27 percent more teeth than the average school kid, anyway. Ed the TV star actually had the cleanest teeth and breath of any horse around. Les Hilton used to brush Ed's choppers with Pepsodent, so they'd look pearly white when he spoke in front of the camera.

Ed constantly lets us know that his stall TV set is put to good use. Television is how Ed picks up news of what's going on in the world, besides his extensive newspaper reading. He always seems to share the paper with Wilbur (his

© *1990 CBS Inc.*
Connie Hines and Edna Skinner emulate Jackie Kennedy's passion for fox hunting in "Ed and the Secret Service," 1962.

© *Orion Television.*

owner can't stand the gooey pages after Ed's through), but his TV viewing is sacred, a real solo hobby. Ed chomps at the bit to share his snide interpretation of current-day phenomena with Wilbur. Take the New York Mets, still a fledgling National League team in 1963. In "Ed the Desert Rat," Ed mocks Wilbur's dismal failure at marital spats: "You lose more often than the Mets," which was pretty awful back then.

And Mister Ed is definitely streetwise when it comes to divorce and lawyers, two budding institutions in the early 1960s. In "Ed's Cold Tail," the palomino thinks twice before instigating trouble between Carol and Wilbur, realizing it will directly affect his own tail: "Hey, Wilbur, guess what I heard on the phone? Well, your wife ... Wait, this could start a fight. You'd split up, she gets custody of me, and I see you only on Father's Day. Forget it, April Fool, I didn't hear a thing." He even jokes about a show designed just for him called *Di-Horse Court.* This is one of the many examples of two-level writing on *Mister Ed,* some lines for kids and some for adults.

"It Pays to Ed-vertise"

Mister Ed, like millions of other TV-watching Americans, refers to popular advertising slogans constantly, having committed them to memory without even trying. The other characters also let us know they're paying attention to ads. Here's a sampling:

○ **Clairol Hair Coloring:**

RALPH THE BLACKSMITH: People are gonna wonder, does he or doesn't he?

WILBUR: And no one will know for sure.

—*"Taller Than She"*

○ **RCA Victor:**

CAROL (*in the distance*): WILBUR!!!!
ED (*to Wilbur*): Your Master's Voice ...

—*"Ed Gets the Mumps"*

○ **National Broadcasting Company (NBC):**

Eᴅ: I may be the first horse to die *in living color.*

—*"Cherokee Ed"*

○ **Generic Ad Speak:**

Eᴅ: Hello, Abercrombe Car Rental? Do you want to put me in the driver's seat?

—*"Ed the Chauffeur"*

"The Medium Is the Schmedium": Spoofing of Television

Mister Ed's writers and producers self-consciously play with and poke fun at "television," not only in the visual tricks (see Chapter 5) but in the way they pay homage to the boob tube—its foibles and virtues, its ability to woo the everyday man into acting ridiculous. Here are some prime cases where Ed is the ultimate TV horse, and *Mister Ed* pure TV:

"The Ventriloquist"

In this very early episode, Wilbur Post's inclination is to share his discovery of Ed's gift with the rest of the world. He urges his horse to make a TV appearance. In his typically cynical, man-of-the-world manner, Ed declines: "I know Trigger. He's a very mixed-up horse." Note how attention to psychological well-being is coming into vogue now (1961), having been given a jump start by out-of-sorts teenage heartthrobs like Marlon Brando and James Dean.

"No Horses Allowed"

Following on the hooves of America's first live-televised political debate, Nixon vs. Kennedy in 1960, this 1962 episode has Wilbur participating in a live TV debate with Mr. Aynsworth, a citizen who wants to outlaw bridle paths. Aynsworth (played by Neil Hamilton, *Batman*'s Commissioner Gordon) just happens to be related to the TV station manager, so Wilbur becomes a stooge in the midst of flamboyant nepotism.

At the TV studio, Wilbur is left high and dry to apply his own makeup. Even his suit jacket is swiped, and he must borrow an oversized one (this was years before David Bowie and David Byrne showed us just how hip big suits could be). So the architect appears before the camera in whiteface and is the laughingstock of the studio . . . and of Roger Addison, who's watching at home. But fear not! Good triumphs over evil eventually (a message we're told again and again in *Mister Ed*), but not before Wilbur Post is subjected to a solid dose of squirming. Aynsworth withdraws his petition, and all is well with horses. From the Nixon-Kennedy debate, we all learned that televised politics was an extension of show biz, and that the importance of a good makeup job could not be overlooked.

A la *Candid Camera*: "Kiddy Park" and "Ed the Race Horse"

In these two episodes, Wilbur pretends to be a *Candid Camera* host. In both cases, he plays off the narcissism of the other characters, who desperately want to believe that they're on TV. They must be on TV, or why else would Wilbur, a stranger, be making such ridiculous demands?! In "Kiddy Park," Wilbur tries to retrieve his runaway horse from the pony rides at the park. The proprietor (played by Richard Reeves) can't imagine that this is a legit request. He figures he must be on *Candid Camera* and says hello to his wife and son at home.

In "Ed the Race Horse," Wilbur tries to buy sneakers (and matching argyles!) for Ed from Dalzell's Shoe Shop. Again, Dalzell concludes that this lunacy must be a TV setup and really hams it up for the "imaginary" camera. (*Inside joke*: Arch Dalzell is the real name of *Mister Ed*'s director of photography.)

HOOFNOTES

I. ED'S TV PICKS

Naturally, a stall potato like Ed frequently refers to other TV shows and characters. Here's a sampling of the horse's favorite tube neighbors. Maybe you remember watching these same shows, right about the time you discovered *Mister Ed*.

○ Palladin (*Have Gun Will Travel*)
○ Trigger (Roy Rogers)
○ Clint Eastwood (*Rawhide*)
○ Ricky Starr (popular comic wrestler who's "on in ten minutes")
○ David Susskind (*Open End*)
○ Perry Mason
○ Bozo the Clown
○ Jack LaLanne
○ Charlie Chan
○ *City Hospital* (no doubt modeled after *General Hospital*)
○ *Lassie*
○ *The Munsters*
○ Lawrence Welk (Ed even blows bubbles and plays a polka on his drum set)
○ Mitch Miller (Ed fantasizes about his own show: *Sing Along With Ed*)
○ Huntly and Brinkley
○ *Di-Horse Court* (Ed's version of *Divorce Court,* in "Ed the Bridegroom")
○ Allen Funt (*Candid Camera*)

II. OTHER TV SHOWS THAT REFER TO MISTER ED

O *Gilligan's Island* (CBS, 1964–67): The castaways refer to the talking horse in their recollections of life back home.

O *Laugh-In* (NBC, 1968–73): There's a Mister Ed joke about Tiny Tim's hairdresser. Incidentally, the goofy ukuleleist does a rendition of the *Mister Ed* theme song on Broken Records which you can purchase through the Mister Ed Fan Club (see Appendix A for photo).

O *Married . . . With Children* (FOX, April 29, 1990): Kelly Bundy is a weathergirl wrought with stage fright. Her brother Bud asks if they can put peanut butter on her mouth to make it move like Mister Ed.

O *The Wonder Years* (ABC, June 19, 1990): Kevin asks, "What would Mister Ed do in a situation like this?"

O *Green Acres* (CBS, 1965–71): (1) Mr. Haney and Oliver Douglas refer to Mister Ed in the course of their conversation; (2) In another 1969 episode, a palomino in Mr. Douglas' barn claims he played Mister *Fred* on TV; He says to Oliver, "Good night, dummy" at the end of the show.

O *The Pat Sajak Show* (CBS, October 20, 1989): Guest Bobby Rivers (from VH-1: Video Hits One cable network) discusses the job of hairdresser for actor Bruce Willis: "It's like choreographer for Mister Ed—what have you got to work with?" Of course, we fans know better—Mister Ed is a dancing fool.

O "It's Garry Shandling's 25th Anniversary Show" (FOX, 1990): Shandling plays a talk show host interviewing several guests, among them Mister Ed.

O *Get a Life* (FOX, September 23, 1990): Chris Elliot accuses Larry's boss of "taking Mister Ed on a joyride through K mart."

III. ED'S TV SNACKS (GUARANTEED OVEREATEN DURING TV SITTINGS)

○ Potato chips (during the evening news with Wilbur)
○ Pizza (during an Italian movie)
○ Popcorn (during an unnamed late-late show)

IV. MAGAZINES/BOOKS THAT ED REFERS TO

○ *Inside Europe:* Wilbur's architectural plans are "Inside Herbert," the goat; Wilbur's book on horses will be called *Inside Mister Ed.*
○ *Reader's Digest:* Ed and Wilbur win the twenty-first prize in a newspaper contest—a miniature horse called Pequito. Ed is tickled with the little guy: "He's a *Reader's Digest* version of me." ("Patter of Little Hooves")
○ *Playhorse Magazine:* a spoof on the obvious.
○ Comics, comics, comics: Ed loves 'em . . . Dennis the Menace "just kills" him.

STRAIN THE BRAIN

1. Why is Clint Eastwood's TV show called *Rawhide,* according to Ed?
2. What kind of movie does Ed feel compelled to watch on TV in "Ed and the Bicycle?"
3. (a) Which contemporary movie does Ed nickname himself after, with slight variations, in two *Mister Ed* episodes?
   (b) What are Ed's two "guilty" nicknames?
4. What is the name of the TV debate show that Wilbur appears on?
5. Just like Hayley Mills, what does Ed have when all four of his feet fall asleep?

ANSWERS

1. Because Mr. Eastwood rides his horses *bareback.*
2. A Charlie Chan movie.
3. (a) *Birdman of Alcatraz* (1962) starring Burt Lancaster.
   (b) "The Birdhorse of Alcatraz" ("Getting Ed's Goat") and "The Horseman of Alcatraz" ("Animal Jury").
4. *Speak Your Peace,* a show devoted to local issues.
5. "A slumber party."

"Cut off My Ear and Call Me Van Gogh"

ED THE CREATIVE SPIRIT

Aside from the obligatory "horse hours" that Mister Ed puts in each day—his rides along the bridle path with Wilbur, for example—the palomino has a lot of downtime. He doesn't work to earn his keep, much to Carol Post's chagrin. In her one attempt to hitch Ed to a wagon, in "Ed Agrees to Talk," she gets nailed by the SPCA. So for better or worse, Ed is really a horse of leisure.

What's a smart horse to do with so much spare time on his hooves? Create art, that's what! In the 143 *Mister Ed* episodes, Ed the dilettante paints two masterpieces, two chairs and one fence; writes and records two hit songs; concocts numerous recipes; extemporaneously composes and recites poem after poem; acts out many diverse theatrical roles, ranging from the classics to a 1960s movie director (spoofing his own director, Arthur Lubin); and applies genuinely creative thought to everything he does.

For the time Ed occupied in TV history, his aesthetic tendencies make sense. He was just another young American in the 1960s who yearned to express himself artistically. He was late-beatnik/pre–Flower Power, yet if the show had lasted through 1969, you can bet he'd have been the first horse on Valley Spring Lane to wear a Nehru shirt (king size) and peace medallion.

Like his creators, Mister Ed can *only* be innovative. As the world's first talking horse, he deals with situations and possibilities not previously available to other celebrity animals. Of his more successful TV canine contemporary, Lassie, Ed boasts: "Dogs smarter than horses! I'd like to see [Lassie] make a phone call!" ("Jon Provost Meets Mister Ed"). Animal feuds aside, no book about Mister Ed would be complete without a thorough peek at each of his artistic disciplines. (As Ed would say, "Think I'll mosey over and nosey around.") Never did a creature so amuse us while dabbling in the stuff of muses. Lou Derman and the other *Mister Ed* writers, as well as trainer Lester Hilton, deserve a great deal of credit for getting Ed to do all those darned, crazy, artful things.

ED THE PAINTER

WILBUR: What got you started on this painting kick anyway?
ED: It's therapy. To relieve my depression.
WILBUR: Hmm. Well, let's take a look here. Well, that's depressing, alright.
                                                    —*"Ed the Beachcomber"*

Ed creates two oil paintings in the series: "Portrait of Carol" (from "Ed the Artist") and "Horseless Headman" (from "Ed the Beachcomber"). Carol Post misconstrues her "portrait," a garish abstract work, to be an unflattering rendering of her by Wilbur, causing an episode's worth of domestic squabbling. "Headman" marks Ed's debut as a socially and politically conscious being. He's a misunderstood youth rebelling against the establishment. As far as his painting technique goes, well ... he holds the paintbrush in his mouth. And when the paint smudges ... no problem, he just eats what's extra.

Frank Lloyd Wright Meets Jackson Pollock

In "Ed the Artist," simple, good-natured Wilbur has a conversation with a brooding, abstract expressionist painter named Schindler. This scene is an example of what happens when a contemporary theme goes through the *Mister Ed* fun factory. Schindler is played by series regular Henry Corden.

WILBUR: That's a beautiful sunset.
SCHINDLER: It's not a sunset. It's my wife.
WILBUR: She's very pretty.
SCHINDLER: No, she's very ugly.
WILBUR: If you feel that way, why did you marry her?
SCHINDLER: Because I'm an artist, and an artist must suffer.

ED THE GOURMET

ED: If there's anyone that's at home on the range, it's a horse.

—*"Hi-Fi Horse"*

Ed's creativity pours into culinary endeavors as well. Here are just a few of the *actual* recipes Ed concocted on the series.

WILBURINI

(This is clearly Ed's most famous recipe, from "Ed's Juice Stand.")

Crescitelli brand carrots
Apples
Day-old Hay

Place carrots in blender and mix until juiced. Ditto for the apples. Combine and strain through day-old hay.

A hit with both kids and adults; distribution through makeshift juice stands.

Wilbur's slogan: "When you eat a red-hot weenie, wash it down with WIL-BURINI."

WILBURINI GIMLET—
WINNIE KIRKWOOD'S RECIPE

4 oz. Wilburini
1 oz. vodka

Combine and serve.

SUNLAMP SANDWICH

(Ed's no dummy when it comes to figuring out ways to jazz up hay.)

Hay
Sliced Carrots

Toast hay under sunlamp. Combine and serve.

Ed, on Hay

The *Mister Ed* series wouldn't be complete without Ed's treatise on hay:

WILBUR: How does hay taste to a horse?
ED: Tastes terrible.
WILBUR: It does? Why are you eating it?
ED: Well, I don't see you offering me pizza.
WILBUR: I guess you get used to hay, do ya?
ED: Oh, yeah, yeah. It's a great, all-purpose food. A horse can stand on it, roll in it, kick it around, sleep in it, and when he's all through, he can eat it. Let's see ya do that with strawberries and cream!
—*"Wilbur Post, Honorary Horse"*

ED THE SONGWRITER

ED: I don't dig writing the blues, pops.
WILBUR: Why not?
ED: I'm like a happy swingin' cat, man. Try Ella Fitzgerald's horse.
—*"Mister Ed's Blues"*

"Pretty Little Filly"

Wilbur Post innocently hums a tune one day in record producer Paul Fenton's office. (See Chapter 2 for a character profile on Paul Fenton, played by Jack Albertson.) Fenton asks Wilbur for the lyrics to the catchy tune, but the architect can't remember where he heard it. Naturally, Mister Ed had been humming the melody that morning, from a song he composed and (yes) wrote lyrics to a while back. It's a pop love song called "Pretty Little Filly," and Wilbur gets credit as the musical genius. Ed performs baritone vocals for this hit recording, behind Wilbur's lip-syncing ("Ed the Songwriter").

"Pretty Little Filly" by Mister Ed

Got a date a little later,
When the moon is on the trail,
With the cutest triple gaiter,
My pretty little filly with the pony tail.

Got a bag of oats to call with,
Hay I'll bring her by the bale,
Want to share a double stall with
My pretty little filly with the pony tail.

Gee, if she would just agree,
She'd be mine today,
But no matter when I ask
The answer's always "Nay, Nay, Nay."

If she'd name that day of wedlock,
I would be there without fail,
Got the ring made for her fetlock,
The pretty little filly with the pony tail.

Incidentally, Ed reprises "Pretty Little Filly" six episodes later ("The Mustache") in his very own shower stall, wearing a size 38 shower cap! Rocky Lane is astute in "stretching out" the lyrics, shower style. Just three episodes after that, in "Wilbur Sells Ed," Ed proudly belts out the same tune to finish the show. And four episodes later, he begins the show with a rendition of the same song ("The Horsetronaut"). Definitely in "heavy rotation" at this point!

Ed the "mezzo barracuda" sings in the shower, 1961.

"Empty Feedbag Blues"

The season following "Pretty Little Filly's" debut, Ed wrote a blues number for Wilbur, called "Empty Feedbag Blues." The source of inspiration for Ed's song was a filly named Sabrina, a fickle gal who chose the stallion Robespierre over the palomino, and left Ed with a broken heart (good blues material).

Once again, Wilbur saves Paul Fenton's fanny from financial ruin with this hit song. We don't see a reprise of Wilbur's lip-sync performance, but hear the whole song, along with Carol, Wilbur and Paul, once it's already recorded. Marlin Skiles is credited with the additional music in this episode.

"Empty Feedbag Blues" by Mister Ed

When I get up for breakfast,
There's no oats in the bin,
'Cause everything is going out,
And nothin's coming in.

Believe me when I tell you,
I've heard the news,
I got those empty feedbag,
Empty feedbag blues.

My pretty filly told me,
To stay away tonight,
'Cause all that I bring with me
Is a healthy appetite.

Why am I so unlucky?
Me with four horseshoes,
I got those empty feedbag,
Empty feedbag blues.

Wilbur gives Ed a jump start to "Empty Feedbag Blues" by improvising his own little blues number. "Eatin' Carrot Blues" clearly shows that horses, not people, have the real talent when it comes to songsmithing.

"Eatin' Carrot Blues" by Wilbur Post

Oh I got the blues,
I got those eatin' carrot blues,
I got those carrot blues,
I got those eatin' carrot blues.

I get the blues when I eat a carrot,
I get the blues when I look at a parrot,
I got those imported carrot blues...

And of course, Ed's always improvising on some traditional tune, like "Jingle Bells" in "Ed's Christmas Story." He opens the show with his own little version of that Christmas classic: "Jingle bells, jingle bells/Jingle all the way/Oh what fun it is to ride/In a one-horse open sleigh/Full o' hay!" Or while charging lots of Christmas gifts for his horse buddies at Tally-Ho Stables, on Wilbur's credit card: "...Jingle all the way/Hope he doesn't get this bill/ Till after New Year's Day!"

ED THE AUTHOR

Mister Ed is a horse of letters, a skilled wordsmith who's always ready to add a dash of horsely pizazz to Wilbur's fairly banal written works. And he's always good for checking the spelling. (It's somehow admirable that Wilbur surrenders himself to the intellect of a horse.)

In "Horse Sense," Ed swipes Wilbur's Letter to the Editor from out of the mailbox and replaces it (right into the postman's sack) with his own, far more eloquent effort:

> On the bridle path, horse and master are alone. Man and beast together, as nature intended it ... a few blades of grass, some oats.... And in conclusion, as we enter the space age, can we not set aside a few feet on earth for man's noble friend, the horse? With deepest conviction, Wilbur Post.

Ed's emotion-packed words do the trick in this particular episode—Roger Addison rescinds his petition to do away with the bridle path.

Regarding lengthier works, Ed's memoirs, *Love and the Single Horse, or the Adventures of a Palomino Playboy,* get packaged as a humorous novel by Wilbur Post. Ed personally hoofprints the first copy for publisher Durvis. Also, the literary-minded equine contributes to Wilbur's more serious nonfiction work, *Our Friend the Horse,* a book that reveals the life of the horse from the inside out. Topics include how a horse turns his ears out, how he sniffs directions and what he thinks about hay.

Ed's Poems

Mister Ed often displayed his gift for rhyme and meter. Here is a selection of the palomino's thought-provoking verses, usually composed and recited all at the same time.

Blessings on Thee

Blessings on thee, Wilbur Post
As a buddy, you're the most,
I promise you I'll never roam,
'Cause where you are is home sweet home.

—*"Horse of a Different Color"*

Ed's Bequest to His Son

Blessings on thee, little fella,
Barefoot colt with cheeks of yeller,
With your bushy, turned-up tail,
Eating oats from daddy's pail.

—*"My Son, My Son"*

Ode to Life

Life is a feedbag without any oats,
A stable that's empty and bare,
I search for the hay in the empty corral,
But how can I find what's not there?

—*"Ed the Beachcomber"*

Ed's "I Feel Loved" Poem (Variation on Above)

Life is a feedbag o'erflowing with oats,
A bag that should never be shut,
And a horse that would leave a sweet guy like you,
Must be some kind of a nut.

—*"Ed the Beachcomber"*

Ed's Christmas Poem

It's the night before Christmas
And Wilbur's my boss,
If he doesn't buy me a present,
He better get a new horse.

—*"Ed's Christmas Story"*

Birthday Poem for Wilbur

Happy Birthday, beloved boss,
Straight from the heart of your little hoss,
I pray together we'll always be,
Like bacon and eggs, the toast is on me.

—"Getting Ed's Goat"

Rock-a-bye Baby: Variation

Rock-a-bye Baby,
On the tree top,
When the wind blows,
Roger's apples will drop.

—"The Blessed Event"

Note: Ed sings this lullaby just moments before knocking Addison's apples out of their tree with a slingshot.

ED THE ACTOR

WILBUR: Ed, you touch that telephone once more and you'll be playing the lead in *Death of a Salesman.*

—"Ed the Salesman"

Ed's played the classics—from Romeo to Hamlet to Robin Hood to Lincoln. Nor is any role too small. He's pretended to be a cat (meowing and playing with a ball of yarn), a dog, and even a lion opposite Wilbur as lion tamer. Plus his great gift for fibbing makes him a natural thespian when it comes to "method fainting" ("It's getting dark, mother . . .") and fake hunting injuries, a la *ketchup.* But the funniest role he performs is that of a Hollywood movie director, spoofing his *own* director, Arthur Lubin. Move over, Cecil B. DeMille . . . there's a new mogul in town.

Ed "directs" Wilbur's *Robin Hood* screen test in the park, wearing the complete director's getup: megaphone, beret, the works:

C'mon, get with it, baby. We're already over budget....
I wonder if Arthur Lubin has all this trouble....
O.K., sweetheart, no hard feelings. The picture's the thing, right?...
Check, baby ... O.K., roll 'em....

—"Robin Hood Ed"

This scene is just another example of how much Ed is a product of the TV generation. His characterizations are always exaggerated and stereotyped, instantly readable for TV. Stock characters are the stuff of sitcoms, though Ed definitely would've appreciated the fact that these archetypes are derived from the ancient Italian theatrical tradition, commedia dell'arte.

ED THE MUSICIAN

Music for Annoyance's Sake

Interestingly, Ed usually performs music not to soothe the savage beast, but to get Wilbur good and mad. Only occasionally does he make music for the sheer joy of it, as in "Ed-a-Go-Go," where he swings with electric guitar and Beatles-type wig. In "Hi-Fi Horse," Ed blasts Wilbur's new high-fidelity system in the middle of the night, unleashing a recorded barrage of air battle sound effects. And he drums up a racket in "Ed the Sentry" so that Wilbur will have no choice but to get rid of him.

Ed is capable, however, of making music for more peaceful pursuits. In "Ed the Musician," he takes up music therapy, becoming a one-horse band to relieve his nightmares. Also, while wearing a Tyrolean hat, he plays accordian for the expectant filly, Gina, in "Ed the Godfather" (she's homesick for Italy, you see). And of course he's always humming some tune, even if it is (wink, wink) the *Mister Ed* theme song!

SCAREDY ED: SUPERSTITIONS AND RITUALS

As sophisticated as you might think Ed is, at least for a horse, he's very much a slave to superstition, astrology and basically unscientific explanations for things. The palomino advocates hypnotism (the scenes of Ed putting Wilbur under a trance are accompanied by "eerie" Chiller Theater music); honors fortune-telling, the zodiac and jinxes; and partakes in typically human good-luck rituals, giving them an animal twist. We, the viewers, are amused because not only is this horse charmed (by virtue of the fact that he talks) but he's also flaky. Maybe there is something to all this superstition junk . . .

ED'S SUPERSTITIOUS EXPRESSIONS

- ○ "Cross my fetlocks and hope to die." ("Ed Cries Wolf")
- ○ "You're a Fink Jinx!" ("Dragon Horse." The whole episode is based on Ed's fears.)
- ○ "She loves me, she loves me not"—Ed's game of carrots and apples, a horsely variation on the human use of daisies ("Ed Visits a Gypsy"). Ed cheats! ("Can't let one old carrot ruin my love life.")

© *1990 CBS Inc.*
Ed gets his hoof read by a crackpot gypsy, Madame Zenda (Belle Mitchell), in "Ed Visits a Gypsy," 1963.

Zodiac Ed

If you're trying to figure out exactly how old the TV character Ed is, or what his sign is, forget it. Only his astrologer knows for sure. Are Ed's "musical birthdays" simply a case of *Mister Ed*'s writers being overcautious about which astrological traits to assign to Ed, or just a matter of delightful inconsistency? You decide...

O Ed was born under the sign of Taurus the bull. Wilbur's a Taurus too. ("Dragon Horse")
O Ed's a Virgo, born on August 28, 1953, celebrating his ninth birthday. ("Horse Party," a 1962 episode. Note: He gets *younger* as the series progresses.)
O He's a Scorpio or a Sagittarius, born in 1957. "My birthday was last November and I'm seven," he tells Wilbur in "The Bank Robbery," a 1965 episode.
O He's also a Pisces. "Us Pisces Gotta Be Careful." ("Hunting Show")

So many horoscopes seemed to bring this horse a great fortune: He has a birthday every other month, and certainly could keep Hallmark Cards in business for a long time!

ED'S "TALL TAILS": THE HOLIDAY FANTASY SEQUENCES

Mister Ed's fantasy sequences, as executive producer Al Simon calls them, were "a great deal of fun." Only three were produced because of their great expense, relative to the average cost per episode. (The cost for a typical show was $55,000, according to director Arthur Lubin.)

These segments involved elaborate costumes, sets and extras, and were enormously popular. "The audience loved them," Al Simon explained recently, "because what you did in a case like that, you brought historic characters back, and Alan Young always was playing the part of the lead, whoever it was. And you found everybody in the show had a part somewhere. And now you can do anything in the world and that's what the audience liked.

When Columbus and Ed saw land and said 'Land Ho,' they saw the skyline of New York. And these were brilliant pieces. But what happens is, you can't do it all the time, it has to feel special." Writer Larry Rhine, who scripted "Ed Discovers America" with Lou Derman, remembers that the makeup, costume and set people "loved Ed's history lessons" (how he and Derman referred to them), because they really got a chance to break out of the typical barn and house mode. "We would do a flashback," Rhine remembers cheerfully. "Ed would say, 'Columbus, it's always a man! That's because men write the history books. You never find a history book written by a horse. But if you did, it would be completely different. The real story is like this. The one Hollywood was afraid to make.' And we'd flashback."

All three holiday shows—Christmas, Thanksgiving, Columbus Day—highlight Mister Ed's great gift for storytelling. Al Simon compares Ed's lies to Baron Munchausen, bigger than life. The horse's clever parables are convenient vehicles for rich fantasy sequences. In typical sitcom fashion, regular cast members are "transported" to an earlier time, playing famous historical and legendary figures like Columbus, Queen Isabella, Santa Claus and the Governor of Plymouth Colony.

In all three episodes, Ed lays the truth on Wilbur: If it were not for the sheer intelligence and cunning of Horse, some of humanity's major achievements and institutions, including the survival of the Pilgrims in Massachusetts, Columbus' discovery of the New World and Santa's annual toy delivery on Christmas Eve, would never have occurred, and the human race would still be floundering in ignorance.

"Ed the Pilgrim"

Ed reveals "the Real Story of Thanksgiving, the one they're afraid to tell."

Year: 1620
Place: Plymouth Colony, Massachusetts

CAST OF CHARACTERS

○ Roger Addison as the Governor
○ Kay Addison as the Governor's Wife
○ Wilbur Post as Chicken Heart, Indian "brave"
○ Carol Post as Indian Princess, Chief Thundercloud's daughter
○ Mister Ed as "the gallant handsome horse"—guess who's narrating!

There's no skimping in this sequence: We get full Indian and Pilgrim costumes; snow-covered ground; teepees; campfires; stocks, the works. Highlights: (1) Action is frozen while Ed does his narration. As soon as he's done speaking, everyone starts to move. (2) The Pilgrims and Indians brainstorming on what to name this day—Appreciation Day, etc., all the way through to Thanksgiving Day. They look and sound like a seventeenth-century ad agency. (3) Wilbur as Chicken Heart trying to tell the Pilgrims how to plant the corn seeds: "First, you plant . . . then you mulch." The Pilgrims, in typically imperialistic fashion, ignoring Wilbur and thinking up methods of torture that they can use, stretching rack, etc., to make him talk, when he's been talking all along! (4) At the very end of the story, Wilbur and Ed are put in the stocks for being witches. Ed's fake front legs are sticking out of the stocks and look great!

© *1990 CBS Inc.*
Ed gets locked in the stocks for witchery
in "Ed the Pilgrim," 1962.

"Ed Discovers America"

Ed tells Wilbur "the Real Story of How America Was Discovered," so he'll understand why the horse, not the eagle, is the true symbol of America.

Year: 1492
Place: Portugal

CAST OF CHARACTERS

○ Wilbur Post as Chris Columbus
○ Kay Addison as Queen Isabella
○ Carol Post as Sam, the mess boy (one of those Shakespearean incognito things)
○ Ed as Queen Isabella's favorite horse, Sir Ed

Once again, Ed narrates the action loftily: "Fortunately for the history of the world, nearby stood a handsome steed of royal blood. There was something about the frustrated Columbus that touched the heart of this highly intelligent animal. He decided to act." Ed is all decked out in Renaissance garb: an ornate blanket, face armor and a plumed helmet.

Columbus is like a spoiled teenager. At the beginning of the sequence, he tells a would-be patron: "I still say the earth is round, and if you say it's flat, then you're a square." And on board his ship, he throws a tantrum because Ed won't let him steer ("We keep going back to Spain," Ed insists). And once he discovers that Sam the mess boy is no boy, he pronounces them man and wife on the spot. They spend the rest of the journey locked in an embrace. Ed picks up the narration: "The horse guided them safely through the storm." Ed yells out the first "Land Ho!" It's the New York skyline, circa 1963! During the voyage scene, painted paper ships flip by in the backdrops.

"Ed's Christmas Story"

It's Christmas Eve, 1963. The barn is decorated with tinsel, miniature trees, and a "Season's Greetings" banner. Ed wants to buy Christmas gifts for his seven horse pals: "I love Christmas. Wilbur is so full of the spirit of giving. And I'm so full of the spirit of receiving." The horse even kisses Wilbur, who's

Ed steers Columbus to the New World in "Ed Discovers America," 1963.

Ed poses as Santa Claus for this holiday publicity shot with Connie Hines and Alan Young, 1963.

standing under the mistletoe. In his efforts to convince Wilbur that his friends deserve gifts, he tells his owner "the Real Christmas Story, the one Hollywood didn't dare make."

Year: Unspecified (the year Santa's Toy Run started)
Place: North Pole

CAST OF CHARACTERS

○ Wilbur Post as Santa Claus
○ Gordon Kirkwood as Ebenezer Kirkwood
○ Mister Ed as Santa's Horse

According to Ed's story, Santa's horse plays a pivotal role in developing the first Christmas Eve toy delivery: (1) He teaches the dolls to say "Ma-ma," (2) he teaches the reindeer how to fly, (3) he acts as foreman in Santa's toy factory (we see stock footage of a 1960s factory and hear "industrious" stock music) and (4) he teaches Santa the obligatory greeting: "HO HO HO, Merry Christmas, Merry Christmas!"

Ed's story works: Wilbur realizes that Christmas is all about giving and allows Ed to buy his friends presents. The highlight of the episode? Without a doubt, the very end: Ed comes out of his stall, dressed as Santa Claus, with white beard and boots. He doesn't even need a fake fat belly. Imagine a Santa suit fitting around a horse's stomach—that's big enough!

ED'S DREAM SEQUENCES/WILBUR'S DREAM SEQUENCES

Ed's Dreams

It's no wonder that a creative horse like Ed would have a colorful subconscious life as well. Human/animal reversal continues in Ed's elaborate dream sequences.

"Ed the Bridegroom"

This late episode is directed by Alan Young. Ed dreams that he's taking Rosita down the bridal/bridle paths of life. Wilbur Post as Justice of the Peace (holding a racing form!) has some funny remarks for the two betrothed horses:

> Friends, we are gathered here today to witness the first legal horse marriage in history. And now, let the ceremony commence. . . . [Ed enters in tux; Rosita enters with veil] Please, Ed, don't kiss her before the ceremony. And now, before I join you two in the bonds of fetlock, let me point out that in the pasture of life, there are many barbed-

wire fences. Face them together, and you will succeed. Back into them separately, and you'll be scratched at the post.

(*Inside joke:* The Justice of the Peace character that Wilbur visits is named Richard A. Greer, played by John Qualen; *Mister Ed*'s production coordinator was Richard Greer.)

"Doctor Ed"

Ed dreams that he's a TV doctor in "Doctor Ed." His character, a noted brain surgeon, is a direct outgrowth of his obsession with medical soap operas on TV, spoofing the likes of Dr. Kildare and Ben Casey. The operating room scene between Dr. Wilbur Post and Nurse Carol is filled with romantic-wit exchanges, and is a startling precedent to *M.A.S.H.* The latter hit show is of course remembered for O.R. scenes filled with sexual repartee between Houlihan (Loretta Swit) and Pierce (Alan Alda), but void of laugh track to keep the gravity of the war message top-of-mind. Special touch: As Dr. Ed enters the O.R. to perform surgery on Addison (for "acute hematosis of the left fibrosis"), we hear a racing trumpet.

Courtesy of Connie Hines.
Connie Hines with Ed in his "Doctor Ed" dream sequence, 1963.

© *1990 CBS Inc.*
Wilbur performs the marriage ceremony of Ed to Rosita in this dream sequence from "Ed the Bridegroom," 1965.

"Dirty Ed" ("Ed's Ancestors")

In this episode, Ed has been chosen to pose for a park statue of "a palomino. To typify the spirit of the American West." Wilbur writes to the American Breeders' Association to learn about Ed's lineage; Roger bets Wilbur fifty dollars that Ed is not descended from royalty and offers to mail Wilbur's letter. Of course, Roger never sends Wilbur's letter, but creates his own "response" from the Breeders' Association.

Addison's letter includes gems like: Ed's great-great-grandfather was named Dirty Ed and belonged to Billy the Kid; his two great-uncles were Eddie the Rat and Evil-eyed Ed, who rode with the Dalton Brothers; his uncle, Mad Dog Ed, was "the first horse ever hung in Arizona."

That night, a devastated Ed dreams that he's an outlaw, based on Roger's practical joke. A policeman wearing a giant star-shaped badge, made of paper, warns officers to "be on the lookout for Mister Ed, alias Shifty Ed, alias Eddie the Dip. Height: 15 hands, 2 fingers; Weight: 900 pounds." We learn that he may be armed and dangerous.

Next we see "Wanted" sketches of Ed in different positions, followed by a police lineup of horses, including Ed, who's wanted for bank robbery. Ed wakes up from his nightmare and decides to "spend the rest of my life at hard work, making up for the crimes of my family." Knowing Ed like we do, we're not surprised that this exercise in martyrdom doesn't last long, and as usual, everything is back to normal within twenty-seven minutes.

Ed's Trial by an Animal Jury for Birdnapping ("Animal Jury")

Ed tries to get rid of Aunt Martha's parrot, Tootsie (who, like Ed, is a big medical soap opera fan), by abandoning her at Glorby's Pet Shop. Wilbur retrieves the bird but reprimands Ed for his actions. Ed insists that "a jury of animals would understand what I did. No jury of animals would convict me." That night, he dreams that he's up for birdnapping in a courtroom with an animal jury. He's got a chimp for a judge ("The Honorable John Jay Monk Presiding"), Wilbur for the district attorney and a pig, hen, duck, goat, owl, skunk, mule and baby chimp for jurors. Ed tries to bribe the baby chimp, the son of the judge, by offering him a banana. Young is superb as the D.A., delivering an eloquent appeal, in most distinguished voice, which convinces even Ed of his own guilt:

Ladies and gentleman of the jury. Birdnapping a parrot is a terrible crime. If we allow this fowl deed to go unpunished, other laws will be broken. Chaos will result. We must not, we cannot allow this criminal horse to go unpunished. (*To hen juror*): You, sir, as a father (*hen lays egg*). I beg your pardon, madam, as a mother, how would you like to have one of your chicks snatched from its roost, torn away from its loved ones, left alone to face a strange and hostile world?

Ed wakes up moaning: "I'm a bad horse, I'm a bad horse, I'm a bad horse."

Other Assorted Nightmares

Besides Ed's lavish dream sequences that were actually produced, we some-times *hear* about the horse's nightmares. These are even more outrageous because we have to imagine them. Usually, he'll call Wilbur up in the middle of the night and tell him to hurry out to the barn. Ed'll be wearing his striped nightcap, scared silly. Wilbur comforts Ed as we hear about the bad dream.

His nightmares are classically Freudian, another sophisticated Lou Derman touch. In "Ed the Musician," he dreams he's falling off a high cliff. Wilbur's at the bottom, waiting to catch Ed, but he drops him. "How could I catch you?" Wilbur asks Ed in self-defense. "You're a horse. You weigh 800 pounds!" Ed justifies: "In my dream, you weighed 8,000!" (How come a horse's weight seems to range anywhere from 800 to 1,200 pounds in these scripts?!)

Wilbur's Two Dreams

Wilbur Dreams He's a Horse
("Wilbur Post, Honorary Horse")

Wilbur spends so much time interviewing Ed for his book, *Our Friend the Horse*, that his wife and neighbors tell him he won't be satisfied until he becomes a horse. That night, Wilbur dreams that Ed's up at a podium, conducting a ceremony in his honor:

Wilbur dreams he's a horse in "Wilbur Post, Honorary Horse," 1963.

Wilbur Post, you will now become a member of the horses of the world. [Wilbur enters, dressed as a horse, flanked by six horses, three on each aisle] Wilbur Post, are you prepared to give up human-hood for horsehood? [Wilbur stomps his foot "Yes"] Good! I hereby declare you "Horse." Okay, fellas, now all together, For he's a jolly good horsie, for he's a jolly good horsie. . . .

Wilbur wakes Carol up with his neighing (he's standing on all fours on the bed, still asleep). She wakes him up, and he instantly snaps his horse obsession. He rushes out to the barn and muzzles Ed so that he can complete his architectural plans on time.

Wilbur Dreams That Ed Becomes a World Hero ("Ed Finally Talks")

Wilbur tries to trick Ed into talking in his sleep so that they can win the $25,000 prize for George Burns' novelty act. Ed turns the tables on his owner, getting him to doze off. While asleep, Wilbur dreams that Ed becomes famous.

Each segment of the dream is introduced by a newspaper headline:

○ "Horse Gets Diploma at Yale" (Wilbur's the Dean).
○ "Mister Ed Elected to Congress" (Wilbur's the Page).
○ "Mister Ed Becomes Army Major" (Wilbur is Private Post).

○ "Mister Ed Captured by Enemy" (two men with Russian-like accents are dangling a carrot in front of Ed, to get him to talk).
○ "Major Ed to Face Firing Squad" (Ed is blindfolded, about to be shot).

Wilbur wakes up shaking, and is relieved to see that Ed isn't a famous horse at all, but just an ordinary talking one.

HOOFNOTES
Ed's Library

How is it that regardless of the story line, Ed always has the perfect book to match the occasion? In numerous episodes, you'll find Ed out in the barn, wearing a gigantic pair of eyeglasses while reading. Notice how the book is always propped up, either on the stall doors or on a reading stand, so that the title is prominently displayed for our benefit. Here is a compilation of the works perused by the palomino through the series. A "Mister Ed Bibliography," if you will:

The Adventures of Robin Hood
Hamlet
Heredity and the Criminal Mind
How to Send Smoke Signals
The Life of Lincoln
Hypnotism Made Easy, by Josef Sullivan
Hypnotism Self-taught
You and Your Will, by Leonard R. Kelton
Live Alone and Like It
Medical Encyclopedia
Medical Textbook
Principles of Human Psychology
Junior Ranger Manual
Thoroughbred Magazine
Playhorse calendar

STRAIN THE BRAIN

1. What will Ed be if Wilbur buys him a paint set?
2. Why does Ed want ice cubes in one episode?
3. Which character always says he's getting ill whenever Wilbur plays the pompous author (as in "Horse Sense")?
4. What instrument does Ed actually play, courtesy of film footage that's repeated and sped up?
5. In "Ed Discovers America," where does Queen Isabella tell Columbus to go for money?
6. What is the name of the spirit that Ed pretends to be in "Ed the Pilgrim?"

ANSWERS

1. The first "Palomino Picasso."
2. So he can drink carrot juice "on the rocks."
3. Roger Addison. He excuses himself in these moments.
4. The accordian.
5. To the Madrid Savings and Loan.
6. The Great Spirit Bingo.

"I've Always Wanted to Let My Tail Grow Wild"

ED THE DAREDEVIL

In case you hadn't noticed, anything's possible in *Mister Ed.* The horse constantly performs amazing feats and stunts, despite the fact that he's a major league coward. The audience delights in the depiction of his death-defying adventures, his thoroughly *bon vivant,* Hemingway spirit. Once you accept the fact that this horse talks, it's not much of a leap to believe that he can scale Mount Everest too. The clever scenarios dreamed up by the show's writers showcase not only the horse star's intelligence but the trainer Les Hilton's patience.

Prime example: Without the benefit of having ever taken a flying lesson, Ed single-hoofedly commandeers an obsolete bomber plane in "Ed the Pilot": "My first solo! My four legs are shakin' like they were the Wright Brothers," he candidly admits. How many horses do you know, or people for that matter, who would undertake such a risky endeavor? At least Fred Flintstone signs up for flying instructions at the Bedrock airport before making an airborne spectacle of himself. Trainer Les Hilton does a great job of getting Ed to walk up the airplane ramp and pose with parachute gear as if he's free-falling.

Reckless Is Raucous!

Ed is always amusing us with his foolhardy approach to life's more harrowing moments. His approach to driving vehicles, however, is particularly reckless, typical of 1960s sitcoms.

With basic prosocial values and humor that still holds up as "funny" today, *Mister Ed* is timeless. But the series participated in a curious phenomenon not unusual to sitcoms at that time—a comic celebration of haphazard driving. Ed's total abandonment while driving and flying a plane wildly is accompanied by raucous laugh tracks. And these moments truly are among the funniest. A contemporary fantasy-sitcom, *My Mother the Car* (NBC, 1965–66), had a similar scene with a drunken Jerry Van Dyke driving out of control. With all the anti-drunk-driving organizations out there like MADD and SADD, we would never get away with stuff like that today. But it was fun while it lasted.

© *1990 CBS Inc.* "Holiday Art" taken by CBS Publicity in 1961, when *Mister Ed* first joined the network.

Here are two of Ed's "wild" monologues. The first is spoken while driving a milk truck (yes, he steps on the gas and the brake pedals with his hoof), and wears a beret, dark glasses and a scarf—real classy. The second scene occurs in the obsolete bomber plane just mentioned. Again, he's got on the whole pilot's garb, even a parachute pack for a safe emergency landing.

Ed the Chauffeur

My first solo. Now I know how Lindberg felt. And awayyyy we go! Hey, watch where you're goin'. [*He hums* Mister Ed *theme song.*] Boy, this beats horseback riding! Oh, my achin' back! YIPPEEE! Oh, Ed, you crazy fool. Look, Ma, no hands! One-way street?! Well, that's okay, I'm only goin' one way.... WHEEEE!!! This is fun! WHEEEE!!! Uh, oh. I'm running out of gas.

Ed the Pilot

Look out! Look out down there! I'd swap this thing for a boat right now. Look out below! CRAZY HORSE! Women and children first! Fasten your safety belts. No smoking. Keep off the grass. WHAT AM I TALKING ABOUT?!

While Ed is flying wildly, we see sped-up stock footage of soldiers scurrying frantically on the runway. We see and hear an airplane (presumably his) flying in reverse, upside down, spinning, etc. In his state of panic, Ed reacts to the situation as if he's a stewardess/shipcaptain/park warden/horse, all rolled into one.

One Part Stoic, Two Parts Panic

ED: Mirror, mirror on the wall,
    Who's the scaredest horse of all?
    You are, chicken!

—*"Ed the Musician"*

Ed gets suited up by a Filmways prop man for his role as space traveler in "The Horsetronaut," 1961.

Some of the biggest laughs in the *Mister Ed* series occur at moments where Ed's panicky lines juxtapose with the supposedly valiant stuff we're seeing. In "Ed's Ancestors," we see Ed doing hard labor, repenting for the imagined crimes of his ancestors. He hauls a hefty load of cargo with a serioso farmer urging him on from the wagon ("Yah, yah!"). The sun is hot and blazing. We hear *Exodus*-like music, far more tragic in scale than Ed's actual toil. Ed looks into the camera: "Oh, my achin' back!" We'll never, *ever* mistake *Mister Ed* for a documentary on animal labor in the twentieth century. This show is pure sitcom all the way.

"Ed the Desert Rat"

Ed's mix of courage and cowardice is at its best in this scene from "Ed the Desert Rat." Ed wanders off to Death Valley to search for "his little green corner of the West," a noble quest. But the horse finds himself surrounded by unfamiliar elements: coyotes, vultures and blinding sun. Here's a couple of his more schtick-laden lines:

ED: Hey, coyotes! [Stock footage of coyotes] It sounds like I'm outnumbered. If you can't beat 'em, join 'em. Whooo! I'm one of yooooou! Whooo! I'm a coyote tooooo! Whoooo!
[Now we see stock footage of swirling vultures.]
ED: Eh, shut up! There'll be no free lunches on Ed! I'd better keep moving. Show 'em I'm alive. Ohhh! That got rid of 'em. Or did they go home to bring back ketchup?

Rocky Lane is great as the panic-stricken voice of the horse.

The Plot "Sickens" . . . Ed the Hypochondriac

ED: I got an earache, Wilbur. Rush over with a couple of hundred aspirin.
—"Ed Cries Wolf"

On the flip side of valor is cowardice, so any true study of Ed's brave deeds must include his not-so-brave ones. Hypochondria, or the imagining of maladies, would fall into this category. Ed commonly believes that he's dying of some rare disease, especially after watching a medical soap opera. And whenever the horse is feeling neglected, he invents a sickness to win back Wilbur's affections. And it works like a charm. The audience looks forward to what type of ailment Ed will concoct next.

Good ol' Doc Evans, a vet who's been caring for sick horses his whole life, is referred to as a "trigger-happy quack" by our favorite palomino. Ed will even climb on top of a roof to avoid a vaccination. Or suddenly, miraculously, recover from his case of dizziness just as the doctor is reaching for the hypodermic. Reversed, sped-up film of Ed sitting down is used to show the horse, now "better," getting up briskly.

Strangely enough, in one show, "Dragon Horse," Ed actually asks for flu shots after a scuba-diving jaunt. Very out of character . . .

Master of Mind Games

When faking an illness just won't do, Ed outsmarts his opponents to avoid the humiliation of defeat. He's even stooped to brainwashing ("mental shampooing," as neighbor Roger Addison puts it). In "Ed the Jumper," Mister Ed meets McTavish, a horse as pompous and obnoxious as his owner, Carl Dickenson (*Gilligan's Island*'s Alan Hale, Jr.). It's a case of animals taking after their owners (a theme revisited much later in episode 110, "Like Father, Like Horse"). Carl's been bullying Wilbur "Dippy" Post since college. This scenario is crying out for poetic justice. Ed will do anything to avoid meeting McTavish at the steeplechase, which they're scheduled to compete in on Sunday. Ed decides to outpsych the other horse, a talent for which he has no peer. Check out McTavish's Scottish subtitles (subtitles are for our benefit—remember, Ed's "talkin' horse" here):

ED: Been jumping long, McTavish?

McTAVISH: Aboot a year, laddie.

ED: Tough racket. Know the average life of a jumper?

McT: No, what?

ED: Four years. How old are you?

McT: Three and a half.

ED: Enjoy yourself. It's later than you think.

McT: Hoot, mon. What d'ye mean?

ED: Let me tell you about my cousin, Pegleg Eddie. Got it at Ainstree. . . .

—"Ed the Jumper"

Ed's ploy works. McTavish is sufficiently spooked and won't go through with the race. Wilbur finally beats Carl at something, gloating: "Oooh, I beat him, I beat him, I beat him."

By the way, Carl Dickenson's wife, a glamorous, vapid former Miss Louisiana, is played by Donna Douglas. Douglas, herself a former Miss Mississippi, finally got her big break from Filmways in 1962, when she won the role of Elly May Clampett in *The Beverly Hillbillies*. Herb Browar remembers the casting of Elly May: "She was the last girl to test, but she was the best."

Wilbur Cries Wolf

Ironically, the one time Ed really does something heroic in the series, saving a little girl on a runaway horse ("Ed the Hero"), the rest of the characters don't believe Wilbur's boasting. It's a classic case of architect crying wolf. Wilbur brags so often about Ed's talents, which are only perceived in his own eyes (and *ours*), that others can't imagine Ed being capable of a noble deed.

HOOFNOTES
Ed's Maladies

Ed seems to have more afflictions than the Bible's Job. "One sneeze and he's ready to write out his will," is how Wilbur describes the four-legged catastrophe. But *we* know better— Ed's just fakin'. Here's some of the pseudo-sicknesses that Ed contracts (not all in the same episode, thank goodness):

Parrot pox
Mumps
Laryngitis
Nearsightedness
Hay fever (he's allergic to hay)
Lameness
Dizziness
You name it, he's got it!

Crime Doesn't Pay

ED: Take one step and you're dead meat!

—*"Ed Cries Wolf"*

Cartoonish criminals are a regular feature in *Mister Ed.* They're some of the brighter, funnier characters in the show, speaking with a wit that's sort of ironic, given their lot in life. For example, when a bank robber pays a visit to Ed's barn, to retrieve the stolen money that he's hidden in Ed's saddle earlier, he tells Ed: "I'd split it with you, but your relatives have taken enough from me at the track." When Wilbur gives the robber a hard time, the shyster laments: "I never liked doing business with married men—they don't care if they live or die."

Throughout the series, Wilbur and Ed crack all sorts of crimes. They foil real estate scamsters, racetrack thugs, con men, run-of-the-mill burglars and prowlers, pool sharks—even card sharks who take over a ski lodge. In that last case, Ed pretends to be an elk head on the wall (the series just wouldn't be complete if Ed didn't pretend to be an elk head at least once) and helps Wilbur win back Roger's scammed money.

The most charming feature of these "crime stopper" episodes are the contraptions that Ed constructs to catch the crooks. He's got nets, pulleys, locked feed bins, the works. Sheer genius, combined with sped-up film, makes for great chuckles in these scenes. And of course it doesn't hurt the comedy when Ed captures a good guy in the trap by mistake, like Wilbur or some policeman or Gordon Kirkwood.

"WILBUR DOESN'T CALL ME OAT-OAT SEVEN FOR NOTHING": THE SPY GENRE EPISODES

The year was 1965. "Red Threat," "the Iron Curtain" and "the Cold War" were commonplace topics of conversation, fueling America's collective imagination. We were obsessed with espionage, reading daily reports on the Missile Crisis, the space race and FBI investigations. Hollywood gave us the chance to fantasize still more about these perils by producing the James Bond series of movies starring Sean Connery (and landing a gold mine in the process). *The Man from U.N.C.L.E.,* NBC's TV entry into the spy field, was ranked thirteenth that season. *Get Smart,* though a spoof on the genre, was im-

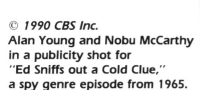

**Alan Young and Nobu McCarthy
in a publicity shot for
"Ed Sniffs out a Cold Clue,"
a spy genre episode from 1965.**

mensely successful that same year, ranking twelfth. The entertainment environment was absolutely ripe for exploring the spy genre, even through a presumably "children's" vehicle like *Mister Ed.* The Filmways team took Hollywood's lead and incorporated themes of espionage into the horse's escapades. These plots offered Ed at the height of his ingenuity and courage. And he took his responsibilities seriously, proudly donning the alias "Oat-Oat-Seven" (again, a movie reference true to his character).

In October 1965 *Variety* announced that *Mister Ed* had "joined the James Bond 'spy' bandwagon by eliminating strife with next door neighbors and sundry domestic problems ... thus far this new plot has paid off very well in the laugh department."

Alan Young had initial hesitations about making these "spy genre" episodes, despite the fact that the American public was primed for it. The actor didn't think international intrigue would be a fitting context for Mister Ed: "But the majority said, 'Look, I think we should get in and do those kind of shows,' so we did about four of them."

The Good Guys

Of course our main heroes are the underdogs, Wilbur and Ed. They are, in effect, free-lancing for the SIA, which stands for Secret Intelligence Agency, a slight variation on the real thing.

The role of SIA Agent J. G. Slattery (played by James Flavin) is recurrent through three of the four spy shows, making them seem more like a crime action serial. Slattery's secretary, Gertrude, is played by actress Sandra Gould, who went on to play busybody Gladys Kravitz in the color *Bewitched* episodes (the ones with Dick Sargeant as Darrin). And she pretty much plays the same character: a woman who sees too much for her own good. In *Bewitched*, she was always witnessing some spectacle of Samantha's witchcraft. In this case, she sees a horse snooping around her boss' office for clues. And of course, everyone thinks she's crazy! Now, that's typecasting. She actually had enough potential work out there with so many "fantasy" TV shows on at the time.

The Bad Guys

These spy episodes are filled with stereotypical, cartoonish depictions of international criminals who speak with generic "Slavic" accents. Even the Chinese waiters are absurd. In "Ed Sniffs out a Cold Clue," Wilbur dresses up as "Roo Fong," a bumbling, *blond* Chinese waiter ("Only my hairdresser knows for sure") at the Flaming Dragon Restaurant, hangout for archvillain Kosh, a.k.a. Coldfinger. When the thugs challenge Wilbur's oriental heritage, he speaks gibberish Chinese to a fellow waiter (Victor Sen Yung), hoping the man won't give him away. The waiter laughs hysterically, as if Wilbur has just told a great joke. Later, when the two are standing a distance from the spies, he admits to Wilbur that he couldn't understand a word he was saying, but it sure sounded funny.

God Bless America

In all four spy shows, Ed and Wilbur's unflappable patriotism is the number one theme. Even Carol is in the dark about her husband's brave doings. The country's security comes before an open marriage—Wilbur's sworn to secrecy. A typically *Mister Ed* way of letting us know how pro-American these two are is through musical touches. Often, we'll hear "Glory, Glory, Hallelujah" (played with fife, etc.) underscoring a dramatic, patriotic comment by Ed, like: "I know it's bad manners to snoop, but it's the least a horse can do for his country." Or else it's used as background music while Ed or Wilbur tries to "guilt" the other into reprising their "Oat-Oat-Seven and Partner" roles just one more time. This same gag was picked up by *Green Acres*, a later Filmways hit. On that show, as Oliver Wendell Douglas (Eddie Albert) waxes poetic on the nobility of the farmer, we hear "Glory, Glory, Hallelujah" loud and clear.

Spy Genre One-Liners

WILBUR: This calls for logic, reason and deduction.
ED: So keep quiet and let me think.

—"Ed Sniffs out a Cold Clue"

ED: Let's see—where would I hide if I was a sneaky human being?
—"Ed Sniffs out a Cold Clue"

KOSH: I don't know . . . when they start sending horses, maybe it's time to get out of the spy business.

—"Ed Sniffs out a Cold Clue"

ED ON EXERCISE

As you might expect, our favorite palomino has a Garfield the Cat aversion to physical exertion. "Some horses were born to run. I was born to eat, sleep, and smooch," Ed confesses. Still, there are moments when even Ed must admit that shedding some excess poundage would be in his best interests. Twice, we see him partaking in light Jack LaLanne calisthenics. But the fanatical stuff, the fitness programs that separate the horses from the colts, takes place in two different shows. In both episodes, Wilbur is coaching Ed in preparation for equestrian events (he is a horse, after all). In "Ed the Race Horse," Ed will take on Cyclone, Gordon Kirkwood's rented horse. In "Ed the Jumper," the horse will try his skill at steeple jumps versus McTavish, the stallion with the attitude problem.

And of course everything in *Mister Ed* has to be larger than life. So a few games of fetch with Wilbur just won't do as a workout. Instead, we get scenes with so much rigor and sweat, they would challenge the likes of Jane Fonda and Richard Simmons. We've got weight lifting (a looped piece of footage of Ed picking up a very light "barbell" in his mouth); Ed wearing a reducing belt (you know, those barbaric contraptions that jiggle one's rump so un-

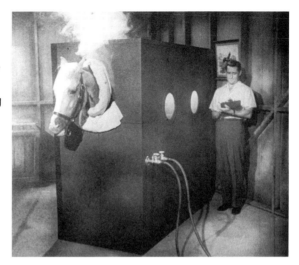

"I want a pony coming out of there!" Wilbur tells Ed during fitness training in "Ed the Jumper," 1961.

abashedly); Ed sweating it out in a steam box (Wilbur tells Ed he wants a pony coming out of there); and Ed jumping rope (this shot is great—Ed's "hind" legs are dark brown, obviously belonging to a different, stunt horse). The best line in these exercise scenes? Wilbur to Ed: "Keep melting that fat away. Pretty soon you'll be fitting Carol's slacks." Is this a farce or what?!

Incidentally, Ed did all the riding scenes himself. "Edna Skinner was the best rider on the set. She really put Ed through his paces," remembers Alan Young, who first learned to ride a horse on Ed.

HOOFNOTES
Ed's Phobias

○ WATER (catalina-phobia)
○ HEIGHTS (acrophobia)
○ FAT MEN WITH WHISKERS (sebastian cabot-phobia)
○ COCKATOOS (claudia-phobia)
○ CATS (felicia-phobia)
○ PROWLERS (shyster-phobia)
○ WOODEN CAROUSEL HORSES (dragon horse-phobia)

STRAIN THE BRAIN

Now, I dare you to answer these questions about "Ed the Daredevil."

1. How come it's so easy for Ed to discover that Coldfinger eats duck chow mein, just by sniffing his glove?
2. What is the first type of car that Ed considers buying in "Ed the Chauffeur"?
3. Why doesn't it matter if Ed gets hurt while driving recklessly?
4. What type of music plays from the top-secret miniature shortwave radio in the second "spy genre" episode?
5. In the fourth "spy genre" episode, what medical "condition" does Wilbur invent to explain the zebra's stripes running together?
6. In "The Bank Robbery," why does Ed lock up Spike the robber in his feed bin?

ANSWERS

1. "Look at my face, Wilbur, it's all nose."
2. A convertible, so he can ride with the top down and blow his horn at all the little fillies.
3. He has "horsepitalization" coverage on his insurance.
4. Hawaiian.
5. Zebritis.
6. Because Spike called him a crummy photographer.

"I Sure Would Love to See Her in a Black Saddle"

ED THE PLAYBOY

WILBUR: Ed, why don't you write a love song?
ED: Who's got time? I'm too busy making love.

—"Mister Ed's Blues"

Mister Ed—America's "mane squeeze"? One thing most everybody remembers about the dashing palomino is his love for the fillies. Some of the biggest laughs in the show come from Ed's clean-yet-oh-so-sly remarks about them, for example, "A horse does not live by hay alone" from "Horse Sense." This was children's television that definitely had an adult bite. Ed the macho stud (in reality a gelding) frequently reads *Playhorse Magazine*. Or waxes poetic about some filly whose photo is tacked up on his wall, always making a rhyme like, "Rosita, no filly is sweet'a, I adore you, chiquita, from your head to your feet'a" (guess he couldn't find a word to rhyme with "hoof'a"). Or else he's gawking at the latest pin-up horse on his calendar. Come to think of it, Ed's stall does sort of resemble a typical gas station.

Photo: Gene Trindl.
**Ed doesn't dig Mae West's bubbly TLC in "Mae West Meets Mister Ed,"
1964.**

A Filly in Every Port

ED: Nothing like taking out a filly in Venice—if she doesn't smooch, she
swims home.

—*"Ed the Godfather"*

Chances are, if you gave this horse a world atlas, asked him to close his
eyes and put his hoof down anywhere at random, no matter where he was
pointing, he'd have some romantic escapade associated with that place to
tell us about ... real or imagined. "I'm just a gay international playboy," Ed
blushingly confesses to his boss from time to time.

Wouldn't Ed have been the perfect guest star on *The Love Boat?* Even
without the benefit of Captain Stubing and crew, Ed manages to be quite
the debonair globetrotter in the course of his own show. He's got a slew of
girlfriends from the Continent, he practically stays in Hawaii to marry Leilani,
and if Japan seems too far off to actually visit, he dreams of bubbly encounters
with a filly named *Fuji.*

© *CBS Photos.*

Ed yearns to globetrot in "The Contest," 1961.

HOOFNOTES
"If It's Tuesday, It Must Be Flossy"

Did Ed know how to skirt-chase or what?! For the first time ever, a complete listing of "the blond bomber's" girlfriends is compiled here. While reading it, you may ask yourself, "How did Ed manage to handle so many fillies, so deftly?" He was a master at the fine art of juggling—never more than one filly per episode. And it worked—after thirty years, the other *horseshoe* still hasn't dropped.

THE ABC'S OF LOVE. ED'S FILLIES, IN ALPHABETICAL ORDER:

○ *Chestnut filly, unnamed:* the filly who "wears her tail on the upsweep" whom Ed sees in the park on Sundays. She's the reason he wants new horseshoes ("Ed's New Shoes").

○ *Chiquita:* Spanish filly who "digs skinny horses." Ed takes a mud bath as part of a reducing program to win her love.

○ *Daphne:* western movie star filly that's smitten with Ed. They meet on the set when Ed shows up as an extra ("Ed the Lover").

○ *Fatima:* foreign spy filly to whom Ed gives the "James Bond treatment," i.e. "SMOOCH, SMACK!"

○ *Miss February: Playhorse* calendar filly. "I'd sure love to park up on Mulholland Drive with you, honey."

○ *Flashaway:* pin-up horse Ed falls for on the Princess Helen rebound. "She makes Princess Helen look like a boy."

○ *Flossy:* pretty chestnut filly with great legs, owned by Mrs. Gordon. "I like the way she's built." "She's got a face that could launch 10,000 ships."

○ *Francesca:* Italian filly whom Ed went with after Suzette and before Chiquita.

○ *Fujiyama:* a Japanese filly in Ed's dream who was scrubbing his back. They "seemed to belong together, like suki and yaki."

○ *Gigi:* French filly that Ed meets for moonlight rides in the park.

○ *Ilsa:* Ed's exotic girlfriend in "Bald Horse." He's embarrassed about losing his hair (really a practical joke by Addison), and afraid she'll find out.

○ *Lady Linda:* While Ed psychoanalyzes her for racing blocks, she falls for him on the rebound ("Horse Doctor").

○ *Lady Sue:* a racehorse that's been slipped a goofball (she said it was "a real gasser"). Ed goes to the racetrack with Wilbur and a walkie-talkie to find out whodunit ("Horse Talk").

○ *Leilani:* Hawaiian filly owned by Sam Manaloa. Wilbur gives Ed to Manaloa so he and Leilani can marry ("Ed the Stowaway").

○ *Little Princess:* A racing filly. Ed gives her owner tips in "Missing Statue."

○ *Penelope:* "800 pounds of cuddly curves" who's three inches taller than Ed, prompting the palomino to get elevator horseshoes ("Taller Than She").

○ *Princess:* Ed dedicates his book about horses to her, which he's ghostwriting for Wilbur ("Horse Sense"). In "Horse Party," Ed invites her to his ninth birthday party. Wilbur advises: "If she can cook, Ed, don't let her go."

○ *Princess Helen:* 68"-47"-68" ("That's a lot of horse to lose"), owned by Mr. Gilbert. Ed wants to ask for her hoof in marriage and makes her a heart from hay.

○ *Rosita:* Mexican filly whom Ed wants to make *the* "Mrs. Ed" in "Ed the Bridegroom."

○ *Sabrina:* The inspiration for "Empty Feedbag Blues," Ed's second hit single ("Mister Ed's Blues"; lyrics, Chapter 8). "Ever see such kissable lips?" "Everything's in the right place." "She's practically Mrs. Ed."

○ *Suzette:* French filly whom Ed went with before Francesca.

○ *Yvette:* Ed wants her to pose for his painting. If she loosens her saddle, she'll "have that impudent, saucy look" ("Ed the Artist"). Five shows later, Yvette is referred to as Ed's "first love" in his memoirs.

Mister Softee: Ed the Gentlehorse

At times Ed may talk like he's into one-stall stands, a confirmed bachelor and womanizer to the end. But in reality, he's a real romancer, a noble admirer who would go to *any* means to win his filly's heart. Case in point: Only a pure gent would bother asking his girl, unseen behind locked barn doors: "Yoo hoo, Sabrina, are you decent?" ("Mister Ed's Blues").

This has got to be one of Rocky Lane's best-read lines, delivered in an almost sickeningly sweet fashion. The fact that Ed mocks Sabrina cruelly mere moments later, when he discovers that "women don't look their best in the morning?" Details!

In the episode "Taller Than She," Ed resorts to an incredible feat, wearing customized elevator horseshoes, five pairs stacked together, to avoid humiliation by his statuesque British sweetheart. Ed coaxes Wilbur into taking him to Ralph's Blacksmith Shop. In order to get Ralph (played by *Mister Ed* regular Henry Corden, whom Alan Young loved working with) to comply with his special request, Wilbur appeals to the blacksmith's sense of noble tradition. He cites Longfellow's immortal poem, jazzing it up a bit for TV comedy: "Under a spreading chestnut tree/the village smithy stands . . . /And no matter what a horse may need/The smith will help him, yes indeed," accompanied by the requisite canned violin music. Pass the bread basket, Giorgio . . .

Ed's Little Black Book

It makes sense that a horse with so many girlfriends would want to find some way of organizing it all. The "little black book," a thorn in the side of many a sitcom bachelor and bachelorette, was invented for just such a purpose. And *Mister Ed*'s writers felt obliged to bestow their star with this device too. But Ed refers to his "little black book" in only one episode, "Bald Horse." Like other swinging singles throughout history, the horse rips up his book in a moment of passion, only to regret it minutes later: "Get the glue, Wilbur. We're going to have to do a lot of pasting."

Let's face it, though. Such a system as the "little black book" is way too crass for Ed, the sophisticate. He aspires to loftier means of recording his love life . . .

Ed's Memoirs

As far as we know, Ed's memoirs, *Love and the Single Horse* (probably named in the spirit of the 1960s "sex farces" that often starred Bobby Morse), represent his most ambitious body of work. According to Ed, the romantic escapades documented therein are just between him, Wilbur (who's sneaked a peek) and "a hundred happy little fillies." Without the pomp and circumstance of Geraldo Rivera opening up a vault, here now is an excerpt from *Love and the Single Horse*:

> *LOVE AND THE SINGLE HORSE, or "The True Adventures of a Palomino Playboy,"* © 1965 Durvis Publishing Co.
>
> ... I will never forget my first love, Yvette. She was only a little French filly, but Ooh, la, la! A kiss from her would melt your horseshoes. And what a shame ... she had so many curves, her saddle kept falling off! ...

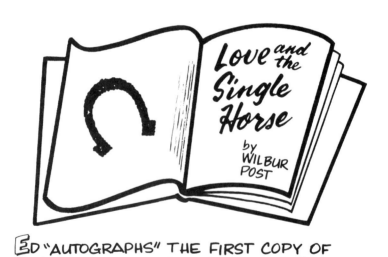

ED "AUTOGRAPHS" THE FIRST COPY OF "LOVE AND THE SINGLE HORSE".

James Spegman.

Although this book did not make *The New York Times* best-seller list, it has been reported that numerous copies were sold at the 1966 Kentucky Derby.

Romance by Subtitles

ED: This horse talk is so limited.

—"Horse Sense"

One of the more ingenious and campy devices employed by Filmways in *Mister Ed* is subtitles whenever there's a scene between Ed and his best filly! Since Ed's girlfriends can't "talk human" like he can, we need subtext to understand what the two lovers are neighing. And the translation is so unbelievably corny—the stuff of Harlequin romance novels, bad violin included.

This tradition of love by subtitles was carried on in *Green Acres*, a later rural Filmways production. On that zany show, you'll see subtitles used to decipher Arnold the Pig's amorous dialogues; for example: "Cynthia, this is madness," Arnold emotes to his canine girlfriend, via printed text on the screen. Of course the major difference between Arnold Ziffel and Mister Ed is that Arnold doesn't even speak English (Ed knew Latin before English, so he had a head start). Only the Hooterville residents can comprehend the meaning behind the oinking.

Matrimony Pony

Since Ed's got an opinion about everything, why shouldn't he give his two cents' worth on matrimony as well? After all, he *is* a ladies' horse ... Most of Ed's comments on marriage, however, derive from his observations of *Wilbur*'s marriage—that is, the mess that he perceives it to be. There's only one episode, "Ed the Bridegroom," in which the palomino actively pursues plans to get married. Usually, Ed's witty remarks on tying the feedbag are from the perspective of a true gigolo.

From the marriage "vows" that follow, the reader will surmise that Ed would not tickle the fancy of any feminist filly.

○ "When I get married, I want to wear the saddle in the family."
  ("Anybody Got a Zebra?")
○ "I've never met the filly I want to share my feedbag with."
  ("Ed the Godfather")
○ "I want a horse just like the horse that married dear old dad."
  ("Wilbur Sells Ed")

Macho Ed

Here are some other examples of Ed's macho temperament:

○ "My name is Ed, not Edwina." ("Mae West Meets Mister Ed")
○ "You want a horse or a housemaid?" ("Lie Detector")
○ "If she doesn't come to me of her own free will, then I say bring her in on a rope." ("Mr. Ed's Blues")
○ Of Carol Post: "For once that blonde gave me a good idea." ("Working Wives")
○ "My mother didn't raise her son to be a doormat." ("Ed Visits a Gypsy")

Come Up and Shoe Me Sometime

Getting Mae West to guest-star on an episode of *Mister Ed* in March 1964 ("Mae West Meets Mister Ed") was quite a coup for Filmways, and quite the pressworthy event. *The New York Times* covered the story on January 22 of that year, speculating that although "many fans of 'Mister Ed' are children ... the average age of the audience may increase considerably when Miss West's performance is televised by CBS on a Sunday evening in March."

It's hard to believe Mae West was seventy-one years young when she filmed that episode. Mae confessed to the reporter that "it is unusual for me to do this kind of show, but I'm doing it to please my fans." Miss West was a tough cookie, and despite her age, knew exactly what she wanted in the script, from wearing her very own wardrobe to using her very own bedroom furniture on the set! "Everything had to be right from her standpoint, and she would change the script if necessary," recalls Al Simon, with respect for Mae's vision. "She knew exactly what she wanted to do, and it was always very, very good. She was excellent, and she never missed a line."

Mister Ed writer Larry Rhine describes his memorable visit to Mae's beach house in Malibu, where Arthur Lubin took him and head writer Lou Derman to review the script they had written for Mae: "We were ushered into this beautiful apartment in Malibu, out of keeping with the area there. It was very clean and air-conditioned and she had a white piano, a beautiful alabaster statue of herself, and a winding staircase you don't expect to see in a beach community, and finally, they gave us Cokes, and said, 'Miss West will see you now.' So we go up to her bedroom and she's laid out on the chaise, in a skimpy kimono, and she says, 'Hello, fellas, what you see is what you're gonna get. I read your script, fellas,' and being Mae West, we had a lot of Mae Westian lines in the thing, we just loaded it, and she said, 'It's not right for me because I don't motivate the plot.' And she also objected to the fact that her leading man, Cesar Romero, was too old for her, and he was probably in his sixties and she was pushing eighty! So we explained to her that Mister Ed had to motivate the plot because it was his show."

Mae West was the talk of General Service Studios while she was performing in *Mister Ed*. Spungbuggy animation director Herb Stott remembers that at the same time they were working on the "intergalactic" Moko animation for episode 93, Filmways was shooting the episode with Mae West (January 1964). George Burns had been talking to Herb Stott, then left him to go see Mae West. Stott followed behind George to see if he could sneak a peek at the glamorous legend, and George was heartbroken—Mae wouldn't come out of her trailer to see him! Her attitude notwithstanding, the episode with Mae West is a gem, and really remarkable when you consider her age at the time.

Publicity Hook, Line & Sinker

On August 21, 1964, CBS issued a master press release announcing Mae West's upcoming appearance in a *second* episode. No such episode was made. "She was very astute when it came to publicity," associate producer Herb Browar pointed out recently. The episode was said to be titled "Mae Goes West," and featured an audience favorite, one of Ed's "history lessons." In this show, a horse gets credit for the discovery of gold at Sutter's Mill in California, 1849. "It does sound like a possible story," writer Larry Rhine now comments, although he wasn't aware of any such script (Rhine was writing the shows that season with Lou Derman, and would certainly have known about such an effort).

"Miss West appears first in modern dress when she calls on Wilbur to approve the plans he has drawn for an addition to her stables," CBS previewed. "Then, in Mister Ed's tall tale she is in the dress of the Diamond Lil era when she plays the part of Lady Belle, the owner of a high-class gambling saloon near Sutter's Mill."

Arthur Lubin was sourced as saying that the episode would be shot at the end of September. Those involved with *Mister Ed* agree that they were fortunate just to work with Mae West on one episode, let alone a second. As it was, Mae's publicist probably got a raise for planting the story.

STRAIN THE BRAIN

Don't mean to tease, but let's see just how much you know about Ed the Playboy:

1. What term would you use to describe Mister Ed in one of his rare moments without a girlfriend?
2. In "Ed the Bridegroom," why does Ed decide against tying the knot in his dream sequence?
3. Why does Ed think that marriage is a God-given right of horses?
4. Why does Ed want a gold filling, in "Ed's Dentist?"
5. In "Wilbur and Ed in Show Biz," which does Ed prefer?
   a) Big round apples and little fillies
   b) Little apples and big round fillies
   c) He's not sure, but he gets a kick out of deciding!

ANSWERS

1. You could say he was *un-a-filly-ated*.
2. His fiancee filly's already married and has two ponies.
3. "Who else but horses have a better right to get hitched?"
4. So the fillies will think he's a rich horse.
5. "C," of course, of course.

"I Wonder if the Peace Corps Sends Horses to Miami"

• •

ED THE SOCIAL ACTIVIST

ED: Wilbur, do you believe a man has the right to stand up for his principles?
WILBUR: Of course.
ED: Well, a horse has the right to lie down for his.

—"Ed and Paul Revere"

It's 1961 and counting ... too early in television history for shocking and politically charged characterizations like those in *All in the Family*. And definitely too late for *Father Knows Best*. If anyone *knows best* in *Mister Ed*, it's you-know-who. For all its glorious innocence, *Mister Ed* has a socially conscious edge that you'd swear is political. The horse is constantly taking a stand (or lying down as in the above quote), leading protests, challenging authority and championing causes.

Practically one third of the 143 *Mister Ed* episodes fall into the category of "Ed the Social Activist," where the horse gets to show off his politically minded, fanatical dimension. In the more graphic beatnik shows, involving "period" costumes and music, Ed is spokeshorse for a new constituency, the under-thirty crowd. These misunderstood and rebellious, nature-loving kids would blossom into the Flower Power generation just a few years later.

Though beatniks are handled farcically in *Mister Ed*, you might say the series, politically correct but screwy, was actually testing the waters with its inclusion of these contemporary themes. Certainly there was never a more political animal than Ed on television. Lassie wouldn't be caught dead ordering the dogs of America to stop fetching their owners' newspapers. Nor would Arnold Ziffel, the pig on *Green Acres*, ever lead a march on Washington to protest bacon consumption.

Mister Ed is a product of its time, early 1960s. America was still on the brink of a social revolution, one that would eventually challenge all preconceived definitions of age, race, gender and even patriotism. Besides, Hollywood always seems to be a few years behind reality in its depictions anyway. Kooky novelty shows were in vogue. Martians, witches, Frankenstein-wannabe's and disembodied hands (the kind that answered the phone and sorted the mail for you). All of these series, when viewed in the context of sitcom history, remain wonderfully innocent. BUT SOMETHING WAS GOING ON! They weren't your average, cookie-cutter domestic comedies.

American imagination, at least that of Hollywood's bright TV scripters, had grown tired of the "same old, same old." We wanted to know more about Mom than the fact that she cooked a mean meat loaf. And how about Dad? Surely he yearned to do something besides trimming the hedges in his spare time. With these fantasy shows, the opportunities for zany and bright writing increased exponentially. "Ed was a unique character. He was irreverent, he could do anything," is how associate producer Herb Browar describes the outspoken hoofer. "Like the Simpsons today because they're animated—they say a lot of things people wish *they* could say. Ed could say or do whatever he wanted." Politically the show may seem tame because it's a horse, not a person, that's giving life such an outrageous interpretation. And our collective social consciousness still lacked touchstone events like Kent State and Martin Luther King's assassination, angry fodder for some of the later, breakthrough shows.

Of Course, Of Course, Ed's Got an Opinion

"You can't do the show unless you really believe that Mister Ed can talk and think along the lines that people do," writer Larry Rhine recently pointed out. "Consequently it led to things like, 'You humans don't have any sensitivity regarding us animals. You let us run around without clothes. You people wouldn't do that.' And also, and this could bring a tear to your eye, the families break up. 'Where's my mother? Where's my father? Who do I get together with on Mother's Day? And Thanksgiving?' It was really a touching kind of thing for a little horsie." All this prosocial sentiment is an example of Ed applying "people sense" to horse situations, one of the Ed Commandments covered in Chapter 4.

It's a Mad, Mad, Mad, Mad World

Ed's soapbox tendencies conveniently allow his writers to explore the "silly man's world" theme. Look what a man will do for a business deal! To what ends will a wife stoop for a mink stole! A fellow will betray his best buddy's confidences (even if that buddy happens to be a horse) in pursuit of the Great American Dream. How compromising, how trivial, when viewed through the more "civilized" eyes of a beast. Ed's convictions are so un-horselike, indeed, they are even too "humane." Maybe there *is* something to be learned from the animal's unique perspective, we're told again and again. For a fantasy-laden sitcom, *Mister Ed* did a pretty good job of depicting the tension between material and spiritual, a very adult theme. Yet the show's producers never really put forth an official *point of view*. Ed expresses his beatnik causes, and Wilbur ultimately approves (the architect always seems to learn something in the process), yet the dialogue is so abundant with camp and schtick as to keep things from ever getting too serious. After all, this was TV comedy for a family audience.

Wilbur Post, Architect of Animal Rights

Inevitably, in the social activist episodes, Wilbur ends up being a loyal supporter of Ed's causes. The writers give us a sense of how "animalized" Wilbur is from the arguments that he gets into with his neighbors.

GORDON: You play with this animal like he was human.
WILBUR: There we go with that prejudice again. Gordon, are animals so different from humans? Don't they feel and see and hear and think like humans? Think, Gordon, think. Maybe in some other world, maybe people will be in cages, and animals will be throwing us peanuts.

—"Ed's Diction Teacher"

Wilbur Post is a regular prophet of the drafting table. To think that within five years of this episode, *Planet of the Apes* would emerge: a shocking, box-office smash with *just* that scenario!

We Shall Overcome

Mister Ed did not go uninfluenced by the social movements of its times. Ed is a true believer in civil rights (both for people and for animals), and freedom is always on his mind. True to the model that Lou Derman established, Ed as rebellious teenager, the palomino calls Wilbur a "fuddy-duddy" and tells him that "young people are taking over the world." He of course includes himself in this group. (If his average age on the show was seven, that would've made him twenty-one in people years.)

Occasionally, there's a pithy statement thrown in, but we're accustomed to it being delivered by the horse. When a down-and-out human speaks with depth and insight, we're really taken aback, as in "Be Kind to Humans" (episode 84), featuring a trio of hobos:

Hobo's Wisdom . . .

The curse of civilization,
Living away from nature,
All herded together like caged animals,
It's no wonder people like [Wilbur] are so confused.

—Stu the Hobo

In this episode, Ed empathizes with the three chaps, and invites them home for some TLC.

Mister Ed, Miracle Worker

Ed has an affinity to all kinds of disadvantaged individuals: hobos, swayback horses, homeless goats, elderly work horses and caged birds. He even tries to rehabilitate the neurotic creatures and give them back their lost sense of self-esteem. No, the producers do not give Mister "Ed-mund Freud" a beard and make him talk with a German accent, although it might have been awfully tempting.

Making Peace With Beatniks

Imagine the stereotypical TV beatnik, circa 1962. Goatee, sunglasses, beret, lots of cosmic references—basically an exaggerated, hammed-up version of Maynard G. Krebs (*The Many Loves of Dobie Gillis*, CBS, 1959–63). These caricatures were positively laughable (the wild laugh track told us so), and a great sitcom ingredient for illustrating generation-gap tension.

Mister Ed has its share of farcial beatniks, brooding shirkers of responsibility who clammer for acceptance by the keepers of art and music, square daddy-o's who don't appreciate their vitally important works of abstract expression. But no matter how obtrusive the young visionaries seem, they end up being the heroes of the story line, true to the underdog form. So when Wilbur insists on performing "Pretty Little Filly" in the stable (the better to lip-sync to Ed's crooning by), three beatniks (one named Fuzzy) back him up on piano, base and acoustic guitar. And in "Ed the Beachcomber," seemingly squaresville next-door neighbor Roger Addison finally agrees to let the beatniks prosper in their artist colony, even if it happens to be on his private beach property. By the end of these "youth celebration" episodes, the stuffy characters have lost some of their stuffing. *Mister Ed*'s beatnik interludes hold a warm place in TV's heart, helping to capture "the way we were."

© *Orion Television.*
Wilbur has a heart-to-heart with his beatnik horse in "Ed the Beachcomber," 1962.

HOOFNOTES

ED'S FAVORITE BEATNIK EXPRESSIONS

○ "I'm real down. Beat. Like depressed. Neglected (*stomps hoof*). Rejected (*stomps hoof*). Befuddled (*stomps hoof*). Bemuddled (*stomps hoof*)." ("Ed the Beachcomber")
○ "Holler, but like, don't hit." ("Ed the Beachcomber")
○ "Wow, dig that crazy transmitter." ("Spies Strike Back")
○ "No, man, I made the scene with one gasser, and I'm, like, through." ("Mister Ed's Blues")
○ "It was like, from the heart." ("Mister Ed's Blues")
○ "This pad's gonna be jumpin' tonight, daddy-o!" ("Ed the Musician")
○ "For every swinger you crush, another hep cat will pick up the bongos and lead the rock-and-roll to freedom." ("Ed-a-Go-Go")
○ "Don't fight it, Pops. We kids are taking over the world." ("Ed-a-Go-Go")
○ "Cinderella ... That kid with the glass slipper is a gas." ("Ed Finally Talks")

Pride Is Progress

This horse is proud! He condemns oppression and slavery of any kind, in a way that transcends animal rights. He would have made a great spokeshorse for Amnesty International. Ed's heroes? Not Trigger or Black Beauty, as you'd expect, but Lincoln and Albert Schweitzer. Here are some of Ed's soapbox speeches which cry out for horsely dignity:

○ If a horse can't have his dignity, he might as well be a human. ("Whiskers and Tails")
○ Steal my feedbag, but not my good name. ("Ed the Hero")

○ You've got a great tradition, Noble Palomino. Now make America proud of you! ("My Horse, the Mailman")

○ There's nothing worse than a horse getting a horse laugh from another horse! ("Ed the Race Horse") (Try saying *that* ten times fast!)

○ I talk for pleasure, not for money. ("Ed Finally Talks")

○ A horse is the noblest animal and we don't like to be ridiculed. ("Ed the Zebra")

Ed is such a good salesman that we believe in the nobility of his causes; however, sometimes we have to dig through the horse's idiosyncratic logic to unearth the nobility. Everything in *Mister Ed* has got to be bigger than life, so it makes sense that his fervor should be just as exaggerated, to the point of ridiculousness. And because it's television, his protest has got to "read" instantly. So when he decides to camp out on the beach with some teenage artists in "Ed the Beachcomber," the producers make sure we "get it" by dressing Ed up in a straw hat and poncho, just like the other kids are wearing.

Dressed for Duress

ED: I'm a horse, not a lamb chop.

—*"Ed the Zebra"*

© *Orion Television.*
Ed is forced to wear a tuxedo against his will in "Ed the Zebra," 1963.

Clothes may make the man, but not the horse. Two *Mister Ed* episodes, "Don't Laugh at Horses" and "Ed the Zebra," poignantly deal with animal dignity, and both use "costume" to drive home the point that "animals are people too." These shows are a perfect example of how *Mister Ed* was written on two levels—a lot of physical gags for the kids, and legitimate thought-provoking issues for the older set.

In the first episode, Wilbur and Paul Fenton dress up as a horse and dance foolishly, offending the palomino. In "Ed the Zebra," Ed is forced to wear a tuxedo for Addison's photo contest, equally humiliating. He protests, "I was born a nudist, and I'll die a nudist," but to no avail. It is actually sad to see Ed standing there in his outfit, surrounded by laughing Roger, Kay and Carol. Trainer Les Hilton did a terrific job of getting Ed to stand there very quietly in his tux; it absolutely tugs your heartstrings. The sad music doesn't hurt, either.

Ironically, even though Ed has the human gift of speech, which we're thrilled about, the minute we see him dressed like a human, we're appalled. To add insult to injury, Addison is blackmailing Wilbur—if Wilbur doesn't pose Ed in the tux, Roger won't discuss Wilbur's plans with Henry Tyler, the builder. The story points out that human ambitions far outweigh concerns for animal dignity. Wilbur is obviously pained by Ed's shameful ordeal. He tries to convince his horse that with the money he earns from Tyler's project, he can buy lots of nice things for him. But it's too late—Ed runs away and pretends to be a zebra at the city zoo, where he can be gawked at professionally. This is one of the only two instances where Ed talks to another person besides Wilbur, this time to a cub scout. Typical of the series, Ed and Wilbur reconcile by the end of the show, Wilbur agreeing never to embarrass Ed like that again.

Just when you're sure you know Ed's attitude toward formal wear, the writers throw in a monkey wrench. In "Wilbur's Father," Ed actually cries at the wedding because he "was the only one without a tuxedo." Obviously a line purely for laughs, without social significance.

The original script for "Don't Laugh at Horses," the other costume episode, was written for Larry Keating in August 1963, but by the time the episode was produced, Keating had passed away. Jack Alberton filled in as the man who shares the horse suit with Wilbur. As a form of protest, Ed calls a strike among the neighborhood horses, starting with Nellie, Pancho and Lightning at Tally-Ho Stables. Under no circumstances are they to carry Wilbur Post. Wilbur punishes Ed by cutting out his TV privileges—"Ed, you'll miss Mitch Miller"—and sends him to obedience training school. Ed replies nobly:

> Do with me what you will, Wilbur, but remember one thing. If I fall, there'll be another horse to pick up the torch and carry on the fight for the preservation of horsely dignity. I thank you (*he bows*).

Of course, Ed's bow tips off the fact that he is, first and foremost, a *ham*, not an activist. He's simply enthralled with being enthralled about something. But you've got to admit, the militant posture makes a good half hour of entertainment.

"Never Ride Horses"

ED: Some must suffer so that others may walk with their tails held high.
— *"Never Ride Horses"*

In "Never Ride Horses," one of the tightest and best-executed *Mister Ed* episodes having a social theme, Ed thinks humans should stop riding equines. This is a silly notion, and even sillier when Wilbur is discovered by Carol and her father out in the barn, test-driving a *cow* (all in the cause of humoring his dear horse). Yet *Mister Ed*'s beef is symbolic of a larger issue, brought up repeatedly in the series: human "exploitation" of the "lesser" animal world.

"One group should not ride another" forms his rallying cry. In the course of the show, he forms the Society for the Prevention of Horseback Riding (SPHR) and has local animals picket the Post house. Their sandwich boards read:

- ○ "Oh my achin' back."
- ○ "We walk, why don't you?"
- ○ "Be modern, drive a car."
- ○ "Take a taxi, spare a horse."

Ed's promotion tools include self-printed pamphlets (he sets up an old-fashioned printing press in the stable); "animated" skywriting; and shortwave radio broadcasts under the name "Radio Free Horse." Abbie Hoffman would have been proud.

Real-life Hero: Ed Visits the Children's Hospital

Despite *Mister Ed*'s success and fame, he was never one to get "on a high horse." At the height of his popularity, CBS Publicity Department received a request for Ed to come visit the Children's Hospital in Los Angeles. "We brought Ed to the grassy area behind the hospital, and he was wearing his blanket so the kids would know who he was," Herb Browar recalls, "and they brought all the kids that they could down to see Mister Ed. It was a very touching thing because there were a lot of kids that couldn't walk, a lot of kids in wheelchairs. All they wanted to do was touch Mister Ed. It brought tears to my eyes. The horse stood there and allowed these kids to touch his snout. They touched his tail. A nurse would lift one to touch his face. And people were looking out from the windows. The horse was really an unusual horse. I'm sure he must have realized that this was some kind of special occasion, because he was just terrific. He didn't become irascible. One kid wanted to get up on him and we lifted him up onto the horse. And there was hardly anything said, except the 'ohs' and the 'ahhs.' The kids didn't scream. They knew they wanted to touch him. And he was there for quite some time. And finally the nurses had to take the kids back in." Kinda gives you a warm feeling inside, doesn't it? Even though we only got to see Ed once a week on our TV sets, it's nice to know that he was putting his "spare time" to good use.

Mister Ed Pickets Hollywood Park Race Track!

Well, actually, it was a publicity stunt by MCA, the original distributors for *Mister Ed*. On May 31, 1966, Mister Ed officially "entered" the "Astronaut Stakes" feature event at Hollywood Park Race Track. The five-furlong race was to be held on June 9, with a prize of $20,000. Top jockeys like Willie Shoemaker and Johnny Longden were asked to ride the talking horse, but the track officials rejected Mister Ed's entry. So come June 9, Ed picketed the racetrack assisted by Connie Hines. Ed, infamous for his placards of protest, wore sandwich boards attesting: "Hollywood Park Unfair to Showbiz Horses!" and "I've been rejected as a racehorse!" In only one *Mister Ed* episode does Ed actually bear the title of "racehorse," wearing sneakers and argyles for the occasion.

Buy U.S. Savings Bonds!

We know that Ed was patriotic in front of the camera, risking hoof and mane to capture treacherous spies. But in real life, the horse was so pro-American that he agreed to star in a short feature for payroll savings bonds in 1964. "Wilbur Gets the Message" was produced by Chrysler Corporation in association with Filmways TV. The film was directed by Arthur Lubin, written by

Mister Ed's original syndicator, MCA, distributed this brochure showing Ed picketing Hollywood Park in a publicity stunt from 1966.

Lou Derman, and ran for 19 minutes—without a laugh track. George O'Hanlon guest-starred with Alan Young and Mister Ed, who orders savings bonds over the phone in Wilbur's name.

HOOFNOTES
Ed's Causes

Ed's activism is multifaceted, everything from wanting the right to vote (he's nonpartisan) to craving Thanksgiving dinner with the family (vegetarian style, of course). Choose the platform you're most partial to and vote "ED!" come next election day.

○ Ed doesn't take lightly to Wilbur's horse suit, nor his burlesque horse dance routine, so he calls a local horse strike. ("Don't Laugh at Horses")

○ Baby animals need care, so Ed leads a picket line of furry tykes in front of live television cameras, to raise money for a kiddie zoo. ("Oh, Those Hats")

○ Ed pretends he's been wounded (the ol' ketchup routine) to make a point about hunting. Very hip. ("Hunting Show")

○ Dressed as Lincoln, Ed frees the birds at the local zoo. ("Ed the Emancipator")

○ "How would you like someone stepping on *your* grandmother?" Ed teaches Wilbur a thing or two about the immorality of bearskin rugs. ("Don't Skin That Bear")

○ An early power struggle between the two blondes of the family: Ed complains to the SPCA when Carol hitches him to a wagon. ("Ed Agrees to Talk")

○ Ed goes right to the source, and calls the White House to complain about Jackie Kennedy's riding craze. ("Ed and the Secret Service")

○ Ed phones the Humane Society and the SPCA to protest an overweight rider who's responsible for Ed's premature curvature. ("The Heavy Rider")

○ Wilbur doesn't respect Ed's privacy and publishes his secret memoirs, so Ed poses as a wax horse to make his point. ("Love and the Single Horse")

○ Ed sympathizes with a group of beatniks who've started an artist colony on Roger's property. ("Ed the Beachcomber")

○ Ed takes in a swayback with an inferiority complex. ("Ol' Swayback")

○ Ed takes in three hobos, who make themselves at home in the barn. ("Be Kind to Humans")

○ Ed abducts Bernadine, an elderly horse that gives rides at the park. He later learns that she loves to work. ("The Other Woman")

○ Ed thinks Wilbur's impoverished, so he steals from the Kirkwoods and gives to the Posts, Sherwood Forest style. ("Robin Hood Ed")

○ Ed thinks the horse is the symbol of America and tells a "history lesson" about the discovery of the New World. ("Ed Discovers America")

○ Ed, "a confirmed bachelor," yearns to be a single parent. Very ahead of his times, very eighties. ("My Son, My Son")

○ Ed learns he's part Indian and wants to scalp a patriotic parrot who's descended from General Custer. ("Cherokee Ed")

○ Ed wants a purpose in life, so he calls up Albert Schweitzer as a "dedicated horse." ("Ed the Artist")

12

"I Went to Bed Naked, and I Woke Up With Polka-dot Pajamas"

•••

EPISODE ODDITIES

Any TV series that lasts for almost six years is bound to have at least a few strange episodes. *Mister Ed* was no exception. The show even boasts its own "Lost Episode," very much in vogue today, as well as spin-off hopefuls galore.

Mister Ed—THE LOST EPISODE!!!

Larry Rhine and Lou Derman were busy at work on a *Mister Ed* script when the series was canceled by CBS in 1966. Tentatively titled "Mister Ed Meets Paul Revere," the script was to feature another of Ed's "history lessons." Cowriter Larry Rhine recently revealed some of the little-known details: "We were working on one story at the end. Paul Revere was a shiftless kind of guy and he either got drunk or was asleep when he was riding the horse. And it was the horse who was yelling, 'To arms, to arms. The British are coming.' It was a relative of Ed's. Never got on the books." Alas, it seems the *Mister Ed* writers were as surprised by events to come as were those original Colonials.

Spin-off Hopefuls

At least three of the 143 *Mister Ed* episodes were actually pilots for spin-off TV shows. And true to the odds facing most TV pilots, none ever became anything more than a volume in the *Mister Ed* library, which is ironic since the focus in these episodes was intentionally *not* on Ed.

Chaos in the Woods

"Pine Lake Lodge" (#26)
ORIGINAL AIRDATE (NYC): June 25, 1961
WRITERS: Lou Derman, Bill Davenport
DIRECTOR: John Rich
GUEST STARS: William Bendix, Nancy Culp (later on *The Beverly Hillbillies*), John Qualen

This pilot for *The William Bendix Show* was barely disguised as a *Mister Ed* episode. It starred William Bendix, who played Chester A. Riley on NBC's *The Life of Riley* from 1953 to 1958. Bendix plays Bill Parker, a kindhearted proprietor of a small rustic lodge, who somehow gets into everybody's business. The *Mister Ed* connection? The scripters made Carol and Wilbur Post friends of Bill Parker, and their visit up to Pine Lake Lodge one weekend sets off a chain of crazy misunderstandings, wrapped up by a happy ending. Mister Ed stays home for this trip, conveniently uninvolved with the plot. The horse does get to vacuum his stall in the opening minutes of the show. What did the critics think of the pilot? Leo Burnett Agency called it "a terrible waste of good talent . . . trite and tiresome." So much for a TV comeback by William Bendix.

Talking Horse Meets Teenage Spin-off

"The Matchmaker" (#50)
CBS AIRDATE: April 29, 1962
WRITERS: Ben Starr, Bob O'Brien
DIRECTOR: Arthur Lubin
GUEST STARS: Noanna Dix, George O'Haulon, Jeff Donnell, Peter Brooks

This episode has the definite feeling of a spin-off pilot. It centers around the trials and tribulations of teenager Emmy Lou Harper, who was based on the

At least Ed gets to vacuum in "Pine Lake Lodge," a spin-off pilot with William Bendix from 1961.

cartoon character created by San Francisco–based Marty Links. Herb Browar happened upon the syndicated cartoon in the newspaper, thought it would be a great idea for a pilot and brought it to Al Simon, who agreed on its potential. Only trouble is, the networks didn't, and except for that one episode, Emmy Lou never made the leap from newsprint to film. Filmways personnel had even flown up to San Francisco to meet Miss Links. Herb Browar attributes the inability of the pilot to catch on to the capriciousness of Hollywood taste. Young actress Noanna Dix does a great job of commanding the limelight. Her character is enraptured by the awkward, apple-munching delivery boy, Arthur. Once again, where's the *Mister Ed* connection? The Harpers move next door to the Posts, and Emmy Lou needs a hair from a horse's tail to complete her love potion.

Episode From Outer Space

"Moko" (#93)
CBS AIRDATE: May 17, 1964
WRITERS: Norman Paul, William Burns
DIRECTOR: Arthur Lubin
GUEST STAR: Moko, the Mischievous Martian
ANIMATION: Spungbuggy Works

This episode is so odd that it doesn't even make sense *unless* you think of it as a pilot for a spin-off series. In the fall of 1963 animation director Herb Stott got a call from his good friend Stan Jolley, who was at that time *Mister Ed*'s art director. Filmways TV had an idea for a new series combining live action and animation, called "Moko and Tatti From Outer Space." The story, which had animated Martians mischievously interacting with real humans down on Earth, had been written by Norman Paul, one of the *Mister Ed* script consultants.

Stott came in to see Al Simon and talk about the project. His newly formed production company, Spungbuggy Works, was awarded the "Moko" animation job. He remembers the details so clearly because it was their very first assignment. "We visited George Burns at his home for lunch and worked on the storyboards together." Although Filmways told Spungbuggy to do the animation cels in black and white, since the episode would be aired that way, they "did them in color anyway—it didn't cost that much more."

TV Martians were definitely *in* that 1963–64 season. There was the Mr. Gazoo character on *The Flintstones* (ABC) and the extraterrestrial hit *My Favorite Martian*. Stott thinks that Hanna-Barbera's success with animation —"Yogi Bear and the Flintstones were very big at the time—was another reason Filmways had the idea to produce "Moko."

Although Filmways' Moko and Hanna-Barbera's Mr. Gazoo are both animated contemporaries from Mars, their personalities are worlds apart. Gazoo is a middle-aged, fairy-godfatherish, Charles Nelson Reilly type who rescues Fred and Barney from sticky situations. Moko, on the other hand, is a young imp sowing his oats, who specifically travels down to Earth to make monkeys out of stuffy, pompous military types.

What makes "Moko" such an atypical *Mister Ed* episode is that the talking horse takes a real backseat. And to boot, he's just as confused as the human characters, extremely unusual for his show. But now we know why. The installment was specifically designed to showcase the new characters, Moko and Tatti. Richard Deacon supplies the voice for Tatti, the elder. Everybody, including Ed, is clueless as to why the stuffed shirts are suddenly so seductive toward Wilbur's femme fatale client, Gloria Laverne (Joan Tabor). What they don't realize is that Moko had stripped the party poopers of their inhibitions, simply by flying into their ears. He makes General Lucius Bromley (Robert Barrat) look especially foolish as the pompous ass who becomes an on-again, off-again playboy. This device of turning uptight characters into swingers was utilized a lot in *Bewitched* (ABC, 1964–72), whenever Endora or Uncle Arthur would use their warped sense of witchery to manipulate events.

The one part of the "Moko" story line that is true to *Mister Ed* is Ed's not becoming Moko's pawn at any time. As it turned out, the pilot never took off the ground. And it's too bad. Al Simon recalls that they even had plans to work Jack Benny into the script: "Jack wouldn't want to spend a quarter, then Moko would take over his mind, and he would spend a hundred dollars without a care." Given Filmways' clout and success by 1964, it is a bit unclear why the pilot wasn't picked up by one of the networks. "I'm surprised that it never took off," Stott remarked. "Filmways was so powerful at the time."

Cast and Crew's Favorite *Mister Ed* Episodes

Even though the last episode of *Mister Ed* was produced twenty-five years ago, most people associated with the show still have a particular installment they consider a favorite.

- ○ **Alan Young (Wilbur Post):** Episode 1, "The First Meeting," specifically the moment when Mister Ed first speaks to Wilbur.
- ○ **Connie Hines (Carol Post):** Also #1. But she's proudest of episode 2, "Ventriloquist," where she received a standing ovation from the crew for filming in one take a complicated physical scene carrying a tray full of drinks.
- ○ **Edna Skinner (Kay Addison):** #4, "Stable for Three," her third episode as Kay Addison. She fondly remembers George Burns' directions, and wearing the mink stole, one of her signature props.
- ○ **Arthur Lubin (Director/Producer):** Doesn't really have a favorite episode, but a very good one is #81, "Leo Durocher Meets Mister Ed."
- ○ **Al Simon (Executive Producer):** #39, "Ed the Beneficiary" because of the way it was constructed. This episode opens on Ed in the barn. After all, "people were tuning in to see Ed," Simon points out. The horse complains to Wilbur that he isn't in the architect's will. Ed's gripe is the catalyst for a good story—Wilbur must go to see a probate lawyer. "You can cut and give that particular scene in the lawyer's office to four or five different writers, and they'll each come up with something very funny."
- ○ **Herb Browar (Associate Producer):** #99, "Ed the Chauffeur," and #114, "Ed the Pilot," for their sheer zaniness.
- ○ **Arch Dalzell (Director of Photography):** #115, "Ed the Stowaway," and #99, "Ed the Chauffeur," both memorable for their rear-projection process.
- ○ **Larry Rhine (Writer):** #136, "Anybody Got a Zebra?" Larry's favorite scene is the one at the zoo where Ed acts as translator between a monkey, a zebra and Wilbur. Here's how it works: Wilbur asks the question. Ed translates it into horse (the zebra can understand since he's half horse). The zebra translates it into Swahili for the spy monkey. The monkey replies in Swahili. The zebra translates back into horse, which Ed, in turn, tells Wilbur in English. Brilliant!
- ○ **Ben Starr (Writer):** #15, "Ed the Songwriter," the episode in which Ed composes the hit tune "Pretty Little Filly" and saves Paul Fenton's career!

THE FAR SIDE   By GARY LARSON

Jimmy meets Mr. Ed.

Alan Young and Mister Ed pose for a CBS time change promo in 1963, when the show moved from Thursdays to Sundays.

"Me I'm So Unlucky, Me With Four Horseshoes"

PUTTING **MISTER ED** OUT TO PASTURE

ED: I pity people. They gotta work for 65 years before they can retire and live like a horse.

—"Like Father, Like Horse"

Mister Ed may have talked as though he enjoyed the life of leisure, but I'll venture that even he was disappointed when CBS canceled his show in 1966, midseason. The last episode produced, "Mister Ed Goes to College," aired on February 6, 1966, and reruns continued until CBS dropped the show from its September 1966 schedule. The personable palomino was replaced by *To Tell the Truth*, another show involving fast talkers.

In its final season, *Mister Ed* had been airing in a somewhat disadvantageous time slot—Sundays at 5 P.M., a tad on the early side for any significant adult audience. Reflecting back on the events surrounding the show's cancellation, associate producer Herb Browar thinks that the decision to cut *Mister Ed* may have been a series of faux pas on the part of network management. "That show could've gone on and on because there was a constantly changing audience—kids," Browar points out. "It was really an adults' show, but if you were in a house with kids and there was a show on about a talking horse, what show do you think would be on in the house? And the network kept changing the time that the show was on, and if there was a football championship, they would preempt us [1964], and we eventually lost our audience, and they canceled us." Since the show was canceled midseason, CBS ended up having to pay out the employees' contracts, a considerable sum.

As a testament to *Mister Ed*'s popularity despite the CBS decision, the show went into immediate syndication, represented by MCA, starting in the fall of 1966. "We had a hell of a run—six years," concludes Filmways chairman, Marty Ransohoff. "The show proved to be very entertaining for a large segment of the population."

But the ratings were not quite good enough to entertain CBS execs. Interestingly, *My Favorite Martian*, another CBS fantasy sitcom, was canceled at the same time as *Mister Ed*, and the next year a third surreal series, *Gilligan's Island*, was axed by the network. Ed's cancellation was perhaps the beginning of the end of the golden age of fantasy and pastoral sitcoms, because in 1970 CBS canceled *Petticoat Junction*, and in 1971 the network put the kibosh on its remaining rural comedies, among them *Mayberry R.F.D.*, *Green Acres* and *The Beverly Hillbillies*, still one of the highest-rated shows of all time.

Talking Horse Underdog in the Ratings!

As unusual and good a show as *Mister Ed* was, it never won an Emmy Award, nor did the show ever rank in the Top 25 Nielsen-rated programs. Even so, the show scored well when measured against other criteria. We know, for example, that the producers were flooded with fan mail, especially from children, and that the American public in general held a real affection for the equine star. The lack of critical accolades for *Mister Ed* may have been partly attributable to snobbery within the TV community itself. "In the days we did this, there was a kind of quiet war going on between the people who were in New York doing television and the people on the West Coast," Al Simon recalls. "And most of the people in New York disliked any of the shows that were coming from the coast, and you had to be lucky to get nominated for an Emmy, and to win, it was one of those things. However, the show was solidly good." (See Hoofnotes, this chapter, for a listing of Ed's awards.)

Hindsight being what it is, there are those who maintain that *Mister Ed* would have done better in the ratings if CBS had placed it *after* the *Lassie* slot on Sunday nights (7:30 EST) instead of as lead-in. By continuing to treat it as "children's" television, CBS missed out, director Lubin believes, on a lot of potential adult viewers. While Ed was talking, America's dinner plates were being washed and dried, leaving Ed with a bad case of dishpan hooves. "We give *Lassie* rating points," Lubin told *Variety* in 1963. "I wish *Lassie* came first and gave us rating points."

Mister Ed's Retirement

How did our favorite animal TV star spend the autumn of his life? Nicolaides, the woman who knew the *real* horse star throughout his entire life, described the horse's last days in her Mister Ed biography (1979):

> Mister Ed retired . . . he was now seventeen years old and deserving of a good rest. He continued living under the loving care of Les Hilton and the studio paid all the horse's expenses such as feed, shoes, vet bills, etc. At the age of 19 [1968], Ed began having kidney problems, along with arthritis, and [had] trouble getting up and down in his stall. The vet, Dr. Harold Dakin, stated he would only worsen with time. Les made the decision to call Carl Ward [Ed's former owner] as a courtesy, and then Al Simon to suggest Ed be put down . . . all agreed. The news was not released to the press [because] the series was still being seen all over the country and many a youngster would have been deeply saddened if they knew the lovable horse they were watching was actually dead.

Interestingly, director Arthur Lubin heard a different story about Ed's final days. Lubin, who also kept in close contact with Les Hilton after the series, claims that Mister Ed broke his leg in 1968, and therefore had to be put to sleep. *World Book Encyclopedia* estimates that one year of a horse's life equals about three years of a man's life, so Mister Ed was fifty-seven in human years when he passed on.

Phony Pony: The Mister Ed Imposter

It's commonly believed that Mister Ed died on February 28, 1979, in Oklahoma. And why not? The news report of the horse's death was in all the papers. Alan Young even got flowers and condolences. The truth is, though, that this palomino was an *imposter*.

Young recalls that during production on *Mister Ed*, a different palomino had been used by Filmways for *one* publicity shot, and Young speculates that perhaps he is the horse that died in Oklahoma in 1979. Only days after the Oklahoma press report, Nicolaides set the record straight. Still, because of the unpublicized nature of the real Ed's death, the majority of *Mister Ed* fans believe that the horse buried in Tulsa, Oklahoma, who had been owned by Clarence Tharp, is *the* Mister Ed.

In July 1990 an Oklahoma radio station sponsored a fund-raising drive over the air to collect money for a Mister Ed monument, not realizing that the 1979 report of Mister Ed's death was a hoax. Despite objections from those in the know, the station persisted, and the statue was erected. It features a relief of Ed looking out from his stall door. More than two hundred people showed up in August 1990 to christen the monument to the imposter Ed.

HOW TO GET OFF A HORSE: AFTER MISTER ED

Ed's trainer, Lester Hilton, was devastated by the death of Mister Ed, his most accomplished pupil. "I used to go visit Lester after the horse died," Alan Young relates. "I'd find a bunch of old wranglers sitting around. And they'd just sit there saying, 'Boy, there was never a horse like that.' And to hear cowboys talk like that, it's quite amazing. . . . I feel Lester died of a broken heart. He said, 'I've done it with the Ed show, I can't do anything better.' Then, when Ed died, he said, 'Alan, I can't watch the reruns.' He was a real hard-boiled old Westerner, too. He was just so soft when it came to Mister Ed." Les Hilton died of pancreatic cancer on October 27, 1976, eight years after Mister Ed passed away.

Script consultant William Burns, brother of George Burns, died in 1966 (the year *Mister Ed* was canceled), at the age of sixty-three.

Allan "Rocky" Lane, the brilliant voice and, in some ways, spirit of Mister Ed, died on October 27, 1973, from a bone marrow disorder. He was living at the Actors' Home in Woodland Hills, California.

The Writers

Several of the *Mister Ed* writers, including head writer Lou Derman, went on to write for Norman Lear during his most creative period, most notably on his breakthrough sitcom *All in the Family* (CBS,1971–83). Lou Derman came on as associate producer for *All in the Family* in the first year, and wrote some of the scripts with fellow *Mister Ed* alumnus Ben Starr. Lou also invited Larry Rhine to write for the show. Rhine considers it a privilege to have worked with the talents of Norman Lear and Carroll O'Connor, whom he considers "a genius." Former horse writer Bill Davenport also gave life to Archie and Edith Bunker. Larry Rhine and Ben Starr both wrote episodes for *The Brady Bunch* (ABC, 1969–74), another favorite show of the TV generation, after *Ed*. Ben Starr also scripted for *Mork and Mindy* (ABC, 1978–82) and wrote pilots for *Facts of Life* and *Silver Spoons*.

Lou Derman died of a heart attack on February 15, 1976, at the age of sixty-one. He had just completed an enormous workweek on *All in the Family*. Colleague Larry Rhine remembers telling Lou to take a vacation, he had been working so hard. Today, Larry and his wife, Hazel Shermet, a character actress who appeared in several *Mister Ed* shows, are travel journalists, contributing pieces to newspapers across the country. Nowadays, Ben Starr writes original plays that are translated into Spanish for production abroad. He respects the writing of TV shows like *M.A.S.H.*, *Cheers*, *LA Law* and *thirtysomething*.

After *Mister Ed*, script consultant Norman Paul went on to write for *Get Smart* (NBC, CBS, 1965–70) and worked as story consultant and executive producer on Norman Lear's comedy, *Good Times* (CBS, 1974–79). He died in 1979, at the age of sixty-six.

Alan Young

In 1967 Alan Young made his Broadway debut in the short-lived comedy *The Girl in the Freudian Slip*. The play closed after just two performances. Young played Dr. Dewey Maugham, a psychiatrist, a switch on his frequent role as psychiatry *patient* on *Mister Ed*. That same year, the Youngs moved to Boston, where the actor established a broadcasting division for the Christian Science Church. He was a church practitioner and lecturer for three years, but eventually returned to show business.

Young began doing cartoon voice-overs for *The Smurfs* (Farmer Smurf and Scaredy Smurf), *Mr. T*, *Spiderman* and *The Chipmunks*. In 1979 he and his partner, Alan Dinehart, adapted Charles Dickens' *A Christmas Carol*

Playbill from Alan Young's
Broadway performance, 1967.

into a comedy record by "the Walt Disney Players," actually Young and Dinehart themselves with their assorted voices. The album featured all the Disney characters, including Scrooge McDuck as Ebenezer Scrooge. In 1983 Disney produced the feature film *Mickey's Christmas Carol*, and Young is credited with both story adaptation and "voice talents." The success of this film led to *Duck Tales*, one of the hottest kids' shows in syndication today. The animated adventures of Huey, Dewey, Louie, Webby and their miserly uncle, Scrooge McDuck, have been a smash in syndication and merchandising for several years (not rivaled until the *Teenage Mutant Ninja Turtles* of 1990).

ALAN YOUNG'S MOVIES SINCE *MISTER ED*

- *Baker's Hawk* (1976)
- *The Cat From Outer Space* (1977)
- *Mickey's Christmas Carol* (1983)
- *Duck Tales: The Movie—Treasures of the Lost Lamp* (1990)

ALAN YOUNG'S TV CREDITS SINCE *MISTER ED*

- *Sitcom* (HBO pilot, 1983)
- *General Hospital* (ABC, 1985)
- *Coming of Age* (CBS, 1988–89)
- *Earth Angel* (Made-for-TV movie, ABC, March 4, 1991)

Today, Alan Young is the most visible of all the *Mister Ed* cast members. He's a speaker at Mister Ed Fan Club conventions, a guest star at Nick at

Nite's TV Land Mall Tours, and does the occasional talk show circuit. He appeared in the CBS sitcom *Coming of Age* (1988–89), and continues to give life to Scrooge McDuck for various Disney projects. Young participates in regional theater as well as a family musical act, Young & Younger, with his wife, Virginia McCurdy, and daughter Wendy. In 1989, Young received the Pioneer award for his contribution to early television. The actor, of course, of course, looks forward to a *Mister Ed* reunion movie.

Other Ed-Alumni

Connie Hines (Carol Post) does some commercial work today, is an avid tennis player and, like Young, hopes a *Mister Ed* reunion movie is made.

Arthur Lubin (director/producer) and Al Simon (executive producer) are both retired. At present, their wish is to make a reunion movie that will rekindle the public's fond memories of Mister Ed who first talked his way into our hearts some thirty years ago.

Courtesy of Connie Hines. Actress Connie Hines today.

Courtesy of Alan Young.
Ed poses proudly with many of the awards he won during *Mister Ed*.

HOOFNOTES

I. *MISTER ED* SCHEDULE SHUFFLE

Season	Program Schedule
Oct. 1961–Sept. 1962	Sundays 6:30–7 P.M.
Sept. 1962–Mar. 1963	Thursdays 7:30–8 P.M.
Mar. 1963–Oct. 1964	Sundays 6:30–7 P.M.
Dec. 1964–Sept. 1965	Wednesdays 7:30–8 P.M.
Sept. 1965–Sept. 1966	Sundays 5–5:30 P.M.

II. EMMY AWARDS FOR BEST COMEDY SERIES DURING *MISTER ED*

1961: *The Bob Newhart Show*
1962: *The Dick Van Dyke Show*
1963: *The Dick Van Dyke Show*
1964: *The Dick Van Dyke Show*
1965: *(You guessed it) The Dick Van Dyke Show*
1966: *The Monkees*

III. AWARDS *MISTER ED* GARNERED DURING ITS ROMP

○ Golden Globe Award (Hollywood Foreign Press Association)—Best Television Show, 1962

○ Television Patsy Awards (Best Animal Actor): 1962, 1963, 1964, 1965 (a clean sweep!)

"Don't Try to Understand, It's Bigger Than Both of Us"

••

MISTER ED'S LIFE IN THE PRESENT DAY

TV theme song historian John Javna maintains that if you are in an elevator anywhere in America with any 10 people and you say, "a horse is a horse," at least one person will reply, "of course, of course."

—*New York Daily News*, 1987

A fitting tribute to the *Mister Ed* theme song perhaps, but what about to the horse himself? Have the past thirty years been good to him? By all accounts, Mister Ed is alive and kicking. In America alone, over 16 million people watch him every week on Nick at Nite, the campy, innovative cable network that can be credited with giving *Mister Ed* new life in the 1980s and 1990s.

The peripatetic palomino can be seen in fifty-two countries, and is dubbed in eight languages. Dawn Synder, who handles international sales of *Mister Ed* for Orion TV, notes that *Mister Ed* has been sold in every country worldwide, and is continually being sold. It does particularly well in the United Kingdom. "They really seem to love it over there." Actor Alan Young today finds himself "a star all over again in England," due to his *Mister Ed* association. The show is also enjoying success in Germany ... "Herr Ed"— hmm ...

"Oddly enough, overseas, the horse is even more popular than here because horses are part of the family life in a lot of these third world countries," explains scripter Larry Rhine. "My wife and I were down in Mexico, and we were talking with the head of a hotel, and he said, 'I have to watch *Señor Ed.*' So we went up to his quarters there, and sure enough, Ed says, *'Hola, Wilbur, como esta usted?'* Wilbur says, *'Estoy bien. Y usted?'* *'Ah, nada de particular.'* They went on in *español.*" It would've done the soul of Mister Ed good to know that he was on TV all over the world. He took great pleasure in contacting Europe with his shortwave radio, and he loved the foreign fillies.

Equus Ubiquitous

The silly yet always noble character of *Mister Ed* has stood the test of time. He's part of our "common body of knowledge" and shows up just about everywhere. Okay, he's not as ubiquitous as Elvis, but he's no stall flower, either. He still gets incorporated into *The Tonight Show* monologue (both

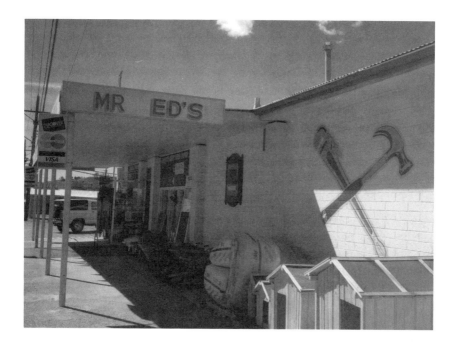

Courtesy of Tom Pomposello.
Mr. Ed's Hardware in New Mexico. Coincidence . . . or something more?

Johnny's *and* Jay Leno's); he's a frequent clue on TV's *Jeopardy* as well as in crossword puzzles; and he gets written into the scripts of contemporary sitcoms like *Married . . . With Children* (See Hoofnotes, Chapter 7). Other evidence of Ed-Mania: A 1986 Doritos commercial actually incorporated *Mister Ed* film footage into the live action, a la *Dead Men Don't Wear Plaid*. But executive producer Al Simon eventually put a halt to this campaign since Frito-Lay restaged their own version of *Mister Ed* (including a different palomino) for a subsequent print shoot, which was never part of the agreement. Another Mister Ed-wanna-be performs as part of the Animal Actors Theater at Universal Studios Florida.

Mister Ed has caught the eye of politicians too. New York Mayor Ed Koch, in the last days of his final term in December 1989, said he might have been treated more respectfully if during his mayorship he had only insisted on being referred to as "*Mister* Ed." Why does our favorite palomino get referred to so much in the media? Because he's come to personify (or "horsify," for you purists) the gestalt of *smart, talking animal*. "He's part of Americana," Larry Rhine believes, "so the show can be referred to in any way. It's recognizable."

Innocence Is Bliss

Given the good clean fun of *Mister Ed*, it's not surprising that the show's creators and stars are critical of current television fare. "I'm very much against all the violence and swearing, and what's going on at the moment," Arthur Lubin admits. "I think there will eventually be a return to normalcy. And people will enjoy a good solid comedy." Connie Hines concurs: "The pendulum swings. People are tired of violence, blatant sex, crudeness. People want that nostalgia. That's why the reunion shows are coming back." And the writers agree—much of today's programming sorely lacks a good story (something *Mister Ed* never deprived us of).

The Devil Made Him Do It?!

Just to keep things interesting, in April 1986 two Fundamentalist ministers from Ohio, Jim Brown and Greg Hudson, claimed that the *Mister Ed* theme song contained satanic messages. Specifically, when the line: "That is of course unless the horse" was played backward, it supposedly came out as: "Someone sang this song for Satan." Theme song composer Jay Livingston countered in December 1989: "Actually, this line backwards is 'Sro Uth Sel

Nish Sroke Vuh Zi-Tah.' Which proves that Fundamentalists have something missing in the brain department."

It's interesting how all this fuss about Ed took place *after* Nick at Nite revitalized the show. It seems that the only thing these two ministers brought to light was their *Mister Ed* viewing habits. Now, it's true that Ed's "devil alter ego" does horse around in a couple of episodes, but futz with the theme song . . . why bother?

The Nick at Nite Connection

Nick at Nite is the perfect TV home for *Mister Ed*, no matter if you're a casual fan or an honest-to-goodness, hard-core "Ed-Head." Since 1985, *Mister Ed* has been the cable network's highest-rated program.

"*Mister Ed* is the quintessential Nick at Nite show," says Rich Cronin, senior vice-president of marketing at the cable network, "because here in TV Land it makes sense for your neighbors to have a talking horse. And Ed is clearly America's favorite horse. The TV generation grew up with him and today's generation discovered him on Nick."

The network does some unique on-air promotion for *Mister Ed*. One promo spot compares Mister Ed to the great actors of the twentieth century—Olivier, Brando—and includes bytes of *Mister Ed* footage where the horse is at his most theatrical, like his resounding recitation of Shakespeare in the barn: "What fools these mortals be."

Another on-air spot, "The Secrets of Mister Ed," divulges truths behind long-held rumors associated with the show, like the use of electric shock treatments on the set. It's commonly believed that Ed was subjected to them on a daily basis so that he would talk. Not so, Nick at Nite informs us. Shocks *were* used, but not for the horse . . . for Wilbur Post! Not exactly the sort of stuff you'd see NBC doing to promote *The Cosby Show.*

Nick at Nite takes their *Mister Ed* show on the road too. A life-size version of the talking horse, named Live Ed, pays visits to shopping malls throughout the country as part of Nick at Nite's TV Land Tour. "When we do local events we find that people from six to sixty know all the words to the *Mister Ed* theme song," Cronin observes, "and most of them can do a reasonable Ed impression." *Mister Ed* memorabilia like board games, comic books, hand puppets and even Halloween costumes are displayed as part of the TV Land Tour exhibit. (See Appendix A for photos of *Ed* memorabilia items.) Alan Young has been known to stop by the tour from time to time—to converse with his equine friend of yore, naturally. Check Nick at Nite for tour locations and dates.

"Live-Ed" attraction at Nick at Nite's TV Land Tour.

As responsible as Nick at Nite is for giving *Mister Ed* newfound respect and relevance, senior vice-president of programming Herb Scannell must admit that *Mister Ed* is thoroughly a product of its time: "I don't think *Mister Ed* could happen again in today's TV landscape. Kids and adults don't expect absurdity from their TV anymore. They've been spoiled by sitcoms that mirror reality and fail miserably. *Ed* happened when TV shows were driven by the question 'what if ...' Now TV shows are driven by the statement 'It's kinda like ...' "

Ed-vertising Works!

Nick at Nite has restored much of *Mister Ed*'s fame and glory through its recent advertising, created by agency Fred/Alan. Since 1988, posters on New York commuter trains have informed riders about "Mister Ed's After-Shave"

Recent examples of Nick at Nite's print advertising for *Mister Ed*.

(yes, there's an obligatory scratch 'n' sniff patch, sans fragrance) and "Mister Ed's Salad Bar" (specializing in oat bran).

Agency cofounder Alan Goodman explains why *Mister Ed* ads are making such a splash with contemporary audiences: "I think the reason Mister Ed lives on today is that unlike all those Disney- and Lassie-type creatures we were force-fed—helpful, heroic, lovable and loyal friends to man—Mister Ed represented what we truly admire in our pets: He was selfish, devious, lazy and only out for Number One. And if you really believe in Nick at Nite, the TV Land where our favorite shows and characters play on, you'll know why Mister Ed After-Shave and Mister Ed's Salad Bar exist. He's just making an honest buck."

Rich Cronin boasts that "Nick at Nite's ads for items like Mister Ed After-Shave and hoof-shaped slippers have won awards and new fans" for the show. And there's lots more fun to come . . .

Hollywood Horse

Now that *Mister Ed*'s renewed popularity is clear, the long-awaited reunion movie may not be far off. Rumors have it that a *Mister Ed* project has been shopped around to various networks and studios, but as of press time, no concrete plans have surfaced.

Sadly, Mister Ed himself passed away in 1968, so a new palomino must be called on to chat it up with Alan Young, who has agreed to reprise his role of Wilbur Post. A tough act to follow, indeed. Series executive producer Al Simon has actually begun the task of casting a new horse for the star role. Whatever horse he chooses, you can be sure that the new one will be just as blond, and just as talkative.

Reunion movie or not, all of Hollywood has been taking cues from the current *Mister Ed* resurgence. Recent examples include Eddie Murphy's CBS pilot "What's Alan Watching?" (1989), which contained a "mockumentary" on the life of Mister Ed. In 1988 the movie *Hot to Trot* starred "Don, the Talking Horse," a rowdy mutation of the ever-decent Mister Ed. Alan Young refused to appear in the flick, based on the rough script. With dialogue such as the lines that follow, is it any wonder?

FRED (BOB GOLDTHWAIT):	What about, like, Mister Ed?
DON (voice by JOHN CANDY):	Mister Ed? (*He spits*) That's what I think of Mister Ed! Every single word of that was dubbed.
FRED:	His lips were like movin'.

DON: Look, you'd move your lips too if some stage-
hand was shovin' a carrot up your butt! Hah,
Mister Ed!

Ed-Heads of the World, Unite!
The Mister Ed Fan Club

The Mister Ed Fan Club, founded in 1975 by Jim "Big Bucks" Burnett,
currently numbers five hundred members and operates out of Denton, Texas.
Celebrity Ed-Heads include British comic troupe Monty Python (a charter

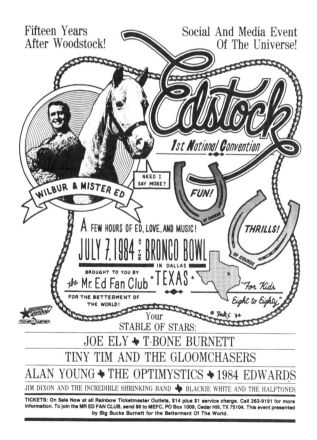

**Flier from the Mister Ed Fan Club's "Edstock"
Convention, 1984.**

**Lassie and Rin Tin Tin have stars on the Hollywood Walk of Fame . . .
why shouldn't Ed have one too?**

member) and musicians Eric Clapton, Ringo Starr and Jimmy Page. If you're wondering . . . yes, Burnett is a musician and runs his own record store in Dallas. His fan club newsletter, "The Horse's Mouth," features interviews with music legends and generally extols the virtues of Ed. It makes sense, somehow, that such an eclectic group of individuals would admire an equally diverse Ed (the horse loved the Beatles, Leonard Bernstein and Mitch Miller).

Since its inception, the fan club has held three Mister Ed Conventions in Dallas nightclubs: "Edstock" (1984), "Live-Ed" (1986) and "Ed-a-Go-Go" (1988), with special guest appearances by Alan Young and Tiny Tim. In addition to music and mirth, Mister Ed Conventions usually include marathon viewing of what else? . . . *Mister Ed* episodes. Burnett would like to hold the next Mister Ed convention at the Los Angeles Palomino Club.

How to Join the Mister Ed Fan Club

To get more fan club information, send a self-addressed stamped envelope to:

M.E.F.C.
c/o Big Bucks Burnett, President
P.O. Box 1009
Cedar Hill, TX 75104

Membership includes a subscription to "Talking Horse," the new quarterly newsletter. Current causes: (1) Project EdStar—getting Ed the Hollywood Walk of Fame Star he so justly deserves; (2) Breaking ground on a Mister Ed Museum in Dallas.

Appendix A

....

MISTER ED COLLECTIBLES

When *Mister Ed* was produced in the early 1960s, the merchandising business was not as sophisticated as it is today. However, the show *was* popular, especially among kids, and several *Mister Ed* items were manufactured, mostly with children in mind. Additionally, magazines such as *TV Guide* gave the show extensive coverage. Between toys and press pieces, quite a few "original" *Mister Ed* collectibles are in existence. They are listed below, some with photos, along with their current price on the "collector's circuit."

ORIGINAL COLLECTIBLES

These beauties were "straight from the horse's mouth"—produced at the time of *Mister Ed*'s original run on CBS. Some are pretty rare, some not so rare. You may recognize them from your own horsing-around days:

Toys, Games and Novelties

1. *Mister Ed Halloween Costume,* circa 1962. Original retail price $2.77. This unusual, hard-to-find, very juvenile trick-or-treat garb is on display as part of Nick at Nite's TV Land Tour. (Price: $125 in its original box).

2. *Mister Ed Board Game,* Parker Brothers, 1962. You can usually find one of these in a stack of TV boardgames at an antique toy convention, varying in condition and price. A not-so-perfect set runs you about $50.

3. *TV's Mister Ed Talking Plush Hand Puppet,* Mattel, 1962. Every antique toy dealer either has one for sale, knows someone who does or has recently sold one. Pat Sajak "wore" one on his late-night TV show, October 20, 1989, the same night in which Alan Young appeared. When you pull its string, the puppet whinnies witticisms like "My girlfriend has a ponytail." It has a luxurious blond wool mane, well worth the $112 it fetches if in good condition, without the original box. (Toys still in their wrapped boxes are in a whole different price league.)

4. *Mister Ed hand puppet,* Knickerbocker Toys, 1962. This simpler Ed representation has a cloth "body" and runs about $75.

5. *Mister Ed record album*: Original TV Soundtracks, Colpix, "*Mister Ed* Sunday CBS 6:30 EST." Includes Mister Ed's two smash singles, "Pretty Little Filly" and "Empty Feedbag Blues." Produced by Howard Berk.

Mister Ed Board Game by Parker Brothers, 1962.

Mister Ed Talking Hand Puppet by Mattel, 1962.

Comic Books, Coloring Books, Paperbacks and *TV Guides*

1. *Mister Ed comic books*: The playful appeal of *Mister Ed* made comic book spin-offs a natural. Most featured color photos of Alan Young and Mister Ed on the cover.

  (a) *Mister Ed the Talking Horse*, 1962 (Dell 4 Color #1295). If you can find a really good copy of the first comic featuring Mister Ed, it could run you $45.

  (b) *Mister Ed the Talking Horse #1*, Nov. 1962 (Gold Key). The first issue of Mister Ed's own comic series might cost about $28 if in great condition.

  (c) *Mister Ed the Talking Horse #2–6* (Gold Key). These subsequent issues are easier to locate, and could range in price from $2 to $15, depending on their condition.

  (d) *Boys' and Girls' March of Comics featuring Mister Ed* (#244, 260, 282, 290). Spiffy copies of this giveaway series don't run much higher than $20 a piece.

2. *Francis the Famous Talking Mule* (Dell 4 Color #335, 465, 501, 547, 579, 621, 655, 698, 710, 810, 863, 906, 991, 1068, 1090). Dell Comics published fifteen issues with Francis the Talking Mule, Ed's celluloid pred-

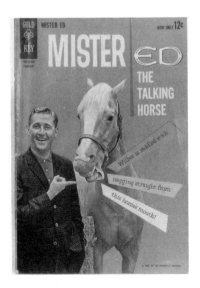

Mister Ed Gold Key Comic Book # 2, 1962.

Dell's Francis the Talking Mule Comic Book #335, 1951.

ecessor. Pictured on page 245 is the very first one, from 1951. A tip-top copy could fetch around $14. The remaining fourteen should cost about $8 each, for copies in great shape.

3. *Mister Ed Coloring Book*, Whitman, 1963. Costs roughly $35.

4. *Mister Ed Little Golden Book*, Golden Press, 1962. This is a 24-page storybook with full-color illustrations and costs about $18.

5. *TV Guide issues with Mister Ed stories.* Cost per copy: $12.50–$25, depending on the condition.
   a. Picture feature, *May 6, 1961*: "Alan Young's Horse Gets the Laughs"
   b. Cover story, *March 31, 1962*: "Mister Ed Takes the Lead"
   c. Picture feature, *June 23, 1962*: "Mister Ed Tries the Twist"
   d. Picture feature, *October 6, 1962*: "Connie Hines and Mister Ed"

Feature story on Connie Hines in the October 6, 1962, issue of *TV Guide*.

e. Picture feature, *February 29, 1964*: "Mae West Meets Mister Ed"
f. Picture feature, *December 18, 1965*: "Who Is the Voice of Mister Ed?"
g. Picture feature, *January 8, 1966*: "The Year of the Stunt"
h. Picture feature, *July 31, 1971*: "Alan Young 10 Years After Mister Ed"

6. *Paperback book: Walter Brooks' The Original Mister Ed*, Bantam Books, copyright 1963. If you're lucky, you can still pick up this book of original Mister Ed stories from the 1930's and 1940's for a mere 25¢ at a garage sale!

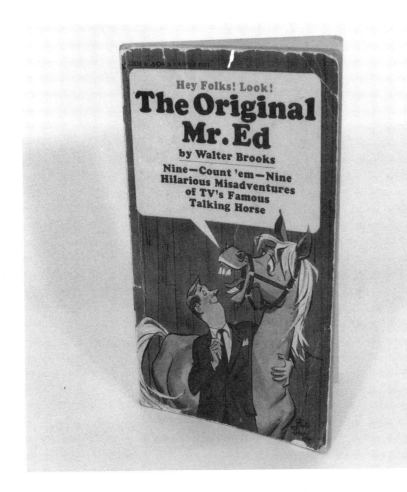

**The original Mister Ed stories
published by Bantam Books in 1964.**

CONTEMPORARY COLLECTIBLES

Modern Memorabilia From Nick at Nite

It wasn't until Nick at Nite revived *Mister Ed* in 1985 that modern memorabilia for the show came on the scene. In the past few years, the cable network has created several zany *Mister Ed* promotional items.

○ *Mister Ed Glue Holder, circa 1988.* Despite the sticky implications of this promotional item, it does not come filled with glue.

○ *Mister Ed T-shirt, circa 1987.* "I Want Cable in my Stable."

○ *Mister Ed T-shirt, circa 1990.* "I Want Cable in my Stable" revisited.

○ *Mister Ed Coaster, circa 1990.* Great for serving potent potables of the palomino order, like carrot juice on the rocks.

○ *Mister Ed Postcard, circa 1990.*

Fan Club Collectibles

In addition to Nick at Nite's zeal, the Mister Ed Fan Club, headed by Big Bucks Burnett in Texas, has been producing amusing *Mister Ed* paraphernalia for years. These souvenirs-in-the-making are available through the Mister Ed Fan Club. Contact Big Bucks Burnett for more information (see Chapter 14 for address):

○ *45 RPM "Tiny Tim Sings Mister Ed"*
  The inimitable "Laugh-In" vocalist tip-toes through the paddock in this priceless recording of the theme song we all know and love.

"Tiny Tim Sings Mister Ed," available through the Mister Ed Fan Club.

○ *"Talk if you like Mister Ed" Bumper Sticker*
  One of several. Fence not included.

Mister Ed bumper sticker, available through the Mister Ed Fan Club.

○ *Official Fan Club Newsletter: "The Horse's Mouth, 1984"*
Features sometimes bizarre letters from members and celebrity interviews. To be replaced by "Talking Horse," the new quarterly newsletter.

"The Horse's Mouth," official newsletter
of the Mister Ed Fan Club, 1984.

Ed models his "siesta sombrero" for Wilbur in "Ed and the Secret Service," 1962.

Appendix B

....

MISTER ED EPISODE SYNOPSES

Mister Ed Pilot

"The Wonderful World of Wilbur Pope"
PRODUCED: 1958 (never aired)
EXECUTIVE PRODUCER: George Burns/McCadden Productions
PRODUCERS: Arthur Lubin, George Burns
WRITERS: William Burns, Bob O'Brien, Irving Elinson, Phil Shuken
DIRECTOR: Arthur Lubin
CAST: Scott McKay as Wilbur Pope, Sandra White as Carlotta Pope

Wilbur Pope, a young lawyer, and his wife, Carlotta, move into their very first home. Wilbur discovers that the horse in his barn, Mister Ed, can talk—no small find. He tries to convince his wife and neighbors, but Mister Ed will talk only to him. The skeptical neighbors alienate the Popes, until Ed comes up with a scheme to save Wilbur's reputation. Wilbur goes to his neighbor's house secretly carrying bird seed and cat food in his pockets, and all the furry and feathered pets leap on his shoulders and arms. Thus Wilbur emerges as a guy who's got a "special" relationship with animals, and the neighbors excuse his momentary lapse of sanity, i.e., thinking his horse talks.

First Season—Syndication
January–September 1961: Thursdays 7:30 P.M., (WNBC, New York)

Note: Original Airdates are as recorded for the New York City area.

#1: "The First Meeting"
ORIGINAL AIRDATE: January 5, 1961
WRITERS: William Burns, Bob O'Brien, Irving Elinson, Phil Shuken
DIRECTOR: Rod Amateau

Wilbur Post, a young architect, and his wife, Carol, move into a lovely Hollywood home. Their display of physical affection whenever neighbor Roger Addison enters the room forms the running gag of the show. Wilbur discovers an abandoned horse in his barn. Once he learns that the horse, Mister Ed, can talk—"How Now Brown Cow"—the series is off and running.

#2: "The Ventriloquist"
ORIGINAL AIRDATE: January 12, 1961
WRITERS: Lou Derman, Phil Davis
DIRECTOR: Rod Amateau
GUEST STAR: Peter Leeds

First episode with Edna Skinner as Kay Addison. Carol wants a new TV set for the bedroom. Wilbur wishes he could put his amazing, magical horse on television. Roger Addison overhears Wilbur and Ed talking in the barn. Wilbur says it's ventriloquism. Roger is impressed. He insists that Wilbur help him win a ten-dollar bet with Hal Robbins. He tells Wilbur to make Beethoven's bust "talk." Ed stands by the window and provides Ludwig's voice. As a reward, Wilbur gets the Addison Clubhouse project and promises to buy Carol a new TV set with the money.

#3: "Busy Wife"
ORIGINAL AIRDATE: January 19, 1961
WRITERS: Lou Derman, Ben Starr
DIRECTOR: Justus Addiss
GUEST STARS: Donna Douglas, Barbara Morrison

Carol joins the Ladies Group to raise money for bus-stop benches. Wilbur feels neglected and decides to make her jealous. He hires a beautiful model

(Donna Douglas) to pose for a "Lady Godiva" painting. Ed in turn feels neglected by Wilbur and decides to take up painting too. Wilbur's scheme works: Carol gives up the Ladies Group. Highlights: Wilbur hiding out from Addison at the supermarket and Ed kicking to see the model undress.

#4: "Stable for Three"
ORIGINAL AIRDATE: February 2, 1961
WRITERS: Ben Starr, Lou Derman
DIRECTOR: Arthur Lubin

Ed eats Carol's vegetable garden ("Oops, caught with my plants down!"), and Wilbur restocks it with less than accurate facsimiles (tomatoes hanging by string, e.g.); Carol sends him out to the barn to sleep, where he and Ed are soon joined by Addison, who recently battled with Kay (and lost) over her new mink stole purchase.

#5: "Kiddy Park"
ORIGINAL AIRDATE: January 26, 1961
WRITERS: Lou Derman, Ben Starr
DIRECTOR: Arthur Lubin
GUEST STARS: Richard Reeves, Bobby Buntrock, James Flavin, Dorothy Konrad, Karen Norris

Ed runs away to the Kiddy Park when Wilbur won't take him on his "men only" fishing trip to Encinada. Ed talks to Bobby Buntrock in this episode; of course, little Bobby's mother doesn't believe him! Highlight: Besides Ed talking to the tyke, the scene where the kiddy park attendant (Reeves) thinks he's on *Candid Camera* ... how else can Wilbur's nutty behavior be explained?

#6: "Sorority House"
ORIGINAL AIRDATE: February 9, 1961
WRITERS: Lou Derman, Ben Starr
DIRECTOR: Arthur Lubin
GUEST STARS: Jack Raine, Norma Varden,Carol Byron, Alex Plasschaert, Michael Monroe

This episode is dying to be called "Sorority *Horse*." Why it isn't is one of life's little mysteries. It features Ed's stint as a football mascot for State University. The boys at Sigma Nu Delta, Roger's old fraternity, hide Ed in the steam room. He's stolen by the opponents, Brighten U, and taken to Alpha Epsilon Mew, a sorority house on campus. Ed calls Wilbur for help from a phone in the basement, and Wilbur comes to the rescue, dressed in drag. The girls mistake him for Mrs. Pentecost, the guest ornithology lecturer, and we get a funny scene between Wilbur and the students, with undone zippers, etc. Ed phones the dean to report the harboring of a stolen horse. The dean calls the sorority house, and Wilbur "volunteers" to clear Ed out of there.

#7: "Little Boy"

ORIGINAL AIRDATE: May 11, 1961
WRITERS: Lou Derman, Ben Starr
DIRECTOR: Arthur Lubin
GUEST STAR: Chris Wayne

This is the first episode with theme song lyrics. The new kid on the block, Peter, is having a tough time making friends. The Posts suggest throwing a party in their backyard and invite all the neighborhood kids. Wilbur performs magic as "Wilburini." The other boys make fun of Peter, and he runs off to Mister Ed. Ed helps Peter win the kids' admiration by rearing up when they all touch him, and making it seem as though Peter is the only one who's brave enough to ride him. Peter's one-shot appearance in the series.

#8: "Ed the Lover"

ORIGINAL AIRDATE: February 16, 1961
WRITERS: Lou Derman, Ben Starr
DIRECTOR: Arthur Lubin
GUEST STAR: Les Tremayne

Ed gets a job as an extra in a western directed by Wilbur's client, Fred Briggs. While on the set, Daphne, the film's star filly, falls in love with Ed. When Wilbur takes Ed away, she becomes too lovesick to work. Ed agrees to return to the set on two conditions: that he be permitted a 9 A.M. call (as opposed to 7 A.M.) and that no overweight cowboys ride him.

#9: "Pageant Show"

ORIGINAL AIRDATE: Feburary 23, 1961
WRITERS: Lou Derman, Ben Starr
DIRECTOR: Arthur Lubin
GUEST STAR: William Fawcett

Ed is using the barn phone all day long, and Carol accuses Wilbur of leaving the phone off the hook. Wilbur punishes Ed by getting rid of the phone.

Meanwhile, the humans are getting ready for the parade. Kay will portray Carmen and Carol will play Guinevere—now they just have to get their husbands to play Don José and Lancelot. Angry Ed pretends to be too sick to carry the Posts in the parade. Wilbur rents a dark horse from Brunswick Stables and calls the vet to horse-sit while they're gone. Ed scares the substitute horse away, and Carol goes out to comfort Ed. When Ed realizes that Carol likes him, he's suddenly all better and ready to carry them at the parade!

#10: "The Aunt"

ORIGINAL AIRDATE: March 2, 1961
WRITERS: Lou Derman, Ben Starr
DIRECTOR: Arthur Lubin
GUEST STAR: Eleanor Audley

The first of two shows with Wilbur's Aunt Martha. In this episode, she visits the Posts with her parrot, Tootsie, who's as much of a TV fanatic as Ed. Martha's wearing out everybody with sight-seeing, and Wilbur even pretends to have a bad back to discourage her. Since she's allergic to the jasmine tree outside the guest room, she has to room with Carol. Wilbur gets rid of the tree so Martha can move back to her own quarters. Ed is annoyed by the loquacious parrot and hides Tootsie in the ash can. But when he learns that the old woman is truly heartbroken, the parrot suddenly reappears. Ed turns out to really miss Tootsie; at least *she* had time to talk to him.

#11: "The Missing Statue"

ORIGINAL AIRDATE: March 9, 1961
WRITERS: Lou Derman, Ben Starr
DIRECTOR: Arthur Lubin
GUEST STAR: Gage Clark

A comedy of errors involving a $50 statue from an antique shop in town. The statue gets bought by Carol, returned by Wilbur, bought again by Kay (for Carol), returned by Roger (who doesn't believe Kay) and bought again by Wilbur. The shopkeeper, who has a "no returns" policy, accuses them of playing a parlor game of musical statues. Ed has a very minor role, placing a bet on his niece by phone, in this episode. He wins $100, which will cover his long-distance phone expenses.

#12: "Ed the Witness"

ORIGINAL AIRDATE: March 16, 1961
WRITERS: Lou Derman, Ben Starr
DIRECTOR: Arthur Lubin
GUEST STARS: Natividad Vacio, Vincent Padula, Nacho Galindo

Location: Mexico. Ed witnesses Arturo banging up Wilbur's car while the Posts and Addisons are eating in a café (that only serves beans). Arturo fixes the dent for Wilbur but once Ed reveals whodunit, Wilbur refuses to pay the bill and gets put in jail. Ed saves the day by proving to the judge that he can read license plates, thus identifying Arturo as the culprit. Highlight: Ed stomping twice to judge's flash card that reads *"Dos."*

#13: "Ed's Mother"

ORIGINAL AIRDATE: March 23, 1961
WRITERS: Lou Derman, Ben Starr
DIRECTOR: Arthur Lubin
GUEST STAR: Henry Norell

A snapshot of Wilbur at the Dowd Farm reveals that Ed's mother, Betsy, works for Dowd as a plough horse (she's in the background). Ed buys his mother from Dowd, but Carol insists that Wilbur return her. Ed bids on his mother at Dowd's auction, and Wilbur buys her so he can give her to a nice family with a couple of kids. Best line: Farmer Dowd says to an eccentric Wilbur: "Excuse me, I have to churn some butter."

#14: "Ed the Tout"

ORIGINAL AIRDATE: March 30, 1961
WRITERS: Lou Derman, Ben Starr
DIRECTOR: Arthur Lubin

Ed picks winning racehorses for Wilbur, who's raising money for the Milk Fund charity. Everybody at the track wants a piece of the action, and track security calls Wilbur inside for an explanation of his "good luck." Similar story line to *Francis Goes to the Races*, a 1951 release starring the talking mule.

#15: "Ed the Songwriter"

ORIGINAL AIRDATE: April 6, 1961
WRITERS: Lou Derman, Ben Starr
DIRECTOR: Arthur Lubin
GUEST STARS: Jack Albertson, Alfred Toigo, Kelton Garwood

The first episode featuring Jack Albertson as Kay's brother, Paul Fenton, and the first of two shows which showcase Ed's talents as a songsmith. Wilbur hums Ed's tune in Paul Fenton's office, and Fenton wants to know the lyrics. Wilbur unsuccessfully tries to write words, but is relieved when Ed tells him they already exist. Ed gets to sing "Pretty Little Filly" from his barn, while Wilbur lip-syncs in front of him. Three beatniks back him up.

#16: "Ed the Stoolpigeon"

ORIGINAL AIRDATE: April 13, 1961
WRITERS: Lou Derman, Ben Starr
DIRECTOR: Arthur Lubin
GUEST STAR: Ralph Sanford

Carol finds a stray poodle, Pierre, and Ed is jealous. He complains to the police about the dog's barking, under the alias of Mr. Thompson, and Wilbur accuses Addison of being the stoolpigeon. "Mr. Thompson" complains a second time, and the police officer has to take the dog away. Just like in *The Wizard of Oz*, Pierre runs from the policeman (Carol and Wilbur: "Run, Pierre, Run!"). Ed confesses to the crime and he and Wilbur shake hands. (Then Ed stretches!) Meanwhile, Roger takes a liking to Pierre and hides him from the cop. The pound calls—they've found Pierre's owner. Ed wants to knit a sweater for the pup.

#17: "Psychoanalyst Show"

ORIGINAL AIRDATE: April 20, 1961
WRITERS: Lou Derman, Ben Starr
DIRECTOR: Arthur Lubin
GUEST STAR: Richard Deacon

Ed has acrophobia—fear of heights—which keeps him from his scheduled ride with Peggy, a little girl who lives up in the hills. Wilbur asks a psychiatrist to make a barn visit and talk to Ed behind locked stable doors. The shrink thinks that Wilbur's schizophrenic, and looks forward to his lead story in *The Psychiatric Journal*. Wilbur takes a blindfolded Ed up into the hills overlooking the San Fernando Valley, to overcome his fear. The horse butts in on two lovers in a parked car. The fella threatens to punch Wilbur, who he thinks is responsible for the rude comments. Ed saves his owner from a fat lip by pretending to be Wilbur's nearby gang. Ed, looking around, suddenly realizes that his fear of heights is licked.

#18: "A Man for Velma"
ORIGINAL AIRDATE: April 27, 1961
WRITERS: Lou Derman, Ben Starr
DIRECTOR: Arthur Lubin
GUEST STAR: Elvia Allman

Based on the Walter Brooks serial *Just a Song at Twilight*, about a man-crazy live-in cook whom Ed serenades by moonlight to keep her cooking. In this TV version, Carol sprains her wrist, so Wilbur hires Velma for the week. Velma bakes a mean cheese soufflé, and her "personal pizzas" for Ed aren't hay. She threatens to leave the Posts for lack of eligible bachelors, so Ed poses as "Walter," a secret admirer. Ed reunites Velma with her butler ex-beau at the end of the episode.

#19: "Ed Agrees to Talk"
ORIGINAL AIRDATE: May 18, 1961
WRITERS: Lou Derman, Ben Starr
DIRECTOR: Arthur Lubin
GUEST STAR: Doris Packer

Carol wants a new car; Wilbur tells her they can't afford one. So Carol hitches Mister Ed to a wagon to make him "earn his keep" (don't you just love that expression?). Ed complains to the SPCA, who in turn sends over Inspector Adams. Ed agrees to tell Mrs. Adams that he's not really abused, but he comes down with laryngitis (how convenient!). Carol promises never to hitch Mister Ed to a wagon again, and Wilbur agrees to buy Carol a car.

#20: "Ed's New Shoes"
ORIGINAL AIRDATE: May 4, 1961
WRITERS: Lou Derman, Ben Starr
DIRECTOR: Arthur Lubin
GUEST STARS: James Flavin, John Qualen

Ed's in love with a chestnut filly he sees in the park on Sundays. He wants to impress her with new horseshoes. Wilbur takes Ed to Kramer the blacksmith, but Axel, the simple hired hand, tells Wilbur that Ed doesn't need new shoes. Kramer fires Axel for his honesty, and Wilbur hires him as a handyman to help fix up his place for a *Home Beautiful* photo shoot. Axel is a schlemiel of the highest order, wreaking absolute havoc. Before the Posts have a chance to fire him, he quits. Wilbur outsmarts Kramer into hiring Axel back at an even higher salary than he was making before.

Note: May 18, 1961 was the last time Mister Ed *aired on Thursdays during the first season. In the New York area, WNBC started running* Mister Ed *on Sundays at 7:30.*

#21: "The Mustache"
ORIGINAL AIRDATE: May 21, 1961
WRITERS: Lou Derman, Ben Starr
DIRECTOR: Arthur Lubin

To help Wilbur land a business deal, Roger Addison encourages the young architect to grow a mustache so he'll look more distinguished. But the mustache goes to Wilbur's brain, and he starts dressing and acting like his older, next-door neighbor. Carol can't stand her newly stuffy hubby and begs him to shave. He'll comply on one condition—that Roger get rid of his mustache too. Kay can't wait to see her husband's upper lip after all these years. Ed bets Wilbur that if he has to shave his mustache, Ed gets a new shower stall. Wilbur ends up shaving, Roger gets to keep his mustache and Ed gets the shower. Highlight: Ed singing "Pretty Little Filly" in the shower.

#22: "The Contest"
ORIGINAL AIRDATE: June 18, 1961
WRITERS: Lou Derman, Ben Starr
DIRECTOR: Arthur Lubin
GUEST STAR: Joe Conley

Wilbur wins "Giant Jackpot," a radio trivia contest, with Ed's help. He qualifies for the $5,000 prize, which he'll use for a trip to Europe if he wins. Ed agrees to coach Wilbur in preparation for the next question, as long as Wilbur takes him to Europe too. They start with presidents' names and birth dates. Wilbur becomes a zombified encyclopedia, reciting random facts and skipping meals. A man from the Giant Jackpot Show arrives at the Posts to explain the rules. It turns out that Wilbur's competing against an elderly couple for the $5,000. Ed decides to let the old folks win the contest and purposely blows the jackpot question.

#23: "The Other Woman"

ORIGINAL AIRDATE: June 4, 1961
WRITERS: Lou Derman, Ben Starr
DIRECTOR: Arthur Lubin
GUEST STAR: Tom Fadden

Ed objects to an eighteen-year-old horse, Bernadine, giving kiddy rides on the grounds that she's overworked. Ed pleads with Wilbur to buy the old horse, but the architect refuses. Carol keeps hearing Wilbur say "Bernadine" every time he's talking to Ed on the phone, and she thinks he's having an affair. Ed takes matters into his own hooves and kidnaps the elderly horse. Charlie Woods, the owner, storms over to the Posts and demands his horse back. Wilbur can't explain why "he" took her, but Woods tells him that Bernadine loves to work, that she was scrawny before he got her. Highlight: Wilbur falling asleep, saying "Bernadine" with a big sexy smile on his face, while Carol looks on, mortified.

#24: "Wilbur Sells Ed"

ORIGINAL AIRDATE: July 2, 1961
WRITERS: Lou Derman, Ben Starr
DIRECTOR: Arthur Lubin
GUEST STAR: Frank Wilcox

Wilbur's client, Fred Gilbert of Gilbert Farms, has a filly named Princess Helen that Ed's sweet on. Ed gives her a heart-shaped bundle of hay—very sweet—and proposes. Ed tries to steal a smooch and upsets the Princess. He calls Gilbert a meathead, and Wilbur gets the blame. Gilbert fires the architect. Ed is so lovesick that he begs Wilbur to give him to Mr. Gilbert. Wilbur agrees, and the deal is back on. When Ed hears that Princess Helen is being shipped to South America, he runs back home. Gilbert finds out that Ed's back with Wilbur, and Addison is furious—he's involved in the deal with Gilbert too and doesn't want Wilbur to blow the deal. On the contrary, Gilbert respects a man who feels so strongly about his horse. All's well that ends well.

#25: "Ed Cries Wolf"

ORIGINAL AIRDATE: June 11, 1961
WRITERS: Lou Derman, Ben Starr
DIRECTOR: Arthur Lubin
GUEST STARS: Rolfe Sedan, Logan Field, Anthony Warde

It's Carol's birthday, and Wilbur buys her the pearl earrings she's been hinting for. Ed is jealous of all the attention Carol's getting from Wilbur and decides to fight back. He tells his owner that he needs an eye exam (even though he can read the legal line at the bottom of the chart), then he feigns an earache and a toothache. A genuine prowler who took down Wilbur's address while at the jewelry shop shows up at the house and steals Carol's gift. Ed calls Wilbur to warn him, but the architect thinks it's a classic case of "Horse who cried wolf." Ed captures the thief ("Take one step and you're dead meat"), and Wilbur gets Carol's jewelry back. That evening at the Addisons, Carol gets a phone call. It's Ed singing, "For she's a jolly good fellow." Carol thanks Wilbur for the wonderful singing telegram.

#26: "Pine Lake Lodge"

ORIGINAL AIRDATE: June 25, 1961
WRITERS: Lou Derman, Bill Davenport
DIRECTOR: John Rich
GUEST STARS: William Bendix, John Qualen, Nancy Culp

This episode was a pilot for *The William Bendix Show* and was never sold. Wilbur and Carol arrive at the rustic Pine Lake Lodge, owned by their friend Bill Parker. Shock of all shocks, Roger Addison is feeding and taking care of Ed in this episode. Bill Parker is trying to raise tree donations so he can build picnic furniture for the children's camp. His friend Milo refuses to help him cut down one of stingy Mr. Thompson's trees. So when unsuspecting Wilbur arrives, Bill selects him to aid in the tree-chopping cause. Guilt-ridden Bill eventually admits to the crime, and Thompson gives him a stern warning. Nevertheless, the not-so-stingy-after-all Thompson ends up donating the cut-down tree for the kids.

Second Season (First Season, CBS Network) October 1961–April 1962: Sundays 6:30–7 P.M.

Note: Mister Ed *aired on CBS from October 1, 1961, to September 4, 1966.*

#27: "My Son, My Son"
ORIGINAL AIRDATE: October 1, 1961
WRITERS: Lou Derman, Bill Crewson
DIRECTOR: Arthur Lubin
GUEST STAR: Jack Mather as Mr. Ogilvie

Ed wants a son, but as a "confirmed bachelor," must consider adopting. He takes Wilbur down to the stables to see his son, Snuffy, who's got a $125 price tag. Ed says, "I'll take it," and Wilbur suddenly has a second horse. The diminutive pony is a favorite of Carol's, but he devours Kay's handbag, and worse still, eats Roger's prize apples. Snuffy is no colt, but actually a Shetland pony, 23 years old. Ed's disillusioned, and Wilbur returns Snuffy to Mr. Ogilvie.

#28: "The Horsetronaut"
ORIGINAL AIRDATE: October 8, 1961
WRITERS: Lou Derman, Bobby O'Brien
DIRECTOR: Arthur Lubin
GUEST STARS: Robert Bernard, Hazel Shermet

Wilbur takes an office in town so he can finish up his plans for an international shopping center. He misses Ed so much, he thinks his secretary, Miss Culbertson, is the horse, and pats her face. Ed feels unwanted and volunteers to be the first horse in space. His intelligence exam at the Lauderback Missile Base is hilarious—Ed gives the doctor his stethoscope, unplugs the wire which sends electric current to the carrot, etc. He's about to take off, but . . . oops, he weighs forty-two pounds too much for the capsule. They send Sparky instead, and Wilbur gives up his office in town.

#29: "Ed the Jumper"

ORIGINAL AIRDATE: October 29, 1961
WRITERS: Lou Derman, Bill Crewson
DIRECTOR: Arthur Lubin
GUEST STARS: Alan Hale, Jr., Donna Douglas

Wilbur's college nemesis, Karl Dickenson, is in town and wants to torment Wilbur "Dippy" Post once again. He challenges Wilbur and Ed to a steeple jump contest with him and his snooty horse, McTavish. Karl is married to a vapid Miss Louisiana, played by soon-to-be *Beverly Hillbillies* star Donna Douglas. Ed wages a massive fitness campaign to prepare for the event but decides to win with his brains instead of his brawn. He spooks McTavish, and Wilbur wins by default.

#30: "Ed the Redecorator"

ORIGINAL AIRDATE: October 22, 1961
WRITERS: Lou Derman, Bill Crewson
DIRECTOR: Arthur Lubin
GUEST STAR: Hayden Rourke

Carol decides to have her place done in Hawaiian Modern, by the fancy interior decorator Beverly Cavell (who never accepts a job for less than $1,500). Wilbur tells her it's too expensive. Meanwhile, Ed phones Cavell and asks him for a price to do his stall in Hawaiian Modern. Carol enters the barn and sees Cavell, who says he'll try to retain the "barnsy flavor." When Carol finds out that "Wilbur" was secretly having the stall done, she fumes. Wilbur takes her down to Palm Springs so they can kiss and make up. While they're away, Ed does his stall in Hawaiian Modern. The Posts return home and Wilbur sees Ed's new decor. He whisks Carol back down to Palm Springs for a couple of days, just to give Ed time to get rid of the furnishings. So much for culture . . .

#31: "Ed's Ancestors"

ORIGINAL AIRDATE: October 15, 1961
WRITERS: Lou Derman, Bill Crewson
DIRECTOR: Arthur Lubin

Ed wants to know more about his forefathers, so Wilbur sends off an inquiry to the Breeders Association. Addison offers to mail the letter for Wilbur and decides to play a practical joke. He sends Wilbur a phony reply which states that all of Ed's ancestors were criminals. Ed dreams that he's "Dirty Ed," complete with a horse lineup and post office sketches. He runs off to a nearby farm, where he can do hard labor as penance. But he's not used to such grueling work and calls Wilbur up to rescue him. Addison confesses to the crime, and Ed gets a nice rubdown.

#32: "Ed the Voter"
ORIGINAL AIRDATE: November 5, 1961
WRITERS: Lou Derman, Stanley Adams
DIRECTOR: Arthur Lubin

Carol makes a TV appearance for the Women's Voters League and volunteers the Posts' home as a polling site. Wilbur tells Ed that his barn will be used as a voting booth, much to the horse's chagrin. Kay will cater the sandwiches to encourage a bigger turnout, and Roger will take this opportunity to meet the mayor and drum up support for his election to office the following year. When the citizens arrive, Roger pretends to love babies and animals and poses for lots of pictures, and when they leave, Ed gets to cast his vote.

#33: "Ed the Hero"
ORIGINAL AIRDATE: November 26, 1961
WRITERS: Lou Derman, Stanley Adams
DIRECTOR: Arthur Lubin
GUEST STAR: Addison Richards

While Ed and Wilbur are riding in the park, Ed saves a little girl named Betsy who's on a runaway horse. Betsy is the granddaughter of real estate mogul Henry J. Thorndike, who owns half of Catalina Island. Ed's fear of water dominates this episode, as the Posts and Addisons get a chance to partake in the parade on Catalina Island. Wilbur rents a boat to help Ed overcome his fear, but Ed plays a practical joke and casts his owner off without him. Roger rents an Ed look-alike from Briarcliff Stables, which convinces Ed to make the trip. Note: Trainer Les Hilton didn't think that Ed could do these water scenes on the boat, but the terrific horse could, and did.

#34: "Hunting Show"
ORIGINAL AIRDATE: November 12, 1961
WRITERS: Lou Derman, Stanley Adams
DIRECTOR: Arthur Lubin

Wilbur and Roger plan a hunting trip to Mammoth Lake, and the girls insist on joining them, to bring a bit of civilization to the outing. Wilbur wants Ed to carry the provisions, but Ed's on a superstition kick—he's a Pisces, and if he leaves town, "disaster will befall" him. This is a real prosocial episode, as a baby duckling who waddles over to the campsite breaks the girls' hearts, and Ed pretends to be dying from an accidental hunting injury (with ketchup). The boys decide to call the whole thing off.

#35: "Mister Ed's Blues"
ORIGINAL AIRDATE: November 19, 1961
WRITERS: Lou Derman, Bill Crewson
DIRECTOR: Arthur Lubin
GUEST STAR: Jack Albertson

The second episode in which Ed writes a hit song for Paul Fenton's music company. This time it's a blues number, "Empty Feedbag Blues," inspired by his sweetheart filly Sabrina, who gives him the cold mane. Ed visits Sabrina at the stables one morning and is shocked at how unattractive she really is. He even wants to warn his archrival, the stallion Robespierre.

#36: "Ed and the Elephant"
ORIGINAL AIRDATE: December 17, 1961
WRITERS: Lou Derman, Robert O'Brien
DIRECTOR: Arthur Lubin
GUEST STARS: Henry Corden, Carole Evern

Wilbur wants to learn the Art of Elephant Levitation from the Great Mordini, thinking he can transfer the skill to Horse Levitation. Mordini agrees to teach him if he'll watch his elephant Bongo for a few days. Wilbur agrees, and lets Bongo share the barn with Ed. Ed isn't thrilled with his new barnmate, who's very mischievous. They play tug-of-war with the light bulb cord and end up staying up all night. Wilbur learns the trick, but it's never revealed to us. Ed splashes Bongo with water, to show the elephant that "horses never forget."

#37: "Ed, the Salesman"
ORIGINAL AIRDATE: December 3, 1961
WRITERS: Lou Derman, Bill Crewson
DIRECTOR: Arthur Lubin
GUEST STAR: Howard Wendell

It's April 12, one year since Wilbur and Ed first "became man and horse." Ed wants a color TV set for the occasion, and Wilbur tells him they can't afford it. Meanwhile, on the domestic front, Carol's racking up a pretty hefty phone bill. She decides to teach the cha-cha to pay her way, which makes Wilbur jealous as heck. Ed starts selling real estate over the phone. Only trouble is, his commissions don't even cover his long-distance phone expenses. Carol quits her job, Ed quits his job and order is restored.

#38: "Zsa Zsa"
ORIGINAL AIRDATE: January 28, 1962
WRITERS: Lou Derman, Bill Crewson
DIRECTOR: Arthur Lubin
GUEST STARS: Zsa Zsa Gabor, Jack Albertson, Berry Kroeger

Zsa Zsa Gabor is the noisy new next-door neighbor, but when Wilbur and Paul Fenton go over to make a complaint, they end up helping Miss Gabor unpack and settle in. A movie producer, Jack Brady, wants Zsa Zsa to star in a western that's filming in Australia, but she's afraid of all horses . . . except "Mister Eddie." Ed tells Wilbur that he wants to go "down under," but in reality, he just wants Wilbur to get the $5,000 so he can buy Carol a mink coat. When Wilbur finds out the truth, he rushes to the pier to retrieve Ed. Zsa Zsa is a good egg and lets the architect have his horse back. Note: This episode ran opposite the FCC Senate Hearings, televised on NBC. *Mister Ed* creamed the elder statesmen, garnering a 47 share of audience. Ed also handily beat out *Maverick*, the other horse show airing on ABC.

#39: "Ed the Beneficiary"
ORIGINAL AIRDATE: January 21, 1962
WRITERS: Lou Derman, Robert O'Brien
DIRECTOR: Arthur Lubin
GUEST STARS: Raymond Bailey, Lee Goodman

Ed wants security after Wilbur's gone (not taking into account that humans outlive horses), so Wilbur draws up a will. Carol finds out and thinks that Wilbur's dying. Roger's doctor friend poses as a golf instructor to examine Wilbur unawares. Ed spills the beans to Wilbur, who tricks everyone into thinking he's got a nervous twitch.

#40: "Ed's Bed"

ORIGINAL AIRDATE: January 14, 1962
WRITERS: Lou Derman, Bill Crewson
DIRECTOR: Ira Stewart
GUEST STAR: Jack Kruschen

Ed comes down with Wilbur's cold, and the architect spoils his horse silly, including chest rub, taking his temperature with a wall thermometer and going into town for a gallon of carrot juice. He gets stopped for speeding by a policeman on the way home and must take sobriety and psychological tests (this section is cut from the Nick at Nite tape). They miss the ballet, and Carol packs to go home to Mother, but Roger gets them to make up. Ed decides to order himself a bed, complete with "gen-u-wine" silk sheets. Roger needs an offbeat subject for his photography contest. Carol is outraged seeing Ed in his new bed and tells Wilbur good-bye. Wilbur tells everyone to calm down—he bought the bed so Ed could pose as Roger's nutty photography subject. We don't see this part, but Kay gets into bed with Ed for the photo. Highlight: Ed pulling the sheets over himself.

#41: "The Wrestler"

ORIGINAL AIRDATE: January 7, 1962
WRITERS: Lou Derman, Bill Crewson
DIRECTOR: Arthur Lubin
GUEST STAR: Ricky Starr

Carol and Kay take up ballet lessons to get in shape. Roger and Wilbur each buy half of a wrestler, Tiger Davis. They take Tiger in while he's in training, but he gains too much weight from Carol and Kay's home cooking. He studies ballet with the girls in order to trim down and turns out to be the next Baryshnikov. Tiger wins his wrestling bout against the Apache Kid by grace and unconventional dance moves and earns himself a position with a ballet company. Ed gets to wash his saddle in this show.

#42: "Ed the Horse Doctor"

ORIGINAL AIRDATE: February 11, 1962
WRITERS: Lou Derman, Robert O'Brien
DIRECTOR: Arthur Lubin
GUEST STARS: Hank Patterson, Robert Carson

Roger Addison buys part of a racehorse, Lady Linda. Only trouble is, she won't race. Something's troubling her, and only Ed can find out what it is.

Turns out she has a broken heart, and after a few sessions with the dashing palomino, she falls for him on the rebound. Addison insists that Wilbur separate the two horses, fearful that Ed might infect his prized beauty. But when Ed leaves, so does Lady Linda's desire to run. Addison has to kiss Ed to get him to come down to the racetrack before the big race. Lady Linda wins, but Addison promptly sells her after the race—"if you think I'm going to spend the rest of my life kissing that old plug, you're crazy."

#43: "Horse Wash"
ORIGINAL AIRDATE: February 4, 1962
WRITERS: Lou Derman, Stanley Adams
DIRECTOR: Arthur Lubin
GUEST STARS: Barry Kelly, Tol Avery, Don Brodie, Herb Vigran

The first episode in which Carol's grumpy father, Mr. Higgins, appears. Higgins is on the verge of a real estate deal with two swindlers, Carmichael and Hogan. Ed's in love with a filly "who digs skinny horses," and takes a mud bath to reduce. Wilbur refuses to clean the disobedient horse, and off to the car wash he trots. This scene was actually filmed at the Cahuenga Car Wash. Wilbur has the ability to read Ed's lips and learns that the men dealing with his father-in-law are scoundrels. He exposes them just as Mr. Higgins is about to sign the contract. Higgins apologizes for treating Wilbur so poorly.

#44: "Ed's Word of Honor"
ORIGINAL AIRDATE: February 25, 1962
WRITERS: Lou Derman, Stanley Adams
DIRECTOR: Arthur Lubin

Ed eats Addison's apples and gets a bad case of hiccoughs. Wilbur cures Ed by breaking a paper bag full of air and scaring him. For Roger's birthday, Wilbur buys a fish pond and fills it with twenty-five-cent goldfish. Addison stocks his new pond with sixty-five dollars' worth of tropical fish. A stray cat eats the fish, but Roger blames Ed. Roger builds a fence to keep Ed out. Wilbur doesn't believe that Ed is innocent, and Ed refuses to talk to Wilbur. When he plans to run away to join the circus. Roger restocks his pond, and when the cats are caught red-pawed in the act, Wilbur apologizes to Ed. He takes his horsie to the circus.

#45: "Ed the Beachcomber"
ORIGINAL AIRDATE: April 1, 1962
WRITERS: Lou Derman, Robert O'Brien
DIRECTOR: Arthur Lubin
GUEST STARS: Larry Merrill, Nancy Lee, Joe Conley

Ed is upset by an editorial he reads in the paper that says horses are extinct. He identifies with the two young beachcombers who form an artist colony on Addison's beach property. Both Ed and the kids feel "rejected, neglected, befuddled, bemuddled," and the horse joins their colony. Addison gets good publicity from helping out the kids, and Wilbur convinces Ed that to be loved is to be wanted. Ed comes home and composes a love poem to Wilbur.

#46: "George Burns Meets Mister Ed" a.k.a. "Ed Finally Talks"
ORIGINAL AIRDATE: February 18, 1962
WRITER: Lou Derman
DIRECTOR: Arthur Lubin
GUEST STAR: George Burns as himself

George Burns offers $25,000 to the person who comes up with a novelty act for his Las Vegas show. Wilbur begs Ed (literally, down on his knees) to be that novelty act, but Ed insists: "I talk for pleasure, not for money." George talks to Ed over the phone: "Hello, Horse" and all that jazz, but doesn't believe Ed's a horse for a minute. Wilbur decides he likes his buddy just the way he is, after having a nightmare about Ed's grandiose accomplishments: Congress, etc. (See Chapter 8 for Wilbur's dreams.)

#47: "Ed's New Neighbors"
ORIGINAL AIRDATE: March 25, 1962
WRITERS: Lou Derman, Stanley Adams
DIRECTOR: Arthur Lubin
GUEST STARS: Willard Waterman, Shirley Mitchell, Jimmy Garrett

Ed's apple-swiping and Addison-hating are at their peak. Kay inherits a mansion in New York, in Hastings-on-Hudson, and they plan to move. Roger sells his house to Mr. Douglas, a humorless inspector for the Internal Revenue Department (pre-IRS), whose son Timmy is "the bad seed," scaring Ed with a snake can. At their weekly gin game with the Posts, the Addisons realize they don't have the heart to move. But Douglas won't let Roger out of the deal. The Posts invite the Douglases to dinner and act like real swingers to get them to change their mind. Alan Young and Connie Hines are terrific as twisting decadents! Highlights: Ed gives Roger a rose; Young playing the bagpipes (that's really him—he learned to play as a kid).

#48: "Bald Horse"
ORIGINAL AIRDATE: March 18, 1962
WRITERS: Lou Derman, Bill Crewson
DIRECTOR: Arthur Lubin
GUEST STARS: Percy Helton, Henry Norell

Kay Addison wants to go to San Francisco with Wilbur and Carol, so Roger plays a dirty trick on Wilbur—he cuts Kay's blond wig and puts some of it on the floor near Ed's tail, telling Wilbur his horse is losing hair. That way Wilbur will cancel the trip. Ed visits the vet, and a blabbermouth horse named Jenny gossips to Wilhelm II and Delores that Ed's going bald. Doc Evans tells Wilbur it's human hair, and Roger fesses up about the prank. They all go to San Fran and board Ed at Briarwood Stables, right next to his love, Ilsa. Highlight: Wilbur talking to Jenny's owner about the plight of bald men, not knowing the man is bald beneath his hat. Also note that in this episode Rocky Lane clearly had a cold, so Ed sounds nasal!

#49: "No Horses Allowed"
ORIGINAL AIRDATE: March 4, 1962
WRITERS: Lou Derman, Bill Crewson
DIRECTOR: Arthur Lubin
GUEST STARS: Neil Hamilton, Olan Soule, Lindsay Workman

Aynsworth takes a petition around to outzone the bridle path. Wilbur challenges him to a live TV debate. Trouble is, Aynsworth's brother-in-law is the station manager, and Wilbur can do no right. He ends up in "whiteface" for the "Speak Your Peace" debate and Ed calls him "Bozo the Clown." When Aynsworth takes the Boy Scouts on a hiking trip at Ferndale Park, one of them, Bobby, gets lost. Mister Ed finds him and Aynsworth is so grateful, he decides to rescind the petition. Guess who got the kid lost in the first place!

#50: "Ed the Matchmaker"
ORIGINAL AIRDATE: April 29, 1962
WRITERS: Ben Starr, Robert O'Brien
DIRECTOR: Arthur Lubin
GUEST STARS: Noanna Dix, George O'Hanlon, Jeff Donnell, Peter Brooks

This episode was a pilot for a spin-off about the trials and tribulations of a love-crazed teenager, Emmy Lou Harper. Based on the United Feature syndicated cartoon by Marty Links, Emmy Lou befriends her new neighbor, Mister Ed, when she realizes that she needs a hair from a horse's tail to complete her love potion. Surprisingly, Ed doesn't talk to her, although she seemed the perfect candidate. Action focuses on her attempts to win the affections of Arthur, the clutzy delivery boy. If this series had made it, it might have preempted *The Patty Duke Show*, which came to ABC in September 1963.

#51: "Clint Eastwood Meets Mister Ed"
ORIGINAL AIRDATE: April 22, 1962
WRITERS: Lou Derman, Sonia Chernus
DIRECTOR: Arthur Lubin
GUEST STARS: Clint Eastwood, Kathleen Freeman, Donna Douglas

Clint Eastwood moves next door to the Posts (same set used for Zsa Zsa's house). His "tall, dark and handsome" horse, Midnight, steals Ed's fillies away, so as revenge, Ed fouls up Eastwood's show biz and romantic dealings via the party line (pre-900 "party lines"). The Posts and Addisons are struggling to come up with a benefit play to raise money for the youth center, so Clint steps in and they pull off a western melodrama. Donna Douglas has a tiny role as Clint's girlfriend.

#52: "Lie Detector"
ORIGINAL AIRDATE: April 8, 1962
WRITERS: Lou Derman, Larry Rhine
DIRECTOR: Arthur Lubin
GUEST STARS: Ben Weldon, Richard Reeves

Addison brings a lie detector test over to the Posts, which leads to domestic strife. Carol's jealousy for Wilbur's brainy college sweetheart, Gladys Hodges, gets ignited, and Carol takes up reading Aristotle to compete. Ed spills ink on the Holbrook plans on Wilbur's drafting table and gets locked in his stall as punishment. The Posts kiss and make up, and plan a big night on the town. But Ed's left home. This is Larry Rhine's first *Mister Ed* script and features one of Ed's great "running away from home" notes with detailed instructions to Wilbur on where to find him! This time, Ed's at the Livestock Shipping Union Truck Terminal, pretending to be a cow.

#53: "Ed and the Secret Service"
ORIGINAL AIRDATE: February 7, 1963
WRITERS: Ben Starr, Bob O'Brien
DIRECTOR: Justus Addiss
GUEST STARS: Robert Hastings, Robert Patten, Barbara Morrison
Note: This episode did not run until the following season, on Thursday 7:30 P.M.

A little piece of history for the time capsule: The Kennedys are in; Jackie is oh-so-chic; women all across the nation, including Carol and Kay Addison, are emulating the First Lady's passion for riding by wearing English garb and joining the Hunt Club. This horse kick has Ed peeved, since Wilbur wants to ride him for the fox hunt. He calls the White House to complain. This brings about a visit from two Secret Service agents, who are trying to figure out what the hay is going on. Great shot of Ed walking into the Posts' living room.

Third Season (Second Season, CBS)
September 1962–May 1963: Thursdays 7:30 P.M.

Note: Mister Ed replaced Frontier Circus, a circus drama starring Chill Wills, the voice of Francis the Talking Mule, in this time slot!

#54: "Ed Gets Amnesia"
ORIGINAL AIRDATE: September 27, 1962
WRITERS: Ben Starr, Robert O'Brien
DIRECTOR: Arthur Lubin
GUEST STARS: Richard Deacon, Lindsay Workman

A tin pail in the barn falls on Ed's head, inducing amnesia. The horse thinks he's human, and Wilbur's a horse. Wilbur pretends to trip and lose his memory so he can get a doctor and learn how to cure Ed. He becomes Vladimir Rabinsky, the great concert pianist, and refers to Carol as "Louise." Dr. Cascard tells Carol that a blow to the same area can cure the amnesia. Wilbur is about to hit Ed when another pail falls on the horse, bringing back his memory. Wilbur "trips" to regain his memory too.

#55: "Wilbur the Good Samaritan"
ORIGINAL AIRDATE: October 4, 1962
WRITERS: Robert O'Brien, Ben Starr
DIRECTOR: Arthur Lubin
GUEST STARS: Jerry Brodie, Kevin Hausner

Joey the paper boy has really bad aim and throws Wilbur's paper on the roof. Ed calls up to complain and gets Joey fired. Wilbur and Roger each think the other one was the grouch who complained. Ed admits that he used the name "Wilbur Post" to lodge his grievance and calls under the alias of three more people to get the kid his job back. Joey gets another chance but busts his bicycle against a tree. Wilbur and Ed finish the paper route but accidentally throw Addison's paper on the roof. Roger thinks Wilbur is a prowler when he goes up on his roof to retrieve it.

#56: "Wilbur's Father"
ORIGINAL AIRDATE: February 28, 1963
WRITERS: Bob O'Brien, Ben Starr
DIRECTOR: Arthur Lubin
GUEST STARS: Doris Packer, Eilene Janssen

Great cinematic tricks, a la *Patty Duke*, in this episode. Alan Young doubles as Wilbur Post and his seventy-year-old Scottish father, Angus (Angus is Young's real name!). Wilbur, Carol, Ed and the Addisons go up to Mr. Post's farm for his wedding. Upon their arrival, they are introduced to the beautiful, young daughter of the bride, but misconstrue her for the bride-to-be. Angus decides to play a practical joke on Wilbur and really plays up the "dirty old man" bit. They finally meet the real fiancée, a proper woman of age, and all is well. The Mister Ed barn is used as the Angus Post barn, shot at different angles. Highlight: Roger milking a cow with *Psycho*-like music playing. Really strange! Great makeup job on Young by Jack Pierce.

#57: "Wilbur in the Lion's Den"
ORIGINAL AIRDATE: November 8, 1962
WRITERS: Robert O'Brien, Ben Starr
DIRECTOR: Arthur Lubin
GUEST STARS: Charles Lane, Samba the Lion

Addison tries to make a real estate deal with the crabby, pill-popping Charles Foster, who works on weekends and has a car phone in 1962! Foster agrees to hire Wilbur to do the designing, but Wilbur refuses to take the job—Foster is mean to Ed. Roger and Carol pressure Wilbur into reconsidering the position with Foster. Meanwhile, Wilbur goes to the park to fly a kite with Ed, and the kite ends up in the lion cage. When Wilbur goes in after it, the lion strips Wilbur of his shirt and pants, and Ed finds a ladder just in time. Carol tells Wilbur not to take the job with the miserable Foster.

#58: "The Bashful Clipper"
ORIGINAL AIRDATE: October 18, 1962
WRITERS: Robert O'Brien, Ben Starr
DIRECTOR: Arthur Lubin
GUEST STARS: Ricky Starr, Barbara Morrison

Carol and Kay are having a hair crisis—Doris Manning, fashion editor of the *Daily Chronicle*, is visiting the Civic Group and they can't find an available hairdresser. Wilbur calls the stables to send a boy over to trim Ed's mane. Chuck Miller arrives and hits it off with Ed. He offers to fix Carol's hair and creates a masterpiece. Kay gets the same treatment. Carol and Kay try to talk him into opening up his own salon, with their husbands as financiers. He confesses that he used to be a beautician before working with animals, but women scare him. Ed purposely kicks Chuck so he'll realize horses aren't so nice after all. When Roger and Wilbur refuse to get involved, they get thrown out in the barn to sleep. Roger buckles under when Ed makes things miserable. Doris Manning is the first customer in the salon, but Chuck has an anxiety attack. Wilbur unsuccessfully tries to fill in, but luckily, Chuck's confidence is restored in time to save the fashion editor's hairdo.

#59: "Wilbur and Ed in Show Biz"
ORIGINAL AIRDATE: October 11, 1962
WRITERS: Robert O'Brien, Ben Starr
DIRECTOR: Arthur Lubin
GUEST STAR: Chick Chandler

Ed gets caught red-hoofed at swiping Addison's apples. Wilbur's new client, Bill Hodges, is in show biz with his elephant, Margie. She specializes in the Twist, just like Ed. Hodges wants a setup just like the one Wilbur and Ed have—office and adjoining stall, with a few added perks: a wading pool and mirror, which makes Ed jealous. Wilbur convinces Ed to go into show biz with him and calls Hodges' agent, Sam Parker. Ed steals Margie's thunder with his tricks, and the elephant becomes incapacitated by envy. Hodges is a wreck—without the elephant, he's got no career. Ed purposely fails in front of a live studio audience, and Margie gets her confidence back.

#60: "Ed and the Allergy"
ORIGINAL AIRDATE: October 25, 1962
WRITERS: Ben Starr, Robert O'Brien
DIRECTOR: Arthur Lubin
GUEST STAR: Isabel Randolph

In this episode, we learn that Roger Addison truly hates his mother-in-law, Dorothy. She comes to visit them (for an unspecified amount of time), but develops an allergy to horse hair ... that means Ed! Addison is the only person who finds out she can't be around horses. Ed knows too: He overheard Roger's call to the doctor. Roger wants to get Ed and "mother dear" together so she'll have to leave, but Ed won't comply. He goes off to Green Valley, where Wilbur was supposed to take him camping. Wilbur, Roger and Dorothy go looking for Ed; her sneezing serves as "a geiger counter." Roger trips on some brush and hurts his ankle. A miraculous transition takes place ... Dorothy is truly worried about Roger. They really do care about each other! Too bad time doesn't allow for a subtle transition in emotion. One minute they hate each other, the next they're "real pals." Highlight: Ed roasting carrots over an open fire, singing "Home on the Range."

#61: "Horse Sense"
ORIGINAL AIRDATE: November 1, 1962
WRITERS: Ben Starr, Robert O'Brien
DIRECTOR: Arthur Lubin
GUEST STAR: Neil Hamilton

Ed writes a Letter to the Editor, under Wilbur's name, to save the bridle path. Mr. Boyd, a publisher, is so impressed with the letter, he sends Wilbur a $2,500 advance to write a book on animals for his spring book line. Ed starts to write the book for Wilbur, dedicating it to his love Princess. Wilbur's newfound success goes to his head, and he alienates Carol and the Addisons. He realizes what a fool he's been and returns the advance so he can go back to being just an architect again. Highlight: An extremely smug Wilbur at the publishing party.

#62: "Ed and Paul Revere"

ORIGINAL AIRDATE: December 6, 1962
WRITERS: Ben Starr, Bob O'Brien
DIRECTOR: Arthur Lubin
GUEST STAR: Hans Conreid

Roger Addison, a descendant of Paul Revere, hires Igor Korzak to sculpt a statue of Paul Revere for the local park. When Ed resists posing as the horse for the statue, Wilbur threatens to use his rival from Tally-Ho Stables, Lightning. Korzak is cartoonishly temperamental and rude; he eats the Posts out of house and home and turns out to be an abstract artist! At the unveiling, Wilbur tells Korzak to put the cover back on!

#63: "Wilbur the Masher"

ORIGINAL AIRDATE: December 13, 1962
WRITERS: Bob O'Brien, Ben Starr
DIRECTOR: Arthur Lubin
GUEST STARS: Coleen Gray, Paul Langton

Ed loves Flossy, a chestnut filly who belongs to beautiful Betty Gordon, a married woman. Ed whistles at Flossy on the bridle path, and Betty accuses Wilbur of being a masher. Ed persists and Betty tells her jealous husband about Wilbur. Wilbur and Ed devise a scheme to clear the innocent architect. Wilbur takes a skeptical Carol to the Gordon's to witness his redemption. He barely escapes divorce and nose rearrangement by having Ed call Mrs. Gordon and whistle into the telephone while he's standing right there, proving that the infamous whistle is *not* Wilbur's. Highlight: Ed and the Addisons do a double double take of each other when Ed walks out of the Posts' living room.

#64: "Horse Party"

ORIGINAL AIRDATE: November 15, 1962
WRITERS: Bob O'Brien, Lou Derman, Ben Starr
DIRECTOR: Arthur Lubin
GUEST STARS: Rolfe Sedan, Joe Conley, Lizbeth Field

It's Wednesday, August 28, Ed's ninth birthday. Wilbur throws him and his friends (Princess, Domino, Flossie, Joy Boy and Frenchie, the Tally-Ho swingers) a party. The ladies' luncheon gets rerouted to the Posts, unbeknownst to Wilbur, and he gets caught in the act by Carol, Kay, the other members and the chair rental delivery man. Highlight: Ed and Wilbur mingling at the horse party.

#65: "Ed the Pilgrim"

ORIGINAL AIRDATE: November 22, 1962
WRITERS: Lou Derman, Bob O'Brien, Ben Starr
DIRECTOR: Arthur Lubin

One of the "holiday fantasy shows" (see Chapter 8 for full details). Ed convinces Wilbur to spend Thanksgiving dinner with him, and tells his owner "the Real Story of Thanksgiving, the one they're afraid to tell," in which a brave, handsome horse saves the Pilgrims from starvation. Great costumes and sets, including Ed's fake front legs in stocks (he's thought a witch!).

#66: "Disappearing Horse"

ORIGINAL AIRDATE: November 29, 1962
WRITERS: Lou Derman, Ben Starr
DIRECTOR: Arthur Lubin
GUEST STARS: Karl Lukas, Ray Kellogg

The Posts and Addisons are rehearsing their routines for the community theater project. Wilbur will "Behead Ed" in a magic act. Ed calls the police to report the mistreating of a horse. The policeman's head gets stuck in the guillotine prop and they have to axe it apart to get him out. Propless, Wilbur will perform "the disappearing horse," another illusion. Ed is too scared to pull the lever, afraid he'll really disappear. Wilbur's act gets mentioned in a newspaper review the next morning, anyway.

#67: "Ed and the Bicycle"

ORIGINAL AIRDATE: January 3, 1963
WRITERS: Lou Derman, Bob O'Brien
DIRECTOR: Arthur Lubin
GUEST STAR: Robert Anderson

Ed ignores the "Keep off the Grass" sign in the park, causing Wilbur to get a ticket. Ed refuses to apologize, so Wilbur takes away his TV set. Kay, Carol and the boys take up bicycling. Roger demonstrates his cycling finesse, courtesy of a stunt man, telling the group he was known as "Mr. Wheels" in college. Ed wants to watch the Charlie Chan movie more than life itself, and sneaks into town to watch the flick through the window of Sullivan's Radio and TV Shop. The jealous horse follows the Posts and Addisons on their bicycle outing to the park, and flattens Wilbur's tires while they're busy picnicking. It starts to pour, and Wilbur has to walk home. When he gets to the barn, soaked and sneezing, Ed shares his blanket and apologizes.

#68: "Horse of a Different Color"
ORIGINAL AIRDATE: December 20, 1962
WRITERS: Lou Derman, Bob O'Brien, Ben Starr
DIRECTOR: Arthur Lubin
GUEST STAR: Hugh Sanders

A bored and restless Ed escapes from his chain (with a spare key he's got hidden in the beams) and goes to the Armstrong Circus, to see Galahad the Wonder Horse. When Galahad gets a cold, Ed decides to take his place. Wilbur helps to paint him so he looks just like the brave circus steed. At rehearsal, just as Ed's about to jump through the perilous Ring of Fire, Galahad's specialty, Wilbur stops him. Ed's relieved and swears he'll never leave home again.

Note: Mister Ed *switched to Sundays, 6:30* P.M., *starting March 24, 1963.*

#69: "The Blessed Event"
ORIGINAL AIRDATE: May 12, 1963
WRITERS: Lou Derman, Ben Starr
DIRECTOR: Arthur Lubin
GUEST STAR: Richard Deacon

Ed's friends, Domino and Chug-a-lug, are expecting a new colt. Ed's as nervous as can be about the birth—while pacing outside Domino's barn, he remarks: "Humans are lucky. They can smoke at a time like this." Kay and Roger overhear Wilbur talking to Ed about Domino on the phone, and think Carol's having a baby. Wilbur overhears the Addisons talking about a baby and thinks Kay is expecting. Dr. Sam Jones (Deacon) delivers the baby boy colt, Ed's nephew. Highlight: barbecue scene where the Addisons fuss over Carol, and the Posts fuss over Kay, each thinking the other is pregnant.

#70: "Ol' Rockin' Chair"
ORIGINAL AIRDATE: January 10, 1963
WRITERS: Lou Derman, Bob O'Brien
DIRECTOR: Arthur Lubin
GUEST STAR: Robert Carson

Wilbur is sentimental about Ed's old horseshoes, which doesn't mesh well with Carol's cleanup campaign. The architect decides to make a rocking chair from Ed's relics, and the objet d'art becomes the laughingstock of Carol and the Addisons. Wilbur places an ad in the paper to sell the chair, and while Addison is in the barn alone, a man arrives with an offer to buy the curiosity for $200. Greedy Addison decides to buy the chair from Wilbur for next to nothing, then sell it to Mr. Farnsworth for $200. Ed decides to put an end to Roger's scheme, so before the neighbor has a chance to sell the chair, the horse drags it to the lake and dumps it there. He and Wilbur retrieve it late that night by scuba diving, and Wilbur dismantles it for good.

#71: "Unemployment Show"

ORIGINAL AIRDATE: January 24, 1963
WRITERS: Lou Derman, Bob O'Brien
DIRECTOR: Arthur Lubin
GUEST STARS: Ralph Erdman, James Flavin, Willard Waterman

Kay Addison's loafing brother, Ralph, is staying with them. Wilbur puts his lazy horse to work at Tally-Ho Stables. Ed applies for a Social Security card and gets one. He pretends to go lame once he learns he's eligible for unemployment compensation. Wilbur devises a publicity stunt which will land Ralph a job as press manager for a movie studio. He takes Ed down to Unemployment, where the horse stands on line for his check. The scheme works—Ed's picture is on the front page of the *Press Herald* the next day.

#72: "Big Pine Lodge"

ORIGINAL AIRDATE: January 17, 1963
WRITERS: Lou Derman, Bob O'Brien
DIRECTOR: Arthur Lubin
GUEST STAR: Benny Rubin

Note: TV Guide *titles this "Pine Lake Lodge," the same name for episode 26.*

Wilbur takes Ed with him to Pine Lake Lodge. Ed learns that two card sharks at the lodge have bilked $110 from Addison. How does Ed save the day? Wilbur challenges the swindlers to a rematch, but this time, Ed impersonates an elk head on the wall, in plain view of their cards. He devises a series of signals to Wilbur, who wins the game, and recoups Roger's money.

#73: "Horse Talk"

ORIGINAL AIRDATE: January 31, 1963
WRITERS: Lou Derman, Bob O'Brien
DIRECTOR: Arthur Lubin
GUEST STARS: Chick Chandler, Emory Parnell, Richard Reeves, Anthony Warde

Addison is having his living room painted by John McGivney, who he learns is accused of doping a racehorse. Ed swears that the former racetrack groom is innocent and vows to clear his name. Wilbur and Ed decide to go to the racetrack, so Ed can talk to Lady Sue and find out who slipped her the goofball (which she says "was a gasser"). Ed will teach Wilbur "horse talk" so he can understand Lady Sue too. When Ed can't get through the track gate, Wilbur sneaks in to see Lady Sue with a walkie-talkie. Ed waits outside with his walkie-talkie and asks her questions. He then translates her answers for Wilbur. Sam Morgan, the gangster who drugged her, returns to the stable just as he's being implicated. Ed saves Wilbur by walking over to the policeman so he can hear the gangster on the walkie-talkie. McGivney gets his job back, and Ed gets a date with Lady Sue.

#74: "Working Wives"

ORIGINAL AIRDATE: February 14, 1963
WRITERS: Lou Derman, Bob O'Brien
DIRECTOR: Ira Stewart

Ed wants Wilbur to take him on a moonlight ride in the park so he can see Gigi, the French filly of his dreams. Carol wants her husband to take her to a movie. Ed hypnotizes Wilbur so he can't get out of his chair—hence, he can't go with Carol. When Wilbur realizes the dirty trick Ed played, he refuses to take his horse on the ride. Kay Addison wants a joint checking account with Roger, who refuses. The women go to the movies by themselves, and the next day, get jobs at a department store. Wilbur and Roger make a shambles of the kitchen and beg their wives to come home. Ed decides to run away so he won't interfere any longer, but Wilbur tells him to stay. Highlight: Carol feeds Ed carrots at the end of the show, and Ed winks to Wilbur.

#75: "Ed the Emancipator"
ORIGINAL AIRDATE: March 24, 1963
WRITERS: Lou Derman, Bob O'Brien
DIRECTOR: Arthur Lubin

Ed gets filled with the spirit of Abraham Lincoln, inspired by the book he's reading. The Posts give Kay a cockatoo named Claudia for her birthday, and Ed teaches her the Gettysburg Address. In the name of Abraham Lincoln, Ed frees Claudia, and she bites Roger on the nose. Roger goes down to Palm Springs until Wilbur gets rid of her. Ed takes his freedom theme one step further, freeing all the birds at Jackson's Bird Farm. He brings his feathered friends to Addison's house, and Roger thinks he's having a nervous breakdown when he sees them. Highlight: the bird scene in Roger's living room, including Wilbur denying there's a chicken on his head.

#76: "The Price of Apples"
ORIGINAL AIRDATE: March 7, 1963
WRITERS: Lou Derman, Bob O'Brien
DIRECTOR: Arthur Lubin
GUEST STAR: Richard Deacon

Ed's addicted to Roger Addison's apples. Wilbur takes Ed to an animal psychiatrist, but the doctor thinks Wilbur is an alcoholic. Wilbur tries peppering one of the apples to deter his horse, but Ed's watching through his telescope. "How naive," says Ed. Roger is the unlucky recipient of the peppered apple and installs barbed wire and alarms to keep Ed away from his apples. Wilbur gets caught planting a baby apple tree in Roger's yard, and the neighbors reconcile. Now that Ed's given up Addison's apples, he's switched to pears. *Inside joke*: Ed's eating the pears from Mr. *Simon's* tree. Of course, Al Simon is the show's executive producer.

#77: "Doctor Ed"
ORIGINAL AIRDATE: March 31, 1963
WRITERS: Lou Derman, Bob O'Brien
DIRECTOR: Arthur Lubin
GUEST STARS: Norman Leavitt, Jack LaLanne

Ed watches a lot of TV, especially hospital soap operas, in this show, which features a great "Ed Dream Sequence." The horse dreams he is the famed brain surgeon, Dr. Ed, who is performing surgery on Roger. The dream turns into a nightmare (Ed is losing the patient), and Ed admits to Wilbur that he knocked down Roger's TV antenna. Roger thinks it was the wind, and Ed and his owner wink to each other. Ed finishes the show by dancing to Jack LaLanne.

#78: "Ed the Zebra"
ORIGINAL AIRDATE: March 21, 1963
WRITERS: Lou Derman, Bob O'Brien
DIRECTOR: Arthur Lubin
GUEST STARS: Frank Wilcox, Lee Goodman, Mike Barton, Ben Weldon, James
    Logan

Roger blackmails Wilbur into posing Ed in a tuxedo for his photography contest. If Wilbur doesn't comply, Roger won't set him up with the Tyler deal. Ed wears the suit, and everyone stands there laughing at him. Ed won't talk to Wilbur. He runs away to the zoo and leans against a freshly painted fence to get zebra stripes. This is one of the two shows in which Ed talks to someone besides Wilbur. He tells a Cub Scout that horses are much smarter than zebras. Ed and Wilbur make up, and Tyler will consider hiring Wilbur.

#79: "Wilbur Post, Honorary Horse"
ORIGINAL AIRDATE: October 6, 1963
WRITERS: Lou Derman, Larry Rhine
DIRECTOR: Arthur Lubin
Note: This episode did not run until the following season.

Wilbur has been awarded the Addison Towers job. He announces to Carol and the Addisons that he's writing a book, *Our Friend the Horse*, for which he interviews Ed extensively on the life-style and habits of a horse. When Wilbur neglects his architecture in favor of his writing, Addison locks him in his study, where he must ring a bell for food. Ed shows up at the window and entices Wilbur to ask more horse questions. Carol, Kay and Roger catch Wilbur trotting around on all fours, learning how to use a "tail," and Roger fires Wilbur. That night, Wilbur dreams he's a horse. Carol wakes him and he rushes out to the barn to salvage Roger's plans.

#80: "Patter of Little Hooves"
ORIGINAL AIRDATE: October 20, 1963
WRITERS: Lou Derman, Larry Rhine
DIRECTOR: Arthur Lubin
GUEST STAR: Leo Fuchs
Note: This episode, the last one in which Larry Keating appeared, did not air until the following season.

Wilbur and Ed win twenty-first prize in a newspaper contest. It's a miniature horse named Pequito, a mischievous sort who eats Roger's prize roses. Roger phones Mr. Rasmussen, the inspector from the Bureau of Animal Regulations, to report Wilbur as having more than one horse. Fuchs is hilarious as Rasmussen, a man who's blind without his glasses, but too vain to wear them in front of other people. Ed and Wilbur pretend that Pequito is a dog, since Rasmussen can't see anything clearly. They call the little horse "Fido," and Ed provides the barking from the window. Addison calls off his complaint when Wilbur tells him that he'll find a nice home for Pequito. He gives Pequito to the Fergusons, a family with kids.

Fourth Season (Third Season, CBS)
September 1963–May 1964: Sundays 6:30 P.M.

#81: "Leo Durocher Meets Mister Ed"
ORIGINAL AIRDATE: September 29, 1963
WRITERS: Lou Derman, Michael Fessier
DIRECTOR: Arthur Lubin
GUEST STARS: Leo Durocher, Sandy Koufax, John Roseboro, Willie Davis, Bill "Moose" Skowron, Vin Scully as play-by-play announcer

Ed helps the Dodgers clinch the National League Pennant in 1963, by providing tips to manager Leo Durocher. He provides hooves-on expertise on location at Dodger Stadium. Wilbur reads Ed's lips and provides pseudo-geometric explanations for the advice. Highlight: Ed hits an inside-the-parker off Sandy Koufax's pitch and slides into home safely.

#82: "Ed Discovers America"
ORIGINAL AIRDATE: October 13, 1963
WRITERS: Lou Derman, Larry Rhine
DIRECTOR: Arthur Lubin
GUEST STARS: Sharon Tate, David Brandon, Ray Kellogg, Joseph Ruskin

The Columbus Day episode. Wilbur has been chosen to plan and construct the American History Museum. Ed appeals to Wilbur to erect a statue of a horse outside the museum. He takes Wilbur through a "history lesson," a fantasy sequence explaining how it was a horse that discovered America. Lots of schtick, including: "You talk, horse?"—"Nay, I talk human." Edna Skinner as vain Queen Isabella; Young as Columbus; Carol as mess boy Sam.

#83: "Taller Than She"
ORIGINAL AIRDATE: December 1, 1963
WRITERS: Lou Derman, Bill Davenport
DIRECTOR: Arthur Lubin
GUEST STAR: Henry Corden

Ed's in love with an English filly who's three inches taller than he ... and she only goes with taller guys. Ed begs Wilbur to take him to Ralph's Blacksmith Shop, to be fitted for elevator horseshoes. At first, Ralph protests: "I'm not an orthopedic blacksmith," but Wilbur instills him with a sense of noble calling. Ed gets Wilbur and Carol out of the house and "borrows" their new living room furniture, so he can create a swingin' bachelor pad out in the barn. He invites Penelope over, but while dancing up a storm, loses his five-decker shoes. The filly leaves in disgust. Highlights: Young and Corden at the blacksmith shop, and Ed's subtitled barn scene with Penelope.

#84: "Be Kind to Humans"
ORIGINAL AIRDATE: October 27, 1963
WRITERS: Lou Derman, Stanley Adams
DIRECTOR: Arthur Lubin
GUEST STARS: Barry Kelly, Stanley Adams

Ed and Wilbur meet three hobos in the park, and while Wilbur's not paying attention, Ed invites them—Stu, Toothpick and Stubby—to stay in his barn. Great timing—Carol's father is also paying a visit. The gents make themselves at home, smoking Mr. Higgins' cigars and hanging their rags on a clothesline. Carol's father discovers them and curses his son-in-law. Carol defends her hubby for feeding the underprivileged men. Highlight: Mr. Higgins reading aloud the hilarious "hobo's life" letter in Wilbur's typewriter, assuming it was composed by his "kook" son-in-law. Stanley Adams plays Stubby.

#85: "Don't Laugh At Horses"
ORIGINAL AIRDATE: November 3, 1963
WRITERS: Lou Derman, Larry Rhine
DIRECTOR: Ira Stewart
GUEST STARS: Jack Albertson, James Flavin, Joe Conley, Butch Patrick
CHOREOGRAPHY: Wally Green

Wilbur and Paul Fenton rent a horse suit for the masquerade ball given by Wilbur's club. Ed is offended by their mockery of horses and runs away from Wilbur on the bridle path. Wilbur locks Ed in the stall as punishment and goes to Tally-Ho Stables to rent a horse "with a sense of humor." Ed saws his way out and calls a lay-down strike among the neighborhood horses. Wilbur sends Ed to animal training school for his disobedience, but Ed outsmarts the instructor. Wilbur and Paul rehearse their horse dance routine for the local kids, and when Ed sees them laughing, he forgives Wilbur and calls off the strike. Butch Patrick became Eddie Munster the following year.

#86: "Getting Ed's Goat"
ORIGINAL AIRDATE: November 10, 1963
WRITERS: Lou Derman, Larry Rhine
DIRECTOR: Arthur Lubin
GUEST STARS: Jack Albertson, Robert Carson, Robert Foulk, Darby Hinton

It's Wilbur's birthday, and Carol, Kay and Paul Fenton are planning a cele-bration for him. When Wilbur enters the house, he's startled by their "Sur-prise!" and lands face-first in his cake. Ed's hiding a stray goat named Herbert in the barn. He temporarily wins his plea to keep Herbert, until Wilbur can find him a home. That night, Herbert devours the Benson Plans, Wilbur's current project. Ed has to redraw them but puts the fireplace on the ceiling. When Benson fires Wilbur, the furious architect takes Ed and Herbert to the animal shelter. Ed incites a riot among the inmates, and a little boy and his mother try to buy Ed. The bratty kid, who went on to play Israel Boone on *Daniel Boone*, kicks Wilbur when he says the horse is his. Ed and Wilbur make up and vow to find Herbert a good place to live.

#87: "Ed the Musician"
ORIGINAL AIRDATE: April 19, 1964
WRITERS: Lou Derman, Larry Rhine
DIRECTOR: Arthur Lubin
GUEST STARS: Richard Deacon, Jack Albertson

Carol is chairwoman of her club's entertainment committee, and she enlists the talents of Wilbur, Kay and Paul Fenton. Ed's having nightmares which reveal his deeply rooted insecurity. Wilbur goes to a psychiatrist, pretending Ed's dreams are his own, so he can learn how to deal with them. The doctor recommends that Wilbur take up a hobby, which Wilbur passes on to Ed. Ed becomes a one-horse band and actually feels better. When Ed wakes up Kay with the racket, Wilbur pretends he was the one playing. Edna Skinner and Jack Albertson perform a lovely ballad at the piano to change the mood from the usual.

#88: "Oh, Those Hats!"
ORIGINAL AIRDATE: November 17, 1963
WRITERS: Lou Derman, Bill Davenport
DIRECTOR: Arthur Lubin
GUEST STAR: Spring Byington

Wilbur's client, Miss Karen Dooley, is a Hollywood gossip columnist with a fetish for hats. Miss Dooley agrees to be the mistress of ceremonies for Carol's fashion show and have it televised from her home. Ed seizes this opportunity for media exposure to raise money for the kiddie zoo. He puts Miss Dooley's hats on the baby animals and parades them by her pool, carrying signs like "We need care" in front of the TV camera. Ed's plan works. The city decides to support the kiddie zoo.

#89: "Ed the Shish Kebab"
ORIGINAL AIRDATE: January 19, 1964
WRITERS: Lou Derman, Stanley Adams
DIRECTOR: Arthur Lubin
GUEST STARS: Harry Blackstone, Peter Leeds, Bill Baldwin, Beverly Wills, cameo by Lou Derman
Note: This episode was scheduled to run on November 24, 1963, but was preempted by CBS news coverage of the John F. Kennedy assassination, which occurred two days earlier.

Wilbur will spend three days in San Francisco for the Magicians' Convention. Carol wants to come along so she can visit her old college roommate. Ed wants to go too, so Wilbur decides to use him in his illusion, "Spears Through the Horse." Carol promises to spend only ten dollars a day, but goes overboard and hides the clothing boxes in the hotel room closet. Ed wants to shield himself from the spears, and lines the magic chamber with Carol's packages. During the act, lingerie bursts from the sides of the chamber on spear tips. When the door is opened, Ed's wearing a mink stole and carrying a handbag in his mouth. The act gets such a laugh, Wilbur is awarded a trophy. The Great Blackstone performs an illusion, assisted by writer Lou Derman.

#90: "Ed the Desert Rat"
ORIGINAL AIRDATE: February 16, 1964
WRITERS: Lou Derman, Bill Davenport
DIRECTOR: Ira Stewart
GUEST STARS: Chick Chandler, Logan Field, June Whitley
STORY BY: Lou Derman, Stanley Adams

Mimi and Jack Hilliard visit the Posts to brag about their new built-in swimming pool. The Posts decide to get a pool too; Ed decides to leave home so he can be around green grass. He scares off a sweet pool salesman, Mr. Callahan, by pretending the yard is inhabited by leprechauns. (Callahan should have been suspicious when Ed introduced himself as *Irving* Leprechaun.) It turns out the Hilliards are miserable with their pool—the neighbors use it constantly. Ed runs off to Death Valley. Wilbur helicopter-rescues his horse from vultures and coyotes, and Ed swears never to leave his cozy little stall again.

#91: "Home Sweet Trailer"
ORIGINAL AIRDATE: December 8, 1963
WRITERS: Lou Derman, Bill Davenport
DIRECTOR: Arthur Lubin
Note: This is the first episode with the Kirkwoods, the Posts' new neighbors.

The Kirkwoods stop by the Posts for a visit in their trailer. Wilbur offers his home to Gordon Kirkwood, his former commanding officer, and his wife, Winnie, while he and Carol will stay in the trailer. Carol's about to go home to Mother, but Gordon buys the house down the block in the nick of time. Highlights: Ed sticks out his front left hoof and trips Kirkwood and poses as a masked rider to bust the trailer's butane tank.

#92: "Love Thy New Neighbor"

ORIGINAL AIRDATE: December 15, 1963
WRITERS: Lou Derman, Bill Davenport
DIRECTOR: Arthur Lubin
GUEST STAR: Sharon Tate

Ever since Colonel Kirkwood moved next door, Wilbur's been spending less time with Ed, who's lonesome for a talking partner. He secretly buys a short-wave radio set and contacts Germany and Liverpool, under the code name "N-A-G." The radio set causes TV interference for Gordon, who thinks Wilbur lied about owning it. The colonel decides to move. Wilbur uses air force nostalgia to win back Gordon's friendship. Sharon Tate plays the attractive phone operator who hangs up on the gabby, talk-starved Ed.

#93: "Moko"

ORIGINAL AIRDATE: May 17, 1964
WRITERS: Norman Paul, William Burns
DIRECTOR: Arthur Lubin
GUEST STARS: Moko the Mischievous Martian, Joan Tabor, Robert Barratt
ANIMATION: Spungbuggy Works

This episode was a pilot for a spin-off series which would combine live action and animation with an outer-space theme. A young Martian named Moko (animated) travels down to Earth to make mischief among the humans. He flies into the heads of stuffy men and makes them swingers. He crashes Colonel Kirkwood's party, which is also attended by the stiffest of them all, General Lucius Bromley. Even the general dances with Wilbur's sexy client, Gloria Laverne, when he comes under the influence of Moko. We see Moko travel back and forth between Earth and Mars, where he is lectured by his elder Tatti, voice by Richard Deacon.

#94: "Ed in the Peace Corps"

ORIGINAL AIRDATE: February 2, 1964
WRITERS: Lou Derman, Larry Rhine
DIRECTOR: Arthur Lubin
GUEST STAR: Miyoshi Umeki

Wilbur decides to hire a secretary, much to Ed's jealous dismay. Ako Tenaka, the exchange student, arrives at the Posts', and turns out to be "the perfect secretary, perfect gardener, perfect cook, perfect everything"—much to Carol and Winnie's dismay. Carol prepares a Japanese feast to compete with Ako, but fails miserably. Ako's too busy with school and has to quit; peace is restored. The running gag through the show: Ed keeps trying to join the Peace Corps, where he'll be appreciated.

#95: "Ed Gets the Mumps"
ORIGINAL AIRDATE: January 5, 1964
WRITERS: Lou Derman, Larry Rhine
DIRECTOR: Arthur Lubin

Ed is jealous of the baby that Wilbur and Carol are looking after, so he concocts a case of mumps (by tying sacks of apples to his cheeks), to win Wilbur's sympathy. The baby turns out to be a real howler (complete with obnoxious sound track) and is only soothed by seeing Gordon Kirkwood's "magic mustache." When Ed's medical fraud is found out, he decides to run away. But stopping to rock Madeline's baby carriage brings out the softie in him.

#96: "Ed's Christmas Story"
ORIGINAL AIRDATE: December 22, 1963
WRITERS: Lou Derman, Bill Davenport
DIRECTOR: Arthur Lubin
GUEST STARS: Gage Clark, Al Roberts

The only Christmas episode produced, it features a great Ed fantasy sequence in which he tells Wilbur the real story of Christmas—how a horse was responsible for teaching Santa's reindeer to fly, etc. Carol and Winnie are angry at Wilbur and Gordon because they have imposed a fifteen-dollar limit on presents, and Ed's mad at his owner because he won't buy gifts for his friends at Tally-Ho Stables. Wilbur gets filled with the Christmas spirit, and Ed dresses up as Santa at the end of the show, ho-ho-hoing to the camera!

#97: "Ed's Dentist"
ORIGINAL AIRDATE: January 12, 1964
WRITERS: Lou Derman, Bill Davenport
DIRECTOR: Arthur Lubin
GUEST STARS: Irwin Charone, George Neise, Tom B. Henry

Ed complains of a toothache, but when Wilbur calls for a vet, Ed hides up on the barn roof. Gordon Kirkwood sees the twosome up on the roof and calls his psychiatrist friend from the military to help poor Wilbur. Both Winnie Kirkwood and the shrink think that it's really Gordon who's in need of a workup, and the colonel sets out to prove them wrong. Wilbur agrees to take Ed to the dentist. Gordon follows them there, but his booby trap backfires. Ed's tooth turns out to be fine.

#98: "Ed Visits a Gypsy"

ORIGINAL AIRDATE: March 1, 1964
WRITERS: Lou Derman, Larry Rhine
DIRECTOR: Arthur Lubin
GUEST STARS: Belle Mitchell, Joe Vitale

Carol and Winnie have their palms read by a local gypsy; Winnie's told that Gordon treats her like a doormat, and she stages a five-minute war of assertiveness. Ed wants Wilbur to take him to the same gypsy so he can have his hoof read, to see if his girlfriend Princess will make a suitable wife. Though unwilling at first, the less-than-busy gypsy agrees to the task; she tells the horse that Princess will treat him like a doormat (sound familiar?) if they marry. Ed dresses up like Arafat in the last scene, pretending to tell Wilbur's fortune.

#99: "Ed the Chauffeur"

ORIGINAL AIRDATE: April 12, 1964
WRITERS: Lou Derman, Larry Rhine
DIRECTOR: Arthur Lubin

Gordon buys a new sports car and refuses to let Winnie drive it. When she threatens to go home to Mother, he gives her the car keys. Her maiden voyage coincides with Ed's raucous test drive in a milk truck: "Look, Ma, no hands!" Ed took up driving because his feet were too sore to go horseback riding. Winnie totals Gordon's new baby, swearing she saw "a horse driving a car." Ed finally figures out how to sleep standing up.

#100: "Ol Swayback"

ORIGINAL AIRDATE: March 8, 1964
WRITERS: Lou Derman, Bill Davenport
DIRECTOR: Arthur Lubin

Ed takes in a swayback horse named Sam who ran away from the carnival, to help him get over his inferiority complex. Wilbur inflates Sam's back in order to ride him, but the horse experiences "a blowout." Ed starts up Gordon's model airplane, creating chaos in the Kirkwood's living room. Sam returns to the carnival: it's a lot safer there than at the Posts'.

#101: "Ed the Donkey"
ORIGINAL AIRDATE: February 23, 1964
WRITERS: Lou Derman, Bill Davenport
DIRECTOR: Arthur Lubin
GUEST STARS: George Petrie, Jay Ose, Jeanne Rainier

Ed's concerned that he might really be descended from the donkey family. "I'm just a four-legged whatchamacallit." Wilbur takes him to a mule farm, but to Ed's dismay and relief, the mules can't understand what he's saying. A visit to his mother at the end of the show confirms that he's all horse. Highlight: Final scene—Wilbur starts to sing, "A horse is a horse . . ." Ed joins in with, "A horse is a horse . . ." as we fade to credits.

#102: "Mae West Meets Mister Ed"
ORIGINAL AIRDATE: March 22, 1964
WRITERS: Lou Derman, Bill Davenport
DIRECTOR: Arthur Lubin
GUEST STARS: Mae West, Nick Stewart, Jacque Shelton, Roger Torrey

Wilbur's new client, the aged yet still glamorous Mae West, asks him to design a luxury stable for her beloved horses. Ed overhears plans for a "rollaway feedbox" and is consumed with jealousy. He pretends to be an abandoned baby on Miss West's doorstep and gets taken into the fold. But bubble baths, perfuming and mane-curling don't agree with this macho horse, and he returns home to Wilbur, promising never to complain again. Ed's two personal grooms at Miss West's house are very similar in style to the grooms in Oz who freshen up the Scarecrow's stuffing.

#103: "Saddles and Gowns"
ORIGINAL AIRDATE: May 3, 1964
WRITERS: Lou Derman, Larry Rhine
DIRECTOR: Arthur Lubin

Carol wants a new gown and Ed wants a new saddle. Ed secretly charges a saddle on Wilbur's credit card. When Carol finds the receipt, devilishly planted by Ed's alter ego, she runs out and buys a gown. Ed feels guilty and returns the saddle, but not before sawing it in half while getting it out of the locked feedbox. One of the two appearances by Ed's devil counterpart in the series.

#104: "The Prowler"

ORIGINAL AIRDATE: April 26, 1964
WRITERS: Lou Derman, Bill Davenport
DIRECTOR: Arthur Lubin
GUEST STAR: Hugh Sanders

A prowler steals Winnie's mink stole and hamburger meat. Wilbur tries to solve the crime, but ends up implicating himself. Ed concocts a surefire booby trap in his stall but captures Wilbur, Gordon and Sergeant Myers instead. Wilbur dresses up as Winnie to fool the prowler, but Winnie thinks he's a home wrecker. The "prowler" turns out to be a dog and her new pups who are harboring in Ed's stall. Query: Why is Ed scared of the prowler too, if he knows that the dog he's hiding stole Winnie's mink and meat?

#105: "Ed the Pool Player"

ORIGINAL AIRDATE: October 11, 1964
WRITERS: Lou Derman, Larry Rhine
DIRECTOR: Arthur Lubin
GUEST STARS: Thomas Gomez, Olan Soule
Note: This episode did not run until the following season.

Winnie Kirkwood wants her interfering husband out of the kitchen, so Wilbur takes Gordon to play pool at the Lawndale Men's Club. Gordon gets hustled for $430 by a Mr. Vernon a.k.a. Chicago Chubby. Ed is determined to win back Gordon's money, so Wilbur rents a pool table for the barn and invites Chubby to a match. Ed wins back all the money, of course, and Chubby swears off pool.

#106: "Ed Writes Dear Abby"

ORIGINAL AIRDATE: October 18, 1964
WRITERS: Lou Derman, Larry Rhine
DIRECTOR: Arthur Lubin
GUEST STARS: Abigail Van Buren, Peter Brooks, Nick Stewart, Horace Brown
Note: This episode did not run until the following season.

Ed wants his own swingin' bachelor pad and writes to "Dear Abby" for advice. He signs Wilbur's name to the note, but forgets to stamp it. Carol opens the returned letter and thinks Wilbur's secretly unhappy. She lays on the romance thick, but Wilbur's too busy thinkin' Ed. He visits Dear Abby, who "advises" him to let Ed move out (she thinks it's one big practical joke). Ed decides he needs "a couple of years" before he makes such a drastic move. Great flashback bit with Wilbur recounting Ed's virtues.

Fifth Season (Fourth Season, CBS) October 1964: Sundays 6:30 P.M.; November 1964: preempted (sports); December 1964– May 1965: Wednesdays 7:30 P.M.

#107: "Hi-Fi Horse"
ORIGINAL AIRDATE: October 4, 1964
WRITERS: Lou Derman, Larry Rhine
DIRECTOR: Arthur Lubin
GUEST STAR: Norman Leavitt

For their anniversary, Wilbur buys Carol the hi-fi set he's been doting on. She's furious. Wilbur sets up a speaker in Ed's stall, and frightens the horse with his "Sounds of Life" sound effects record. Carol leaves for Mother, but changes her mind and comes back. In the middle of the night, Ed feels like a little music, so he turns on the hi-fi set (bomber-plane sound effects).Wilbur has to pay a repairman twenty dollars to turn the blasted thing off.

#108: "Tunnel to Freedom"
ORIGINAL AIRDATE: October 25, 1964
WRITERS: Lou Derman, Larry Rhine
DIRECTOR: Arthur Lubin

Wilbur locks Ed in his stall for stealing Carol's pie and brownies from the windowsill. Ed digs a "tunnel to freedom" from the barn that leads all the way to the Posts' living room. Wilbur falls into the hole, causing it to cave in. He crawls out, but Ed's stuck down below—that is, until a bumblebee gets caught in Ed's tail and catapults him to the surface. Highlight: shovel heaving dirt onto the barn floor; we're supposed to imagine it's Ed digging.

#109: "John Provost Meets Mister Ed"
ORIGINAL AIRDATE: June 9, 1965
WRITERS: Lou Derman, Larry Rhine
DIRECTOR: Arthur Lubin
GUEST STAR: Johnny Provost

Johnny, the star pitcher for the Hawks, Wilbur's Little League team, breaks Gordon Kirkwood's window while delivering papers. To pay off the damage, Gordon makes Johnny do chores around his house on Sunday, the day of the big game. Wilbur appeals to the Colonel's soft side so Johnny can pitch in the game. Highlight: Opening shot—Ed dressed as a catcher, with giant chest protector. Wilbur pitching. Ed catches the first ball with the glove in his mouth. He catches the second one with the glove in his *tail*! Great trick photography!

#110: "Like Father, Like Horse"
ORIGINAL AIRDATE: February 10, 1965
WRITERS: Lou Derman, Larry Rhine
DIRECTOR: Arthur Lubin
GUEST STAR: George Barrows

Ed reads a newspaper article about animals taking after their owners and tries to emulate Wilbur. Gordon is thinking up inane slogans for Crawford's Bird Seed so he can win a trip to Hawaii. As a practical joke, Ed pretends to be the president of the bird seed company and tells Gordon that he won the grand prize. Wilbur finds out what Ed did and tells Gordon it was a hoax. But Gordon really wins, and when the real Mr. Crawford arrives with the tickets to Hawaii, Gordon kicks him in the pants. In episode 115, the Kirkwoods actually take their trip to Hawaii, accompanied by the Posts.

#111: "Ed the Race Horse"
ORIGINAL AIRDATE: January 27, 1965
WRITERS: Lou Derman, Larry Rhine
DIRECTOR: Arthur Lubin
GUEST STAR: Irwin Charone

Gordon rents a horse named Cyclone and challenges Wilbur and Ed to a series of races along the bridle path. Only trouble is, Gordon's cheating, taking a shortcut and beating Wilbur. Carol isn't too happy—the men keep betting each other home-cooked meals by their wives. Wilbur buys Ed sneakers and argyle socks at Dalzell's Shoe Shop. This show features one of Ed's great "fitness campaign" sequences, complete with reducing belt and steam box. Gordon is discovered and has to buy a fine meal for the Posts. *Inside Joke*: Arch Dalzell is the name of *Mister Ed*'s director of photography.

#112: "My Horse, the Ranger"

ORIGINAL AIRDATE: June 16, 1965
WRITERS: Lou Derman, Larry Rhine
DIRECTOR: Arthur Lubin
GUEST STARS: Flip Mark, George Neise, Keith Taylor, Robert Nunn

Carol takes the Girl Rangers on a hike, and when Jay Walsh, the Boys' Troop leader, sprains his ankle, he asks Wilbur to take the inner-city boys on their outing too. Ed wants to go along, and his spunky devil alter ego purposely fouls Wilbur up by putting a magnet near his compass. Ed continues his mischief and steals the boys' uniforms. They put on the girl rangers' outfits, and we get a very funny dialogue between extremely street-smart kids and perplexed Wilbur. When they get home, Wilbur makes Ed write "I am a bad horse" on the blackboard. Ed tells Wilbur his devil made him do it, and when Wilbur says there's no such thing as the devil, his devil alter ego appears to close the show.

#113: "The Heavy Rider"

ORIGINAL AIRDATE: December 30, 1964
WRITERS: Lou Derman, Larry Rhine
DIRECTOR: Arthur Lubin
GUEST STAR: Mike Wagner

Poor Ed! He must carry Wilbur's new client, Herbert Banning, a 300-pounder, through this episode. That's more than Carol and Wilbur's weight combined, we're told. Ed complains, "If you put the two of us on a see-saw, my feet [he means *hooves*] would never touch the ground." Ed calls the Humane Society to report a suffering horse, then disguises himself as the SPCA and calls Banning, who's out on the patio. Highlight: To avoid Banning further, Ed plops himself in the wet patio mortar, dubbed "Operation Cement." But when Banning says he must have put on twenty pounds from Carol's dinner last night, Ed rips his way out of the foundation! Banning has to rent another horse, and Wilbur doesn't get the $10-million deal.

#114: "Ed the Pilot"

ORIGINAL AIRDATE: January 6, 1965
WRITERS: Lou Derman, Larry Rhine
DIRECTOR: Arthur Lubin
GUEST STARS: Robert Patten, Gene Tyburn, Harold Gould

Gordon wants Wilbur to chip in on a surplus government plane. But Wilbur fails the required psychiatric exam when Ed tags along to cheer him up, wearing silly hats and making him laugh uncontrollably. This scene in the psychiatrist's office is among the funniest in the series. Ed goes to the 146th Air Transport Wing and commandeers an obsolete plane. Wilbur arrives at the airport, runs up to the control tower and navigates Ed down to a safe parachute landing. Only problem is, Ed lands on his tail!

#115: "Ed the Stowaway"
ORIGINAL AIRDATE: February 17, 1965
WRITERS: Lou Derman, Larry Rhine
DIRECTOR: Arthur Lubin
GUEST STARS: Jack Bailey, Tiki Santos

Ed sneaks aboard the ship with the Posts, who decide to join the Kirkwoods on a trip to Hawaii. Carol demands that Wilbur ship Ed home. Ed decides to make his home on the islands and marry the filly Leilani, who's owned by Sam Manaloa, hotel proprietor. Wilbur dresses up as a hula girl to steal Ed back from Manaloa. His dance is hilarious, including the Charleston. Highlight: but of course . . . Ed surfing!

#116: "Animal Jury"
ORIGINAL AIRDATE: January 13, 1965
WRITERS: Lou Derman, Larry Rhine
DIRECTOR: Arthur Lubin
GUEST STARS: Eleanor Audley, Byron Foulder

Once again, Wilbur's Aunt Martha leaves her parrot, Tootsie, with the Posts while she goes on a trip to the Orient. The parrot is hooked on medical soap operas. Ed abandons Tootsie at Glorby's Pet Shop, and Wilbur identifies her by turning on a medical TV show in the shop. When the parrot says, "Take out the gall bladder," he knows he's found Tootsie. Ed feels guilty and dreams he's being convicted by an animal jury. Wilbur is great as the district attorney in Ed's dream.

#117: "What Kind of Foal Am I?"
ORIGINAL AIRDATE: January 20, 1965
WRITERS: Lou Derman, Larry Rhine
DIRECTOR: Arthur Lubin
GUEST STARS: Barry Kelly, Hugh Sanders

Ed hires a detective to search for his long-lost father. They find him at the carnival by identifying his tattoo—a "Ship Ahoy" anchor on the left flank.

Wilbur buys him and gives him to Ed's mother so his parents can be together. Highlight: Wilbur and Ed singing "Oh, my papa, to me he was so wonderful," in harmony.

#118: "Ed's Juice Stand"
ORIGINAL AIRDATE: February 3, 1965
WRITERS: Lou Derman, Larry Rhine
DIRECTOR: Arthur Lubin
GUEST STARS: Neil Hamilton, Ben Weldon, Richard Reeves

Parallel plots in this episode: Both Gordon Kirkwood and Mister Ed are preoccupied with growing old. Ed decides to provide for his old age by going into the beverage business. He orders a barnful of carrots and apples, and creates Wilburini. Mr. Rogart thinks the drink is sensational but pulls out of a business deal with Wilbur once he learns the juice is strained through day-old hay. This show features that great bit at the Livestock Shipping Yard with Charlie and Joe, also seen in episode 52.

#119: "The Dragon Horse"
ORIGINAL AIRDATE: March 31, 1965
WRITERS: Lou Derman, Larry Rhine
DIRECTOR: Ira Stewart

Ed has to share his stall with a carousel horse until Sunday when the girls will auction it off. Ed calls it a "fink jinx" and sets out to destroy the bad-luck charm. Wilbur catches Ed with a saw in his mouth. The horse sleeps on Wilbur's living room floor that night. He brings the dragon into the house the next day, but Carol insists it go back in the barn. Ed drags it to the lake and dumps it below. He becomes the first "frog-horse" and scubas to retrieve it. Once he sees the dragon looking so wet and scared, he's no longer afraid.

#120: "Never Ride Horses"
ORIGINAL AIRDATE: February 24, 1965
WRITERS: Lou Derman, Larry Rhine
DIRECTOR: Arthur Lubin
GUEST STARS: Barry Kelly, Joe Conley

Ed and Wilbur go to the children's playground, but Ed's frustrated—he can't go on the swings or the seesaw. He tells Wilbur that people shouldn't ride horses. Carol's father is spending a week with the Posts, and of course Wilbur arrives home late after his disagreement with Ed. Ed wages an all-out fight against horseback riding, starting up the SPHR (Society for the Prevention of Horseback Riding). He hires a skywriter and operates a shortwave radio under the name "Radio Free Horse." He prints anti-horseback-riding pamphlets, pickets the house with his friends and catches the attention of the *Valley Gazette*. Ed brings home a cow wearing a saddle and tells Wilbur to try her out. Wilbur decides to ride her and make Ed jealous.

#121: "Ed the Sentry"

ORIGINAL AIRDATE: March 3, 1965
WRITERS: Lou Derman, Larry Rhine
DIRECTOR: Arthur Lubin
GUEST STARS: Nick Stewart, Peter Hobbs, Bill Edelson, Robert J. Stevenson

Ed finds a straw hat in the park while playing hide-and-seek with Wilbur, and wears it home. Carol is allergic to the hat, but they all think Ed is the cause of her sneezing. The air force has asked Gordon out of retirement to help them test animals for jungle sentry duty. He brings a mischievous chimp home who makes a monkey out of Ed, but the horse gets even. Since Carol's allergic to him, Ed will become a sentry. He shows up for intelligence testing at the air force base and outwits his two testers. Wilbur arrives to take him home. He tells Ed that Carol was allergic to the hat, not to him, and they pretend to the doctors that Ed's allergic to plants—no good for jungle work.

#122: "Ed's Diction Teacher"

ORIGINAL AIRDATE: March 10, 1965
WRITERS: Lou Derman, Larry Rhine
DIRECTOR: Arthur Lubin
GUEST STARS: George Ives, Don Brodie

Ed thinks he overhears a plot by Gordon Kirkwood to have him stuffed (it's actually a comment about a little stuffed horse Winnie got at the carnival). Ed is so scared, his speech gets all screwed up. He calls his owner "Wilrub." Professor Pettigrew arrives to cure Ed of his speech condition. Ed stands behind a screen so the professor can't see it's a horse talking. Ed overcomes his speech problem when Gordon shows him the toy horse, now fixed. *Inside joke*: Pettigrew asks Ed to say, "How Now Brown Cow," one of the very first things that Ed says to Wilbur in the premiere episode.

#123: "Ed the Godfather"
ORIGINAL AIRDATE: March 17, 1965
WRITERS: Lou Derman, Larry Rhine
DIRECTOR: Arthur Lubin
GUEST STAR: Frank Wilcox

Ed's friend Gina, an Italian filly who belongs to Bill Johnson, is expecting. Ed will be the godfather. He tells Wilbur that Gina wants her baby delivered by Dr. Chadkin, the obstetrician who delivered the Johnson children. Wilbur goes to Dr. Chadkin's office to try to convince him to deliver a horse, but the doctor thinks he's crazy. Wilbur even goes into town to get pizzas for Gina late at night. Ed calls Chadkin when Gina goes into labor, and the doctor delivers the colt.

#124: "Ed's Contact Lenses"
ORIGINAL AIRDATE: March 24, 1965
WRITERS: Lou Derman, Larry Rhine
DIRECTOR: Arthur Lubin
GUEST STARS: Benny Rubin, Howard Wendell, Roy Stuart

A park attendant laughs when he sees Ed wearing glasses. Ed stomps on his specs in disgust and tells Wilbur he wants contacts. He bumps into things to convince Wilbur and Carol that he's nearsighted. Wilbur indulges him and takes Ed for an eye exam. The young optometrist, Herbert Fosdick, has been given the helm while his father's on lunch break. When Fosdick Sr. returns and sees his son examining a horse, he blows his stack. Ed gets over his contact lens obsession—in "horse size" they would cost a fortune.

#125: "Ed's Cold Tail"
ORIGINAL AIRDATE: April 7, 1965
WRITERS: Lou Derman, Larry Rhine
DIRECTOR: Arthur Lubin

Carol wants a new refrigerator, and Ed wants a heating system for his stall. Wilbur scientifically demonstrates how to fit all their food into the tiny fridge, and innocent Winnie Kirkwood has to rip out the temperature control to get Carol on her way to a new model. The Posts keep their food at the Kirkwoods, and we get a great scene of Winnie, Gordon and Wilbur fussing over whose food is whose. Ed sticks his tail in dry ice and shows Wilbur his tail is "frozen stiff." This is a great special effect—Ed's tail looks like a clothesline. Carol bets Wilbur a new refrigerator that Ed's tail isn't frozen. When she goes out to the barn, Ed has already defrosted his tail, and Carol gets her fridge. Ed pretends to be sick and have laryngitis to make his point about the heating system. Wilbur goes to the Kirkwoods to get his milk for the "sick" Ed, and Gordon thinks he's a burglar.

#126: "The Bank Robbery"
ORIGINAL AIRDATE: April 14, 1965
WRITERS: Lou Derman, Larry Rhine
DIRECTOR: Arthur Lubin
GUEST STARS: Marc Lawrence, Harry Swoger, Lizbeth Field

Wilbur buys Ed a camera and tripod to celebrate their fifth anniversary. We see a flashback to "The First Meeting," the very first episode. Wilbur rides Ed into town to the bank. We get a funny scene with the tellers closing their lines and an impatient bank robber waiting to be served so he can hold someone up. The robber stashes the loot in Ed's saddle and takes down Wilbur's address, nicely printed on a plaque in the leather (only time in the series we see this). Ed photographs "Spike" when he comes to the barn to retrieve the money. Spike holds a gun to Wilbur to get the photo. Ed rigs a rope around Spike's feet and pulls him into the feedbox.

#127: "My Horse, the Mailman"
ORIGINAL AIRDATE: April 28, 1965
WRITERS: Lou Derman, Larry Rhine
DIRECTOR: Arthur Lubin
GUEST STARS: Nick Stewart, Mickey Simpson, Richard Collier

Ed decides to deliver the U.S. mail, in the proud tradition of the Pony Express. First, he takes a letter from Gordon's living room. Next, he swipes the postman's mail bag. Finally, he yanks the mailbox off its pole and takes it home. Highlights: Ed wearing a dunce cap and Wilbur walking a straight line for the police officer.

#128: "Whiskers and Tails"
ORIGINAL AIRDATE: May 5, 1965
WRITERS: Larry Rhine, Lou Derman
DIRECTOR: Arthur Lubin
GUEST STARS: Sebastian Cabot, Hazel Shermet, Meg Wyllie

The Posts' new neighbor, a chubby bearded archaeology professor, makes Ed nervous. Ed believes that all fat men with beards are horse-haters. Carol tries to fix up the arrogant Professor Thorndike with her single girlfriend, and the effort is a disastrous flop. Wilbur dresses up like "Thorny" to rid Ed of his phobia. Highlight: Ed literally rolling on the floor with laughter, at the end of the episode.

#129: "Robin Hood Ed"
ORIGINAL AIRDATE: May 12, 1965
WRITERS: Lou Derman, Larry Rhine
DIRECTOR: Arthur Lubin
GUEST STAR: Karl Lukas

Wilbur wants to audition for the part of Robin Hood in Mr. Ransohoff's new Sherwood Forest flick. Ed decides to become a Robin Hood in his own right. He steals living room furniture from the Kirkwoods and gives it to the Posts. Ed helps Wilbur do a screen test in the park. Highlights: Ed's show biz lingo as a Hollywood director, and the police officer's humoring of "crazy" Wilbur: "Let's go, Robin, we musn't keep the King waiting." End: Wilbur must report to the city psychiatrist once a month; Tony Curtis gets the movie role! *Inside joke*: Marty *Ransohoff* was the CEO of Filmways TV Productions.

#130: "Ed the Artist"
ORIGINAL AIRDATE: May 19, 1965
WRITERS: Lou Derman, Larry Rhine
DIRECTOR: Arthur Lubin
GUEST STARS: John Banner, Henry Corden

Ed wants to be remembered after he's gone, so he sets out to become the first "Palomino Picasso." He paints an unflattering "Protrait of Carol," which Carol finds and assumes her husband did. She makes Wilbur sleep out in the "barnsy warnsy," and only resumes dialogue with him once Professor Myerhoff critiques the painting as having everything *wrong* with it. Best line: Ed declares, "In the sea of life, I'm just a piece of driftwood with four legs and a tail." Highlight: Wilbur's conversation with Schindler, an abstract painter. Notes: (1) *Lost in Space* replaced *Mister Ed* during this time slot the following season. (2) This was the last episode featuring the Kirkwoods. The remaining shows (1965–66) featured only Ed, Carol, Wilbur and Carol's father, Mr. Higgins, and aired on Sundays from 5 to 5:30 P.M.

Sixth Season (Fifth Season, CBS)
September 1965–September 1966: Sundays
5 P.M.

#131: "Ed the Counterspy"
ORIGINAL AIRDATE: September 12, 1965
WRITERS: Lou Derman, Larry Rhine
DIRECTOR: Arthur Lubin
GUEST STARS: Barry Kelly, Jacqueline Beer, Mike Mazurki

The first of the spy genre episodes. Ed discovers spies at the bridle path and uses James Bond sex appeal to lure details of their scheme out of the spy's filly, Fatima. In their attempts to return the stolen microfilm to the U.S. government, Wilbur and Ed are captured and taken to a deserted beach house. They use "horse code" to contact the Coast Guard, who rescues them and captures the spies.

#132: "Ed-a-Go-Go"
ORIGINAL AIRDATE: September 19, 1965
WRITERS: Lou Derman, Larry Rhine
DIRECTOR: Arthur Lubin
GUEST STARS: Johnny Crawford, Frank Wilcox
CHOREOGRAPHY: Wally Green

"Mister Ed Meets the Beatles . . ." Jeff Kerrigan, the teenage boy next door, keeps Carol and Wilbur up with his loud rock-and-roll music. No problem for Ed, who's out cavorting all night anyhow. Ed becomes a swinger just like Jeff and invites two hep-horses over to his pad to dance, play guitar and wear wigs like the Beatles! Wilbur tutors Jeff on algebra the rock-and-roll way, with bongos and dancing. Jeff gets an A and Wilbur gets to design Mr. Kerrigan's new apartment buildings. Dances featured: the Froog, the Monkey, the Swim, the Mule.

#133: "Ed Sniffs out a Cold Clue"
ORIGINAL AIRDATE: September 26, 1965
WRITERS: Lou Derman, Larry Rhine
DIRECTOR: Arthur Lubin
GUEST STARS: Nobu McCarthy, Oscar Beregi, Henry Brandon, James Flavin, Victor Sen Yung, Logan Field

The second of the spy genre episodes. While Wilbur and Ed are watching the news, they learn that the new army shortwave radio has been stolen. Ed dubs himself "Oat-Oat-Seven" and offers to crack the case for a bale of hay and fifty bunches of carrots. Ed sniffs a black glove left at the scene of the crime and picks up the scent of duck chow mein. There's only one restaurant in town, the Flaming Dragon, that serves this dish. Wilbur impersonates a Chinese waiter so he can discover who in the restaurant is wearing gloves. They find the shortwave radio hidden in the stockroom and barely escape the clutches of Kosh (a.k.a. Coldfinger) and Derek. Great sound effects of Ed galloping away from the scene of the crime.

#134: "Spies Strike Back"
ORIGINAL AIRDATE: October 3, 1965
WRITERS: Lou Derman, Larry Rhine
DIRECTOR: Arthur Lubin
GUEST STARS: Nobu McCarthy, Oscar Beregi, Henry Brandon

The third of the spy genre episodes. Kosh and Derek have checked out Wilbur Post, and find he's just an architect, not an SIA agent. Brachman is flying in to buy the top-secret rocket fuel formula (Space Race overtones). Wilbur goes to the Flaming Dragon disguised as an Englishman, but is immediately recognized. Ed eavesdrops on a plot to kill Wilbur and warns him. They escape just in time. That evening, they return to the restaurant to find Brachman. He is taking notes being transmitted to him via Mei Ling's elaborate hip dance. The SIA translates the message as: "No deal tonight. Jerk at window is Wilbur Post." Kosh kidnaps Ed and leaves a note for Wilbur to meet them at 2 A.M. They throw knives at the architect to make him talk, and Ed saves the day by making Wilbur out to be a sorcerer. "Wilbur" makes it rain with a hose, and Derek surrenders, spooked by his powers.

#135: "Love and the Single Horse"

ORIGINAL AIRDATE: October 10, 1965
WRITERS: Lou Derman, Larry Rhine
DIRECTOR: Arthur Lubin
GUEST STARS: Irene Ryan, Raymond Bailey

This episode serves as a nice cross-promotion for *The Beverly Hillbillies*, featuring two of its stars. Ed's at work on his memoirs, *Love and the Single Horse*. Wilbur sneaks a peek and begs Ed to let him finish reading the manuscript inside the house. Carol finds it and thinks Wilbur is the author. The next morning, she rushes off to a publisher to have it printed. With the advance, Wilbur buys Carol the diamond ring she wanted, and nice gifts for Ed. Ed refuses the trinkets and runs off to the Hollywood Wax Museum to make a point about Wilbur's lack of respect for his privacy. Wilbur poses as a wax Indian to get Ed back. Highlight: the scene in the museum with Irene "Granny" Ryan.

#136: "Anybody Got a Zebra?"

ORIGINAL AIRDATE: October 17, 1965
WRITERS: Lou Derman, Larry Rhine
DIRECTOR: Arthur Lubin
GUEST STARS: Percy Helton, James Flavin, Victor French, Sandra Gould

The SIA calls on Wilbur to help them discover who's stealing classified information from their files. Wilbur will only assist on the condition that Ed be allowed to snoop around for clues. He smells "pennies and fur," and concludes the culprit is an organ-grinder monkey. Wilbur poses as an organ grinder and swaps monkeys with Jocko, the spy, when he's not looking. They take the spy monk to the zoo and set up a fascinating translation system: from Wilbur to Ed to zebra (who translates from horse into Swahili) to monkey, and back the other way. They learn that the monkey has been climbing through the window and taking information from the files. Percy Helton is great as the bewildered zookeeper who falls for Wilbur's story about the zebra having "zebritis," a condition when the stripes run together.

#137: "TV or Not TV"

ORIGINAL AIRDATE: October 24, 1965
WRITERS: Lou Derman, Larry Rhine
DIRECTOR: Alan Young
GUEST STARS: Barry Kelly, George Neise, Joe Conley

Ed wins the jackpot prize, a color TV set, from "Strain the Brain," a radio phone-in contest hosted by Happy Hannegan. The TV gets delivered to Wilbur Post, who won the contest "under an assumed brain." Since Wilbur's "so smart," Carol's father challenges him to a chess game. If Wilbur wins, Mr. Higgins will give the kids a second honeymoon and *matching luggage* (wow). The architect expects Ed to stand outside the window and dictate his chess moves, but the horse is peeved—he wants the new TV set inside his stall, since he won it. Wilbur loses the match and Ed sneaks the TV set into his stall late at night. Wilbur catches him while watching an Italian movie and eating pizza. So do Carol and her father, who think Wilbur brought the set out there. Ed tells Wilbur he can take the TV back, for two reasons: (1) because he loves him, and (2) he found out he's color-blind. Note: This is the episode where Ed's stand-in double, Punkin, was actually used. It's in the opening shot of a horse from the back, sitting up and talking to Wilbur, who's in a hammock.

#138: "The Horse and the Pussycat"

ORIGINAL AIRDATE: October 31, 1965
WRITERS: Lou Derman, Larry Rhine
DIRECTORS: Ira Stewart, Alan Young
GUEST STARS: Hazel Shermet, Rolfe Sedan, Henry Corden

Carol's friend Selma Peterson leaves her Siamese cat, Felicia, with the Posts during her trip to Hawaii. Ed is jealous of the feline and tries various ways to get rid of it, including painting a skunk stripe down its back. Ed competes with the cat and jumps into Wilbur's lap, causing the architect to fall and wind up in the hospital. When Ed comes to visit, the doctor tries to transfer Wilbur to the psycho ward for basket-weaving class. Highlight: Ed sitting on the living room floor playing with dangling yarn, pretending to be a cat. He even meows.

#139: "Ed the Bridegroom"

ORIGINAL AIRDATE: December 26, 1965
WRITERS: Lou Derman, Larry Rhine
DIRECTOR: Alan Young
GUEST STARS: John Qualen, Les Tremayne, Barry Kelly

Ed asks Wilbur to serenade him as he asks for Rosita's hoof in marriage. The filly says yes, but the Justice of the Peace says no. Ed dreams he gets hitched, only to learn that Rosita has ponies from another horse. He awakens from his nightmare, relieved that horses don't really get married. Wilbur does a good job of convincing a psychiatrist that horses in love should be betrothed.

#140: "Don't Skin That Bear"

ORIGINAL AIRDATE: November 7, 1965
WRITERS: Lou Derman, Larry Rhine
DIRECTOR: Alan Young
GUEST STARS: Barry Kelly, Les Tremayne

Carol's father buys the couple a bearskin rug as a sign of gratitude (yikes) for putting him up for the past six weeks (which explains why he's been in many of the episodes since #131). Wilbur reminds everyone it's been 126 meals. Ed scares Wilbur into getting rid of the rug by enlisting a zoo bear, Sadie, in his cause. Highlights: Wilbur in the psychiatrist's office with Sadie parading by the window; the carnival-like scene in Wilbur's living room where people are trying to swap piranhas, surfboards and bagpipes for the bearskin rug.

#141: "Ed and the Motorcycle"

ORIGINAL AIRDATE: January 2, 1966
WRITERS: Lou Derman, Larry Rhine
DIRECTOR: Alan Young
GUEST STAR: Barry Kelly

A young motorcyclist is disturbing Carol's father with his noise. Ed insists that Wilbur ride him bareback. To make Ed jealous, Wilbur rents a motorcycle. Mr. Higgins is shocked to discover that his son-in-law has a motorcycle too, and treats him like a Hell's Angel. Ed decides to give up his bareback-only policy.

#142: "Cherokee Ed"
ORIGINAL AIRDATE: January 9, 1966
WRITERS: Lou Derman, Larry Rhine
DIRECTOR: Arthur Lubin
GUEST STAR: Barry Kelly

Ed goes to visit his mother for her birthday. She tells her son that he has Indian blood, that he was a "palomino papoose." Ed becomes militant and refuses to march in the Pioneer Parade (carrying a parrot that's the grandson of General Custer!). Ed realizes he couldn't scalp the parrot if he tried, and backs down from his protest.

#143: "Ed Goes to College"
ORIGINAL AIRDATE: February 6, 1966
WRITERS: Lou Derman, Larry Rhine
DIRECTOR: Arthur Lubin
GUEST STAR: Barry Kelly
Note: This was the final episode produced. Ed goes to medical school to become an animal doctor. He wants his Ph.D. (Palomino Horse Doctor), but faints during an appendectomy. The horse sets up his own "Dr. Ed's Animal Clinic" in the barn, and soon has a multitude of furry, feathered patients. Carol's father sneaks a peek through the barn window and falls from the shock, passing out. When he comes to (Ed advises Wilbur on how to treat him), all traces of the clinic are cleared away, and Mr. Higgins thinks he's been seeing things.

Final Note: From February 13, 1966, through September 4, 1966, Mister Ed reruns aired on CBS, Sundays at 5 P.M. The final episode to air was a repeat of "Ed's Juice Stand" (#118). CBS filled the time slot with To Tell the Truth.

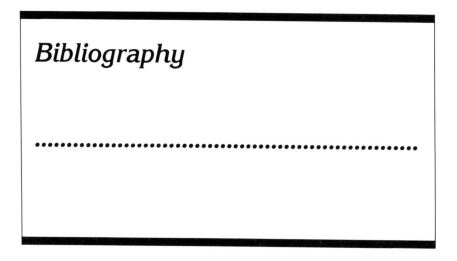

Bibliography

The following books and periodicals provided valuable links and clues in piecing together the *Mister Ed* legacy.

Classic Images, #136, 1986. "Allan Lane" by N. Nicholls.

Classic Sitcoms, Vince Waldron. Collier Books, 1987.

The Complete Directory to Prime Time Network TV Shows, 1946–present (revised edition), Tim Brooks and Earle Marsh. Ballantine Books, 1988. A gem of a resource book.

Cult TV, John Javna. St. Martin's Press, 1985.

The Great Movie Series, edited by James Robert Parish. A. S. Barnes and Co., 1971.

The Great TV Sitcom Book, Rick Mitz. Perigee Books, 1988.

Holy Mackerel! The Amos 'n' Andy Story, Bart Andrews and Ahrgus Juilliard. E. P. Dutton, 1986.

The Original Mister Ed, Walter Brooks. Bantam Books, 1963.

Rocky Lane Western, No. 1. AC Comics, 1989.

Say Goodnight, Gracie! The Story of Burns & Allen, Cheryl Blythe and Susan Sackett. E. P. Dutton, 1986. Excellent book!

Total Television, Alex McNeil. Penguin Books, 1980.

TV Guide: 1952, 1961–66.

TV Movies and Video Guide, 1988 Edition, Leonard Maltin, editor. New American Library, 1987.

TV Turkeys, Kevin Allman. Perigee Books, 1987.

Unsold Television Pilots, Lee Goldenberg. McFarland, 1990.

Whatever Became Of . . . ?, Richard Lamparski. Crown Publishers, 1985.

Index